Bird's-Eye Views

Queer Queries About Activism, Animals, and Identity

pattrice jones

Published by VINE Press; 158 Massey Road; Springfield, VT 05156 USA

ISBN: 979-8-9896172-0-3 (paperback) 979-8-9896172-1-0 (e-book)

SOCIAL SCIENCE / Activism & Social Justice

NATURE / Animal Rights

NATURE / Animals / Birds

Contents

Introduction

Every year, the folly of human supremacy becomes more clear. Problems that have plagued our communities for centuries persist. New catastrophes of our own making compound existing injuries and emergencies. We fight about identity. We cannot agree on what the facts might be.

For thirty years, as an activist and a scholar, I've been writing essays as a way of assaying the interactions among elements of problems that vex or perplex me. In the 1990s, I wrote as an AIDS activist, anti-racist educator, and tenant organizer. Since 2000, I've written from the grounds of an animal sanctuary, doing my best to incorporate what I have learned from nonhuman animals and the larger-than-human world into my analyses. This has sometimes required me to rethink everything I thought I knew.

Since human-centered interventions into human misdeeds have so far failed to solve intra-species problems such as warfare, poverty, or inequality, much less human-engendered planetary catastrophes like the climate, water, and pollution crises, the need for more ecological analyses and truly new strategies feels urgent to me. I offer these essays, old and new, not as *the* answer to anything but as contributions to our collective process of problem-solving and imagination.

I've grouped works that follow by broad theme. If you want to create your own arc instead, feel free!

I. BIRD'S-EYE VIEWS

Shortly before Miriam Jones and I moved to a peninsula where the poultry industry kills and cuts up more than a million birds each day, rescued an industry escapee from a roadside ditch, and thereby accidentally founded what would become VINE Sanctuary, I read a book about the folklore of birds. I'd convinced myself that this book, which I'd happened upon in a used bookstore in Ypsilanti, Michigan so packed with haphazard stacks that the only way to browse was to give oneself over to serendipity, was somehow relevant to my dissertation research on the psycho-history of white racial identity. That research did require me to dive deeply into European imaginaries, but the truth was that I just wanted to read that book.

Despite the dullness of its dusty details, the book absorbed me. Not for the first time, deiform birds appeared in my dreams. Meantime, migratory birds flocked to our weedy yard, each with the ability to see colors I could not see. The beliefs and practices I was reading about seemed both right and wrong: Correct in their recognition of birds as beings who offer glimpses of a larger-than-human world and to whom we might have some obligations, incorrect in their projections of human preoccupations, such as gender stereotypes and heteronormativity, onto other animals.

Not long afterward, our migration to the Delmarva peninsula launched me into what has become a multi-decade odyssey of efforts to flip the script by looking at myself, other humans, and human constructions from an avian point of view. It started at sunrise the morning after we brought the rescued chicken home. I let her out of the makeshift coop we had created in the garage, and she immediately began scratching in the fallen leaves from the autumn before, knowing to look in the damp earth beneath for minerals I couldn't see without a microscope. I scattered birdseed and chicken scratch in my wake as I returned to the house and then turned back to see her—a big white chicken surrounded by grackles and red-winged blackbirds—neither a deity nor a commodity, just a bird among birds.

The essays in this section are all rooted in, or at least include, some effort to adopt an avian point of view. Today, as two-thirds of North American birds are at risk of extinction and migratory birds worldwide confront the existential challenge of mistiming[1] due to climate change, it seems more urgent than ever to do so.

1. Marcel E Visser and Christiaan Both, "Shifts in Phenology Due to Global Climate Change: The Need for a Yardstick," Proceedings of the Royal Society B: Biological Sciences 272, no. 1581 (December 22, 2005): 2561–69.

1

Property, Profit and (Re)Production

This essay was originally published in 2017 in *Animal Oppression and Capitalism* edited by David Nibert. It is a true "essay," in the sense that I was trying very hard to figure something out. In preparing to write the piece, I spent a lot of time asking myself questions like "how would I explain property to a cow?" and "what do pigeons know about us that we might not know about ourselves?" I hope you will find the process of asking such questions as invigorating as I did.

Property, Profit & (Re)Production

A Bird's-Eye View

I wish I knew how to think outside of capitalism.

I was born in 1961, on the cusp of the current era of capitalism wherein consumer 'goods' multiply at warp speed. I can still remember—barely—the days before there were 37 different varieties of orange juice[1] in a typical U.S. supermarket.

In that year, Rachel Carson must have been putting the finishing touches on Silent Spring, published in 1962. Reading it decades later, I gaped at her description of flocks of birds in urban and suburban backyards, the disappearance of which prompted women all over the United States to sound an alarm, eventually leading to the discovery that DDT and other poisons were to blame for the sharp decline in the populations of their feathered friends.

What? There were many more birds in the sky only a few years before I was born?

I can almost imagine an urban skyscape with many more songbirds than when I was a child, but I can't know what effect(s) more color, more sound, more life might have had on my developing brain. Nor can I change the fact that comparatively barren skies feel normal to me. Two or three times, I have had the good fortune to be among trees in which flocks of migrating birds have stopped to rest, and this has given me a glimpse of the days before deforestation, before billions of birds were shot out of the skies. But that felt exceptional to me, while machine-generated transmissions (radio waves, microwaves, wifi) occupying

---

1. That's the number I counted one day in one store. Since the brand Minute Maid alone offers 11 varieties — Premium Original Orange Juice; Pulp Free Orange Juice; Orange Juice with Calcium & Vitamin D; Pure Squeezed No Pulp; Pure Squeezed Some Pulp; Pure Squeezed No Pulp with Calcium & Vitamin D; Country Style; Heart Wise®; Home Squeezed with Calcium & Vitamin D; Kids+; and Low Acid — in both liquid and frozen form, and since other brands are similarly prolific in devising variations of the same product, the true total of available varieties of orange juice must be much higher.

airways that once thrummed with birdsong and the beating of wings is what feels usual.

It's similar for me with late capitalism, by which I mean the current cultural-economic state of affairs in which those machine-generated transmissions thrum with advertisements for the exponentially expanding swarm of consumer 'goods' that have come to seem normal in this era of hyper(re)production and consumption in which no relationship or idea, no clever phrase or dance craze, escapes commodification. The other day, I counted more than 60 varieties of mints and chewing gum arrayed above the conveyer belt at the grocery store check-out line. Until boredom provoked me to count, that felt normal to me. And I probably wouldn't have been quite so bored by a brief wait were it not for the constant stimulation that the internet has taught my brain to expect.

All of which is to say that my ability to think about capitalism must be presumed to be compromised. Even if there were some site outside of capitalism from which to stand and survey it, significant features might seem so 'normal' as to be unremarkable. I might be unable to imagine alternatives to aspects of the situation that feel 'natural' because they have been ever-present within my own lifetime. I might not ask important questions about capitalism's unspoken assumptions... because I make those assumptions myself.

And so I ask myself: Who might be better able to notice the most salient aspects of capitalism? What might we see from their standpoints?

Nonhuman Animal Standpoints

In its most basic form, feminist Standpoint Theory reminds us that "one's social situation enables and sets limits on what one can know."[2] Given the degree to which my own colonized and commodified mind may be unlikely to perceive important things about capitalism, it occurred to me to ask: What can nonhuman animals tell us about capitalism?

As Alison Wylie summarizes it, Standpoint Theory holds that "...those who are subject to structures of domination that systematically marginalize and oppress them may, in fact, be epistemically privileged in some crucial respects. They may know different things, or know some things better than those who are comparatively privileged."[3]

2. Harding, "Rethinking Standpoint Epistemology," 54-55.

3. Wylie, "Why Standpoint Matters," 26.

Some nonhuman animals, such as cows held captive on for-profit "dairy" farms, subsist entirely within capitalism, with every aspect of their lives (including their very bodies) shaped by its machinations. Other nonhuman animals, such as free-flying birds, cannot escape the climate change, pollution, and incessant encroachments on their habitat caused by capitalism but are not ensnared by its property relations. Nonhuman animals who might be considered inquilines in relation to humans—rats, raccoons, pigeons, and others who find ways to survive within human homes and communities—have yet another standpoint vis a vis capitalism, having carved out their own niches within it even as others of their kind (in the case of rats and pigeons) remain commodified captives.

Sandra Harding, who has perhaps done more than anyone to demonstrate the utility of Standpoint Theory, argues that "the activities of those at the bottom of such social hierarchies can provide starting points for thought... from which humans' relations with each other and the natural world can become visible. This is because the experience and lives of marginalized people, as they understand them, provide particularly significant problems to be explained."[4]

Could this be true for nonhuman animals as well? Could consideration of capitalism from the vantage point of nonhuman animals fundamentally (and fruitfully) change the question?

Indeed this has been the case for me. When I set out to imagine what nonhuman animals might tell us about capitalism if they could, I ended up with more questions than answers. At first that felt like failure, but then I noticed that these were different questions than critics of capitalism usually ask. In seeking to answer those questions, I hit upon a few ideas that might be useful foci for future investigations — or, even better, interventions — into capitalism.

The Pigeon Point(s) of View

As related by zoologist John McLoughlin,[5] the story of how pigeons came to be so plentifully among us reminds me of the entanglement of animal exploitation, colonization, and capitalism: The rock doves who were the ancestors of modern pigeons lived amidst the people of the Mediterranean for millennia, in one of those mutually beneficial cohabitations so common in nature. But then, here and there, people got the idea to reshape the birds

4. Harding, 54.

5. McLoughlin, The Animals Among Us.

to better meet human wishes and began to deliberately interfere with their reproduction. Some sought heavier birds with bigger breasts, others wanted lightweight long-distance messengers, and still others wanted feathers of specific colors for aesthetic or symbolic purposes. By the first millennium B.C.E., Egyptians used specially-bred homing pigeons for communication, Hebrews sacrificed specially-bred doves by the thousands in temple rituals, and people around the region raised pigeons for their flesh in structures called dovecotes. Roman soldiers picked up these practices and spread dovecote culture, along with the birds themselves, across Europe, using homing pigeons to report back to Rome on their imperialist adventures. Similarly, the Arabs who took up the task of world conquest upon the decline of the Roman Empire spread dovecote culture into South Asia, maintaining precise genealogical records of the homing pigeons they used to communicate across their expansive domain. Doves had become soldiers, conscripts in imperial wars.

By World War I, the use of pigeons in warfare was so common that 100,000 birds were used as military tools in the course of that conflict.[6] At about that same time, the new science of experimental psychology discovered a new use for pigeons, as subjects of experiments. Meantime, within the United States, raising pigeons for "meat" began to be promoted as both a pastime and a commercial endeavor.

Today, many pigeons remain captive. "Meat" markets around the world sell plump young pigeons as "squab." In the United States, rural communities stage festive "hunts" by releasing captive-born birds to be shot out of the sky during their first real flight. Urban enthusiasts raise racing pigeons on rooftops, using the mates and offspring of bonded birds to lure partners and parents into exhausting efforts to get back home. Unconstrained by any animal welfare laws at all,[7] researchers subject pigeons to every imaginable kind of experimentation. Vendors make money selling pigeons to scientists and hobbyists. And, at least in France, pigeons remain military conscripts, ready to be drafted into conflicts not of their choosing.[8]

Therefore, pigeons have had the opportunity to observe capitalism from every angle. What do they see?

---

6. Wallop, "Animal Soldiers."

7. Pigeons and other birds (along with rodents) are not classified as "animals" under the minimal federal nonhuman animal welfare regulations in the United States, leaving the vast majority of other animals in laboratories entirely unprotected.

8. Parussini, "In France, a Mission to Return the Military's Carrier Pigeons to Active Duty."

First, it seems to me that pigeons might not make such a sharp distinction between capitalism and the practices that paved the way for that particular mode of exploitation and accumulation. Each of the key catastrophes of capitalism—private ownership, production, profit—were visited upon pigeons by people long before accumulated assets coalesced into a configuration that political economists sprang up to call 'capitalism. Understanding these continuities might help critics of capitalism to avoid analytic errors that have led some communist economies to become as heartless and environmentally ruinous as any capitalist endeavor.

Again and again in the process quaintly called 'domestication,' free-flying pigeons were lured into human-constructed nesting places only to be dispossessed of their offspring or made captives themselves. That is one way that 'property' comes into being.

A pigeon considered to be property would know, instinctively if not through some process of cognition that we could understand, that the problem is not private ownership but ownership itself. To be owned and exploited by some egalitarian collective of unrelated people would not be less onerous than to be owned and exploited by some person or family of people.

In both cases, reduction to the status of property is the problem, which is then compounded by being utilized as a means of (re)production. The ruthlessness of production—in this case, either having your offspring taken from you to be made into "meat," if not being made into "meat" yourself—remains, regardless of the relations among the various makers, vendors, buyers, and users of the products.

Just as I find it difficult to think outside of late consumer capitalism, champions and critics of capitalism alike find it difficult to conceptualize a culture not centered on production. In the The Mirror of Production, Jean Baudrillard notes "the virtual impossibility of thinking beyond or outside the general scheme of production."[9] This difficulty arises, in part, from the entanglement of the ideas of humanity and productivity.

In The German Ideology, Marx and Engels assert that men "begin to distinguish themselves from animals as soon as they begin to produce their means of subsistence."[10] Like me, Baudrillard wonders, parenthetically, "Why must man's vocation always be to distinguish himself from animals?"[11] More im-

9. Baudrillard, The Mirror of Production, 18.

10. Marx and Engels, The German Ideology, 7.

11. Baudrillard, 21.

portantly, Baudrillard describes a link between productivity and human identity, as experienced by men —and I do mean 'men'— living in cultures centered on the ethos of dominion of nature.

Baudrillard critiques the way of thinking that "hallucinates man's predestination for the objective transformation of the world,"[12] finding in this widespread fantasy a key to the reduction of people to their labor power within both capitalist and communist political economies as well as a source of the reckless exploitation of nature, such that "production subordinates Nature and the individual simultaneously."[13] People under the spell of this way of thinking see themselves reflected in the products of their labors, and "through this scheme of production, this mirror of production, the human species comes to consciousness in the imaginary."[14]

This brings us back to the pigeon point of view. Recall that Europeans often rationalized the forced displacement of Native Americans and other indigenous people by asserting that the original inhabitants had not made productive use of the land. Both as indigenes themselves[15] and as captives brought along on voyages of conquest, members of the extended pigeon family witnessed the migrations of European humans from the lands they had so '"productively"' deforested to these new environs. Pigeons also have had a bird's-eye view of the accelerated expansion of the population of both people and farmed animals subsequent to the imperialist expansions that led ultimately to the globalization of capitalism. Historian and geographer Alfred Crosby imagines that "one who watched the Caribbean islands from outer space during the years from 1492 to 1550 or so might have surmised that the object of the game going on there was to replace the people with pigs, dogs, and cattle."[16]

I'm not so sure what pigeons would have surmised. Surely, native pigeons and doves would have noticed the unfamiliar animals and reshaped landscapes that followed the European invasion. Perhaps they did notice that the people waging wars on forests were lighter-colored and differently ornamented than

---

12. Ibid., 19.

13. Ibid., 54.

14. Ibid., 19.

15. Collectively, pigeons and doves compose the family Columbidae, which includes more than 300 extant and extinct species. (The birds commonly called "pigeons" are member of the the "rock dove" branch of that family.) The broader order of Columbiformes includes not only pigeons and doves but also the unlucky indigene known to Europeans as the dodo.

16. Crosby, The Columbian Exchange, 75.

the humans to whom they were accustomed. Perhaps they thought of the difference in the same way as we distinguish between African and Asian elephants. If so, I wonder which behavioral differences might have seemed salient to them.

Hyper-reproductivity comes to mind. Like indigenous peoples everywhere, the native peoples of the Americas tended to keep their populations well below what the land could support. This makes good social and environmental sense, as it allows for there to be enough for everybody, even in the times of comparative scarcity that weather fluctuations sometimes present. The Catholic Iberians who first invaded the Caribbean and the Protestant Northern Europeans who later immigrated into what would become Canada and the United States had different ideas and practices. The flip side of the denigration for non-reproductive sexuality that they famously brought to the Americas was a valorization of profligate reproduction that has subsequently come to seem so normal as to appear natural. They went forth and multiplied as recklessly as they cut down trees. Over the centuries, this irresponsible habit (in combination with the despicable practice of importing captive people as laborers) added up to explosive human population growth.

And then passenger pigeons met profit. These peripatetic pigeons had been hunted, in deliberate moderation, by various Native Americans and thus must have perceived people as among the many predators of which to be wary. Immediately upon their arrival, the firearm-toting European immigrants must have seemed to be a different kind of animal. Over time, the foreigners subjected these avian indigenes to three new injuries: captivity, sport hunting, and (most lethally) commercial hunting. Some settlers converted wild birds into property, in order to monetize their offspring. Others promoted pigeon killing as a wholesome form of recreation for boys and men. With the coming of refrigerated railroads, high-volume commercial hunting of passenger pigeons became such a lucrative endeavor that tens of thousands of birds were killed at a time. Not long after, the last passenger pigeon died alone in a zoo.

Let's look at that sorry story from the pigeon point of view. We can't! The closest matches, within human experience, are genocides from which there were few if any survivors, and records of these might help us to begin to empathize with the combination of horror and incomprehension surviving birds might have experienced surveying stacks of the dead bodies of their flock mates and family members. But this is more like if bears, who sometimes do kill people, suddenly became able to kill people by the thousands, and did so, gradually emptying our cities as they spirited the bodies off to some unknown place for some unknown purpose.

I hope that imagining such a scenario can help to make profit seem strange, because this is the question that I think may have reverberated, in whatever way that queries ring in bird brains: Why take so many more than you can eat? Not just a few more, to take home to your nestlings or store for the winter, but more than you could consume in a lifetime? Those of us who have grown up within capitalism may tend to see the wish, or even the perceived need, for profit to be natural. Considering the question from the pigeon point of view, the profit motive becomes something that needs to be explained.

Live 'Stock' Looks Back

One day, a cow jumped over a "beef" farm fence to birth a calf in the forest, far from the grasping hands of humans. She and her son then found their way to a friendly person who conveyed them to a sanctuary. The mother's fierceness in protecting her son from perceived threats made them a poor match for a sanctuary offering tours to the public, and so they both came to VINE Sanctuary, where they eventually joined the hardy herd in our back pasture. The cows in that community organize their own affairs as they see fit. They often choose to sleep in the forest rather than in the barn and to drink from a brook or pond rather than water troughs. Other than eyeballing everybody twice each day, just to ensure that nobody is ill or injured in any way, sanctuary staff stay out of the way.

Jan and her calf Justin have flourished in that setting. As Justin has grown up into a sweet-tempered young adult with a fondness for bird-watching, Jan has made friends with cows her own age. She no longer glares and prepares to charge any person who might dare to look too lingeringly at her son, but she still becomes visibly wary when strangers appear.

I've endured more than a few uncomfortable moments under the searchlight of Jan's gaze, hoping she will see that she need not charge at me to protect herself or her son. At such moments, it seems to me that she is both mad and mystified, angered and confused by what she has seen people do to cows. In Jan's expression when she looks at people, even when she is comparatively relaxed, I perceive a combination of challenge and question, as if she is prepared to fight an enemy she cannot fathom.

Maybe I'm wrong in this, but let's imagine that my empathic imagination is in this case correct. What is Jan mad about? What questions does she have?

I don't know enough about the farm from which Jan escaped to know whether she was artificially inseminated while chained into immobility or placed in a situation from which she could not escape a bull brought in for the purpose of impregnating her. Either way, she was not free to refuse to become pregnant with a child destined to be made into "meat." Depending on whether or not the small-scale farm from which Jan escaped was one of the increasingly common (and ostensibly 'humane') slaughter-on-site facilities beloved by locavores, Jan would have either heard the screams as other cows were killed or simply witnessed cows wrestled from the herd and never seen again. Some of the victims were her children; others were her friends.

And for what? A cow or other ungulate who witnesses a herd member taken down by a predator also sees the reason for the attack. However upsetting, the incident 'makes sense' to creatures whose auroch ancestors evolved in relationship to truly carnivorous fellow forest denizens. But wholesale slaughter and dismemberment (or disappearance) of relatives and other community members must shock the minds as well as the hearts of these exquisitely social nonhuman animals whose brains (like ours) evolved to be attuned to the experiences of others in the social group.

So, one question Jan might have is: Why?

Another question Jan might have is: How? What kind of creatures are people, that they can do such things?

Yet another question Jan might have is: What other horrors might you people be capable of committing?

Cows can't understand capitalism. They feel its effects all too well, and they certainly know that people are the proximate cause of their woes, but it would be difficult for them to imagine the rationales used by people to explain any sort of nonhuman animal exploitation to themselves, much less the preposterous mathematics of of an economic system that requires incessant growth to avoid collapse.

Those of us who understand, or think we understand, the logic of capitalism can exercise both empathy and solidarity by taking Jan's questions seriously. We can ask ourselves afresh: Why? How? What else? Instead of accepting 'profit' as an easy answer, we can consider the profit motive a questionable phenomena requiring some explanation. We can notice the sexual violation at the heart of "meat" and cow milk production, and we can join Jan in wondering what other obscenities might be forthcoming from people accustomed to perpetrating such perversities.

Multiplication and Division

Ecofeminist philosopher Lori Gruen stresses the importance of empathy as an essential cognitive tool for nonhuman animal advocacy.[17] Feminist anthropologist June Nash calls for us to use "peripheral vision" when seeking to understand the machinations of globalized capitalism.[18] Having tried to follow that advice in considering capitalism from the perspectives of pigeons and cows, I end up with questions about several of the foundations of that socio-economic system: property, profit, and (re)production.

Ownership and Identity

Nonhuman animals under the control of people don't experience themselves as property but as captives. Empathizing with this perspective makes property strange and draws attention to the violence implicit in it.[19] Nonhuman animals contest captivity in many ways.[20] They flee, fight back against their captors, and sometimes even free other animals.[21] Thus, it seems safe to conclude that many nonhuman animals experience captivity as a kind of continuing assault.

The problem, for nonhuman animals, is not only that they themselves are liable to be violently converted into property (if not hatched or born into that status) but also that their habitats are considered by people to be property. Nonhuman animals also contest this, sometimes exercising notable ingenuity in organizing both individual and collective resistance to 'development.'[22] But sit-ins by baboons are no match for bulldozers. Hence, even if nonhuman animals were magically emancipated from the category of property, many misfortunes would remain. Property itself is problematic.

I've often imagined how I would explain property to somebody, like a pigeon, who is unfamiliar with the notion of ownership. Of course, a pigeon might understand very well the notion of exclusive use of a nesting cavity. Many birds who build nests certainly do defend them from interlopers and might well

17. Gruen, Entangled Empathy.

18. Nash, "Globalization and the Cultivation of Peripheral Vision."

19. jones, "Stomping with the Elephants: Feminist Principles for Radical Solidarity."

20. Gruen, The Ethics of Captivity.

21. Hribal, Fear of the Animal Planet.

22. jones, "Sharks Bite Back: Direct Action by Animals Around the World."

endorse the Lockean idea that mixing your labor with found materials entitles you to claim the resulting object as your own.

Most people think of 'property' as things owned, but property theorists within philosophy and legal studies tend to use the word to refer to the relationships among people codified and enforced by laws regarding ownership. In this way of thinking, property is most frequently conceptualized as a 'bundle of rights' enjoyed by owners, along with perhaps some responsibilities.[23] While there may be some argument about whether this or that tangible or intangible item (such as an amputated body part or an idea) rightly falls under the reign of particular property regulations,[24] and while scholars will quibble (as scholars do) about whether 'bundle' is the best metaphor, we should not miss the central insight: *Property is a relationship among people.* Property is ruthless in relation to nonhuman animals and other entities claimed as possessions because property is, in the minds of people, all about people.

Perhaps termites could understand our presumed license to seize a homestead without regard for others who might already be living there, but I wonder whether any nonhuman animal could understand the feeling of violation experienced by some human home-owners when some other-than-human animals happen into their suburban backyards. At first this feeling seems absurd: Nonhuman animals aren't party to the agreements people make with each other in order to establish private property, and so it is silly for any person to expect nonhuman animals to respect property boundaries drawn up by people. Still, the feeling of trespass is real, and tends to occur even when the nonhuman animal in question poses no threat.

Thinking about that leads me to notice two aspects of property that often go unremarked:

1. The affective components of the notion of property are wider and deeper than those usually acknowledged by property theorists, even when the objects of ownership are not of particular sentimental value.

2. Speciesism is implicit in the very notion of property, whether or not nonhuman animals are the property in question.

These aspects are related by the degree to which property ownership figures into 'human' identity. While it of course makes sense for social nonhuman animals of any given species to make agreements among themselves about how they will share the various essential features of their habitats, people go further

---

23. Penner, The Idea of Property in Law.

24. Morales, "The Property Matrix"

than this in the ideas and practices that constitute property, simultaneously elevating and alienating themselves in the process of claiming ownership.

A pair of Canada geese nests, every year, at the edge of a pond past which I frequently drive. When they are nurturing eggs or nestlings, they certainly do defend themselves and their home from any perceived encroachment. Nonetheless, I've seen nothing to suggest that these geese consider themselves to be anything other than two of the many denizens of the pond. In contrast, the people on whose 'property' the pond sits certainly do consider themselves to be the owners of the pond. In so doing, they set themselves above and apart from the waterfowl, frogs, insects, and turtles (not to mention the marsh grass and the water itself) who co-create the ecosystem that is the pond and thus might be considered to have even more of a claim to it.

I am suddenly reminded of the ranchers who feel furious when a wolves consume a cow, considering the natural behavior of a handful of indigenous nonhuman animals to be a crime worthy of the death penalty for the whole species. Why such fury? Is it only the slight decrease in profit associated with the loss of one piece of 'stock'? Or do the ranchers recognize the threat as more existential? Like the raccoon who tips over a suburban trash bin while committing the crime of rescuing food scraps from a landfill, those wolves are saying, "we don't recognize your system of property. We do not concede the earth to you."

When nonhuman animals contest property, they also challenge the very basis of 'human' identity. We should join them, however we can, and not only because property is so hurtful to them. To the degree to which our identities are bound up with what we own, we are alienated from our animal selves as well as the ecosystems upon which we depend for everything.

The Superfluity of Surplus

In currently common parlance, to be 'extra' is to behave in an excessive manner. In the preceding exercises in empathic imagination, both pigeons and cows noticed and were mystified by the 'extra' character of predation by people. From a human standpoint within capitalism, we can see that some of the people who shot hundreds or thousands of passenger pigeons at a time intended to sell their bodies for a profit. However, this leaves much unexplained, such as superfluous killings in the course of sport hunting. Moreover, why a person should want profit, which is just another way of saying excess, remains unclear. To people in profit-seeking cultures, the wish for more, if not the willingness to commit injuries up to and including killing for that non-essential pleasure, seems natural, but many other animals (including other humans) are collectively content with enough.

If we consider 'enough' to mean both (1) sufficiency of resources necessary for livelihood, including an adequate reserve against hard times, and (2) equity within exchanges, then the impulse to accumulate more than that really does need to be explained. From an ecological standpoint, the incessant alienation and appropriation of as much surplus as possible from a finite planet seems suicidal, especially given another remarkable habit of the humans who created capitalism: overpopulation.

Reproduction and Duplicity

If the pigeons and doves indigenous to Europe were able to communicate with those elsewhere in the world, then they would collectively be able to tell a birds-eye tale of one group of apes depleting one part of the world, literally shipping off the surplus people that the deforested land could no longer support, and then starting the process all over again in other places.

If the pigeons who first were '"domesticated"' could shout a warning about into the future, they might say, "Watch out! They seem nice at first, but then they steal your babies!!" Both human population explosion and the process of making other animals into property revolves around forced reproduction. And that brings us to patriarchy.

Ascent of Man

How did some humans become the kind of animals who identify themselves via ownership, monomaniacally pursue a fantasied infinite surplus, and center their cultures on incessant (re)production? To begin to answer the questions nonhuman animals might have about capitalism, we must trace some of the many intersections among sexism and speciesism, noticing the pathways by which patriarchy set the stage for an economics of hyper(re)production in the service of appropriation and accumulation.

From the pigeon point of view, patriarchy might look like the males of one species of ape battling each other—individually and in gangs—for control of females, land, and other animals. Each male fights on several fronts, deploying physical force not only in the competition with other males but also in the subordination of human and nonhuman animals as well as in the never-ending quest to administer the workings of the world. They raze forests, dam or divert waterways, and even sometimes chop the tops off mountains. They also wage war on any nonhuman animals who in any way impede their endeavors.

Why did they start fighting with each other? Did they first subordinate the females of their own kind and then extend that practice to other animals... or vice versa? Those are good topics for another day, as are many other aspects of patriarchy that ecofeminists such as Carol Adams and Lori Gruen have identified as correlates of speciesism.[25] But, in order to understand how patriarchy paved the way for capitalism, we need only parse this simple phrase: man versus man over resources.

Let's come back to what 'man' might be after looking at the other terms.

Versus

The centrality of competition to patriarchy can be missed when we (quite understandably) focus on the subjugation of women, nonhuman animals, and 'nature' by human males. In addition to contributing to many of the more toxic aspects of masculinity, a combative rather than cooperative approach to the mutual use of material resources tends to create stockpiles and scarcity, both of which increase the likelihood of continuing conflict.

Whether due to insecurity, arrogance, or some combination of the two, males in a social system patterned by fights about property will tend, if they can, to amass weaponry and hoard resources. Hoarding by some creates scarcity for others, heightening the tension if not outright fighting and therefore setting the stage for never-ending warfare. Thus does the competition within patriarchy help to supply one of the keystones of capitalism: Desire for surplus.

Surplus means more. In order for there to be more, reproduction of many kinds must be fostered or even forced. Thus does the wish for surplus that is a function of patriarchy contribute to the obsessive and coercive focus on reproduction known as reprocentrism,[26] which is a central element of capitalism.

Competition itself is, of course, another central element of capitalism. In addition to fomenting divisions of all kinds, cultures based on conflicts over

---

25. Adams and Gruen, Ecofeminism.

26. In their germinal 2010 anthology, Queer Ecologies, Catriona Mortimer-Sandilands and Bruce Erickson critique the "repro-centric" (11) logic that presumes reproduction to be the prime aim of all animals. I use the term more broadly, to include not only such misunderstandings of animal behavior but also the monomaniacal focus on reproduction that is a defining feature of sexism, homophobia, and capitalism alike.

property tend toward a fractured rather than holistic view of the natural world. Seeing forests or islands as made up of divisible entities to be assigned to various owners makes it difficult to think ecologically.

Resources

Within patriarchy, males compete with one another to obtain the kinds of exclusive control over resources that are now codified in property law. Thus does patriarchy pave the way for another central element of capitalism: ownership. The conversion of everybody-other-than-men (or, in subsequent racist cultures, everybody-other-than-men-like-me) into potential property has other important consequences.

Within patriarchy, not only female and juvenile humans but also land and other animals are reduced to the status of resources to be exploited by 'mankind.' Living beings become mere inventory or 'live-stock.' The violence by which this demotion is accomplished fosters callousness, which then facilitates further violence.

Reprocentrism becomes rape when animals, human or otherwise, are the stock to be accumulated. Repeated violations of the bodies of others both requires and reinforces callousness and a feeling of entitlement to dominion over others. These central aspects of toxic masculinity feed into and are fortified by the competitive aspects of patriarchy described above, forming an ever more vicious circle.

Man

Within patriarchy, the social identities of adult males depends upon their competent performance of masculinity. Manhood is defined, in part, by participation in the competitions described above. 'Real men' demonstrate their ability to control the women and other animals under their dominion. In many patriarchal cultures, only men may own property, and only property owners are considered real men.

I've often said that pastoralism and patriarchy are two sides of the same coin, with that coin being the profits of controlling somebody else's body.[27] Inherently hurtful to human and nonhuman animals, patriarchal pastoralism also set the stage for two of the most central components of modern-day

27. jones, The Oxen at the Intersection: A Collision.

capitalism: reprocentrism and the entanglement of identity and ownership. Hence, any efforts to undermine capitalism, or speciesism, must be mindful of the interconnections. Neither self-consciously 'militant' nonhuman animal rights activism that embraces toxic masculinity nor vegan consumerism that encourages people to buy their way to animal liberation of other animals are likely to succeed in undermining either capitalism or nonhuman animal exploitation. Similarly, efforts to improve the standing of other animals within the existing legal framework, which ensnares all of nature in property relations backed up by state firepower, may bring some temporary relief of some forms of oppression but are unlikely to lead to true liberation.

Animality as Antidote

Here are some things that pigeons and cows might or might not have noticed about humans:

They like color. A lot. They decorate themselves and their dwellings, often experiencing such frivolity as absolutely essential. They plant flowers with no food value just for the pretty colors—and for their scents, which can have almost intoxicating effects. They like intoxication too, seeking out sensations that feel freeing by an ingenious variety of means, including not only chemistry but also art and music.

While best known (among themselves) for their pronounced tendency to communicate by means of self-generated sound-symbols shaped into words and structured into sentences, these talking apes also use color and other kinds of sound to convey emotions and ideas. Many of them are able to denote sound-symbols visually, thereby increasing the distance across which they can communicate. Tool makers among them have invented various devices that increase that distance even further, so that their exchange networks now encircle the globe.

In other words, these are pleasure-seeking creatures who signal to one another incessantly. This extreme sociality makes sense in the light of their extreme vulnerability as neonates and their comparative lack of muscular strength, relative to other apes, even as adults. Not one of them could survive without some others.

However did such weaklings colonize an entire planet? The fact of that colonization offers a clue. Think of all of the different climates in which these virtually hairless apes abide. Think of all of the different ways they have fed, clothed, transported, and sheltered themselves. Think of all of the different tools, both material and conceptual, they have devised along the way and all of the different practices common in different places.

Quiet as it's kept, this diversity was once much more breath-taking than it is today. For all of the pseudo-variety on ostentatious display on the supermarket shelves of late consumer capitalism, the process of trade globalization has hastened the demise of languages and cultures begun by European imperialism. Nonetheless, the fact remains: Behavioral plasticity is a defining feature of the human species.

Behavioral plasticity refers to changes in behavior arising from an organism's circumstances, including "adaptation, learning, memory and changes in adult behavior as a result of experience during development."[28] Animals and other organisms vary in the flexibility of their repertoire of responses to environmental circumstances. Noting that all behavior is, to some degree, both innate and learned, Mery and Burns suggest that we see behavioral plasticity as "an interaction between evolution and experience."[29] Most importantly, for our purposes, Morris highlights the role of behavioral plasticity in allowing organisms to persist in changing environments as well as colonize new environments.[30]

In colonizing so much of the planet mostly by means of cultural rather than physical evolution,[31] human beings as organisms have demonstrated a remarkable degree of behavioral flexibility. This accounts for not only the diversity of personalities, abilities, and proclivities among humans as individuals but also for the diversity of cultures that have arisen as groups of people have developed cultures in response to varying ecological circumstances.

We're at this juncture, standing amidst the clutter of consumer capitalism as polluted seas rise around us, because certain kinds of cultures—cultures that solve problems with violence, stripping habitats of resources and then moving on to do the same elsewhere—tend to reproduce themselves. But the behaviors encouraged by those cultures are no more (or less) 'human nature' than more pacific and sustainable ways of being in the world.

28. Binder, Hirokawa, and Windhorst, Encyclopedia of Neuroscience, 372.

29. Mery and Burns, "Behavioural Plasticity," 571.

30. Morris, "Plasticity-Mediated Persistence in New and Changing Environments."

31. In those cases where humans eventually evolved new physical characteristics in response to new environments, this was made possible only by the persistence of people in those environments long enough for those changes to occur. That persistence was due to behavioral plasticity.

People build concentration camps... and nonhuman animal sanctuaries. People amass war profits... and divest themselves of all wealth in order to aid others. Most people do a bit of both.

What makes the difference? In every case, a complex conjunction of social and material factors stretching back before birth and continuing throughout the lifespan. Capitalism constricts consciousness, favoring some ways of seeing the world and making others seem impossible, but other ways of thinking and being are not only possible but already present.

In his critique of the concept of 'man-the-producer' that inflects both capitalist and communist thought, Baudrillard asserts that "it is impossible to think this non-growth, this non-productive desire."[32] I respectfully disagree. Lesbians, gay men, and otherwise queer people know all about desire that is not centered on reproduction, and our persistence in pursuing that desire despite social and state repression demonstrates its abiding power.[33]

People of all sexualities know, at some level, that our most heartfelt desires are not for the 37 varieties of orange juice and 60 kinds of chewing gum that consumer capitalism offers us. Let us tap into those desires. Let us allow Afrofuturists and anarchists and artists of all stripes to teach us to imagine heretofore unthought-of aims and strategies that take our current social and material ecologies into account. Let's liberate all the animals, including ourselves, from the tyranny of property, profit, and production.

Works Cited

Adams, Carol J., and Lori Gruen, eds. *Ecofeminism: Feminist Intersections with Other Animals and the Earth*. New York: Bloomsbury Academic, 2014.

Baudrillard, Jean. *The Mirror of Production*. St. Louis: Telos Press, 1975.

Binder, Marc D., Nobutaka Hirokawa, and Uwe Windhorst, eds. *Encyclopedia of Neuroscience*. Berlin: Springer, 2008.

Carson, Rachel. *Silent Spring*. Greenwich, CT: Fawcett Crest, 1962.

Crosby, Alfred W. *The Columbian Exchange: Biological and Cultural Consequences of 1492*. Westport, CT: Greenwood Publishing Group, 2003.

Gruen, Lori. *Entangled Empathy: An Alternative Ethic for Our Relationships with Animals*. New York: Lantern Books, 2015.

———. *The Ethics of Captivity*. Oxford University Press, 2014.

Harding, Sandra. "Rethinking Standpoint Epistemology: What Is 'Strong Objectivity'?" In *Feminist Epistemologies*, edited by Linda Alcoff and Elizabeth Potter, 49–82. Routledge, 1993.

Hribal, Jason. *Fear of the Animal Planet: The Hidden History of Animal Resistance*. AK Press, 2011.

jones, pattrice. "Eros and the Mechanisms of Eco-Defense." In *Ecofeminism: Feminist Intersections with Other Animals and the Earth*, edited by Carol J. Adams and Lori Gruen, 91–106. New York: Bloomsbury, 2014.

———. "Sharks Bite Back: Direct Action by Animals Around the World." *Satya Magazine*, April 2007.

———. "Stomping with the Elephants: Feminist Principles for Radical Solidarity." In *Igniting a Revolution: Voices in Defense of the Earth*, edited by Steven Best and Anthony Nocella, 319–29. New York: AK Press, 2006.

———. *The Oxen at the Intersection: A Collision*. New York: Lantern Books, 2014.

Marx, Karl, and Friedrich Engels. *The German Ideology*. International Publishers, 1970.

McLoughlin, John C. *The Animals Among Us: Wildlife in the City*. New York: Viking Press, 1978.

Mery, Frederic, and James G. Burns. "Behavioural Plasticity: An Interaction between Evolution and Experience." *Evolutionary Ecology* 24, no. 3 (November 26, 2009): 571–83.

Morales, Francisco J. "The Property Matrix: An Analytical Tool to Answer the Question, 'is This Property?'" *University of Pennsylvania Law Review* 161, no. 4 (2013): 1125–65.

Morris, Matthew R. J. "Plasticity-Mediated Persistence in New and Changing Environments." *International Journal of Evolutionary Biology 2014*, 16497, (2014).

Mortimer-Sandilands, Catriona, and Bruce Erickson. "A Genealogy of Queer Ecologies." In *Queer Ecologies: Sex, Nature, Politics, Desire*, edited by Catriona Mortimer-Sandilands and Bruce Erickson, 1–47. Bloomington, IN, USA: Indiana University Press, 2010.

Nash, June. "Globalization and the Cultivation of Peripheral Vision." *Anthropology Today 17*, no. 4 (2001): 15–22.

Parussini, Gabriele. "In France, a Mission to Return the Military's Carrier Pigeons to Active Duty." *Wall Street Journal*, November 11, 2012.

Penner, James E. *The Idea of Property in Law*. Clarendon Press, 1997.

Wallop, Harry. "Animal Soldiers: Hannibal's Elephants to Ukraine's Killer Dolphins." *The Telegraph*, March 31, 2014.

Wylie, Alison. "Why Standpoint Matters." In *Science and Other Cultures: Issues in Philosophies of Science and Technology*, edited by Robert Figueroa and Sandra G. Harding, 26–48. New York: Routledge, 2003.

2

Harbingers of Silent Spring

This piece was originally published in 2010 in *Spring: A Journal of Archetype and Culture*, which was edited by Gay Bradshaw and also published as a book entitled *Minding the Animal Psyche*. *Spring* is a Jungian journal and, while I am not a Jungian, I appreciated the opportunity to engage with Jungian ideas in thinking through the ways that ideas about birds flitter within human brains as well as what might be going on within the minds of my feathered friends.

Harbingers of Silent Spring

Archetypal Avians, Avian Archetypes and the Truly Collective Unconscious

Laid low by sorrow, I crouched in the dust, gathering strength against grief at midday. Suddenly, I saw a flurry of feathers and felt a wobbly weight on my shoulder. The ungainly white bird swayed to maintain his balance while peering at me inquisitively. "Yes," I said, "I do need a friend right now." We swayed together for a moment, regarding each other and the day. After a moment, he alit and I went into the afternoon, soothed.

While the helpful bird is a well-traveled inhabitant of the lands of mythology and reverie,[1] that was no dream and that bird no mere symbol. The dust was that of a foraging yard at the Eastern Shore Sanctuary where, for nine years, I offered shelter and care to avian survivors of factory farming and cockfighting. The bird was a juvenile "broiler" chicken who had leapt or fallen from a slaughterhouse-bound transport truck and had arrived at the sanctuary only the week before. I no longer remember the specific source of the seemingly unsupportable grief that weakened me that day, but I will never forget the young rooster who so intrepidly leapt to comfort me. I called him "Heartbeat," and he was my little friend.

Birds' hearts beat more rapidly when they are afraid. Eyes narrow. Muscles twitch. In the midst of a full-fledged fight or flight response, a bird unable to escape a perceived threat may begin to pant in panic. We know this fear. We've felt it ourselves. Terror jolts through our limbic system like lightning, just as it does through theirs.

Full-fledged. Fight or *flight*. Our long associations with birds of all kinds linger in our language as allusions and figures of speech. Our earliest alphabets

1. Edward A. Armstrong, The Folklore of Birds (London: Collins, 1958).

and pictograms used birds to depict sounds and concepts.[2] Birds dwell at every level of our collective unconscious as well. But the beating hearts and wings of birds are not symbols. Birds feel real fear, real joy, real hope and disappointment and, probably, other real feelings the nuances of which we may not be able to imagine.

The question then becomes: Has our long-standing use of birds as psychological symbols facilitated our ever-escalating appropriation and abuse of their bodies? And, given how deeply our fantasies about birds permeate our *own* psyches, is it even possible for us to conceive what life feels like to them? Thus, before we can begin to think about bird psyches, we must first alert ourselves to the birds fluttering in our psyches. Put another way, before we can think clearly about birds' brains, we must think critically about "birdbrain" and other derogatory notions.

In the days following our encouraging encounter, I got into the habit of calling "Heartbeat! Heartbeat! Where's my little friend?" whenever I went into the yards to refill water basins, replenish feed bowls, or put fresh straw in the coops. He always came running to greet me, charging enthusiastically from the underbrush.

The so-called "broiler" chickens raised for meat in factory farms across the globe spend their short lives in otherwise empty sheds, shoulder to shoulder with thousands of others of the same age and sex. They never nestle under their mothers' wings nor ever spread their own feathers in the sun. Bred to grow unnaturally large unnaturally quickly, the young birds are trucked to slaughter when only about eight weeks old. Human avarice for chicken flesh is now such that billions of birds suffer this foreshortened and impoverished life cycle terminated by a terrifying death shackled upside-down to a slaughter machine.

Every one of those birds is an individual. Despite their genetic similarity and the social and environmental poverty of their early lives, birds lucky enough to escape the whirring blades of the poultry processing factory vary markedly in habits and personality. Some are shy, others sociable. Some are timid, others bold. Some are high-strung, others easy-going. Some are quick-witted, others dull. Some are curious, seizing every opportunity to try new things; others hang back, waiting for somebody else to be the first to venture into new territory or try new food.

2. Andrew Robinson, The Story of Writing (Thames and Hudson: London, 1995).

Not long after Heartbeat's arrival at the sanctuary, a young hen I would come to call "Octagon" appeared in our driveway. Though shaken and bruised from her own fall from a transport truck, she wasn't so injured as to require isolation in the infirmary. Still, I hesitated to leave her to fend for herself in the foraging yard. What she needed was a friend. A-ha! "Heartbeat! Heartbeat! Where's my little friend?" Heartbeat came running but stopped short at the sight of the battered little hen. He circled her slowly, peering closely at each bruise and scrape. Then he sidled next to her until their wings were touching and lowered himself to the ground while making the sound that mother hens use to soothe their chicks. Octagon sighed, the tension leaving her body with her breath, and settled down beside him. I stood, stunned by the empathy and generosity displayed by a young bird who had known little but suffering in his own short life.

During its nine years in rural Maryland, the Eastern Shore Sanctuary provided refuge to poultry industry and cockfighting survivors and offered habitat to ground- and tree-nesting wild birds such as woodcocks and cowbirds while also serving as a home-base for evolving flocks of feral chickens who had "rewilded" themselves, eschewing domestic life to live among the wild birds, foraging widely during the day and roosting at night in tree-branches. For many years, chickens and other birds have been subjects of both naturalistic observation and scientific experimentation. Hence, there are extensive data about their brains, minds, and bodies in the literature of psychology, ethology, and neurobiology. The ideas here integrate that data with my own conclusions based on years of observation of and interaction with both psychologically healthy and severely traumatized birds.

Speaking of Birds...

Birds express themselves fluently through motion and sound. Language is one of the capabilities human beings like to reserve for ourselves, forever narrowing what we mean by "language" as one or another non-human animal proves capable of manipulating sounds as communicative symbols. However, the fact remains that birds communicate with one another and, as the need arises, with members of other species quite adequately and often complexly. As we do, birds use sounds as symbols. Among chickens, for example, the alarm cry for an aerial predator is distinct from the sound that symbolizes a threat on the ground.[3] As we do, birds inflect sound symbols with emotion.[4] The alarm vocalizations of magpies vary in volume and intensity depending on the degree of perceived danger.[5] Again as we do, parrots, hummingbirds, and songbirds learn and use complex vocal sequences structured by syntax[6] and develop distinct regional dialects.[7]

But would it be possible for a skylark to sing something meaningful about our dreams? If not, how can we presume to speak about avian psyches?

Like birds, we use combinations of gesture and sound to convey meaning. Just as the communications of other animals are delimited by need and anatomy, human languages are shaped by the brain,[8] which evolved in interaction with ecosocial environments.[9] The word "unspeakable" notwithstanding, we tend to assume that human languages are capable of saying everything, of accurately symbolizing whatever anyone might like to express. Of course this is not true, as our frequent recourse to music, dance, and graphic arts demonstrates. More troubling is the tendency of language to shape perception and perhaps constrain thought. If my language tells me, as English does, that "corporal" is an antonym of "cerebral," I may find it hard to conceptualize cognition as a biological process. If common usage places "animal" on a different and decidedly lower plane than "human," I may have difficulty reconciling myself

---

3. Christopher S. Evans, Linda Evans, and Peter Marler, "On the Meaning of Alarm Calls: Functional Reference in an Avian Vocal System," Animal Behaviour 46 (1993): 23-38.

4. Mei-Feng Cheng and Sarah E. Durand, "Song and the limbic brain: A new function for the bird's own song," Annals of the New York Academy of Sciences 1016 (2004): 611-627.

5. Deborah Buitron, "Variability in the responses of black-billed magpies to natural predators," Behaviour 87, no. 3/4 (1983): 209-236.

6. Timothy Q. Gentner et al., "Recursive syntactic pattern learning by songbirds," NatureErich D. Jarvis, "Learned birdsong and the neurobiology of human language," Annals of the New York Academy of Sciences 1016 (2004): 749-777.

7. Timothy F. Wright, Christine R. Dahlin, and Alejandro Salinas-Melgoza, "Stability and change in vocal dialects of the yellow-naped amazon," Animal Behaviour 76, no. 3 (September 2008): 1017-1027.

8. Morten H. Christiansen and Nick Chater, "Language as shaped by the brain," Behavioral and Brain Sciences 31, no. 05 (2008): 489-509.

9. Juan D. Delius et al., "Cognitions of birds as products of evolved brains," in Brain Evolution and Cognition, ed. Gerhard Roth and Mario F. Wulliman (New York: Wiley-Spektrum, 2001), 451-490.

to my own animality and will almost certainly tend *not* to notice evidence of animal equality.

Speakers of different languages have different ways of conceptualizing such basic elements of life as space[10] and time.[11] Even people with words in common may struggle with more than semantic differences in the meanings of terms related to psyche. Conceptually and experientially, "self" is very different for people of collectivist versus individualist cultures, so much so that cross-cultural conversations about "self" can sometimes be confounding.[12] People from individualist cultures tend to conceive and experience each "self" as a unitary and discrete entity while people from collectivist cultures tend to conceive and experience selves as relational and overlapping; these different conceptions of "self" (and, therefore, "other") influence not only emotion and social cognition but also aspects of cognition, such as perception and inferential reasoning, that are often assumed to be culture-free.[13] If people from individualist cultures must struggle to grasp what the interaction between self and world feels like to a person from a collectivist culture, how much more difficult must it be to imagine what the interaction between self and world that we call "psyche" feels like to a bird? Thus, our ability to speak accurately of avian psyches must be considered dubious at best. Yet speak we must, because our existing ideas about birds and their brains have been and continue to be so hurtful to them.

Flights of Fancy

We can't even imagine, those of us alive now, what it was like when the skies were black with birds. Reports filter down from the days before the triple trauma of hunting, smog, and DDT left us a world that our ancestors would find shockingly bereft of birds. I caught a glimpse of that past, a couple of times at the sanctuary, when migrating flocks descended, overflowing the trees and saturating

---

10. Jurg Wassmann and Pierre R. Dasen, "Balinese Spatial Orientation: Some Empirical Evidence of Moderate Linguistic Relativity," The Journal of the Royal Anthropological Institute 4, no. 4 (1998): 689-711.

11. Lera Boroditsky, "Does language shape thought?: Mandarin and English speakers' conceptions of time," Cognitive Psychology 43, no. 1 (2001): 1-22.

12. David Myers, "Hazel Markus and Shinobu Kitiyama on cross cultural communication," in Social Psychology, 10th ed. (New York: McGraw Hill, 1991), 46.

13. Hazel Rose Markus and Shinobu Kitiyama, "Culture and the self: Implications for cognition, emotion, and motivation," Psychological Review 98, no. 2 (1991): 224-253.

the soundscape for just a few hours before bolting off again, my heart pounding crazily along with their departing wings. Now, living in a city after nine years at a bird sanctuary, I apprehend our collective loss acutely. The city sounds silent rather than noisy to me. Empty tree branches seem naked. The few birds I hear sound lonely. My heart leaps then crashes when I see a gamboling group of crows or a fluttering flock of morning doves

Homo Sapiens emerged in a world full of birds. Those of us living under comparatively barren contemporary skies can only extrapolate from the historical record to imagine what it might have been like to coexist with birds before the combination of hunting, pollution, and deforestation emptied the airspace above us. As recently as the late 1800s, for example, billions of passenger pigeons in North America migrated in flocks a mile wide and hundreds of miles long, passing overhead for hours or days.[14] Wherever they rested, they filled the trees with movement and the air with sound.

That's just one kind of bird just over a century ago, long after firearms, smog, and tree-cutting had decimated many avian populations and driven others to extinction. Imagine, then, if you can, the degree to which bird bodies and bird song filled the perceptual fields of our hominid ancestors as they came out of the trees and into the grasslands, where the warning cries of songbirds alerted them to danger at the watering hole and the hovering of corvids directed them to potentially fruitful scavenging sites. In late winter, the return of migrating birds presaged the rebound of spring.

Our brain architecture, including the structures and pathways associated with archetypes, evolved in this context. We may be evolutionarily predisposed to see birds and think spring. Such associations are not inherently hurtful. An upsurge of birds often does mean that warmer weather is around the corner, just as the sight of the postal carrier rounding the corner often does mean that bills will soon be in the mailbox. But if we begin to associate the postal carrier — or, worse, people of his race — with the unpleasant sensation of receiving a demand for payment, our relations with people who look like him may begin to go awry. The key difference is between signal and symbol. When we recognize birds or mail carriers as signals, we see them clearly and accurately, noting the implications of their appearance or behavior for us within a shared ecosocial environment. When we use birds, other animals, or other people as symbols, we reduce them to objects to be manipulated in the realm of fantasy.

14. Geoffrey Sea, "A pigeon in Piketon," The American Scholar 73 (2004): 57-84.

The fine line between archetype and stereotype is easily seen in the facility with which we project our feared and despised shadows onto people of other races and ethnicities (Fidyk, 2008; Reeves, 2000).[15] The same process of projection can lead to abuses of birds and other animals. People around the world associate vultures with death and persecute them accordingly. While vultures are protected species in the United States, people made uneasy by their association with death feel free to blast them from treetops with shotguns, hanging their corpses from the trees as warnings to others.[16]

Bird protection ordinances date back at least to Deuteronomy,[17] evidence of both our sympathy for and lethality towards our feathered kin. Both bird watching and bird hunting remain popular sports.[18] These two opposite acts mirror opposite conceptions of birds dating back at least as far as we have evidence of human thought. Depictions of birds in rock art around the world illustrate both "a connexion between birds and death" and "an association between birds and reproduction."[19]

Birds populate the human psyche. Because birds spring so readily to mind, we reach for birds — both literally and metaphorically — to symbolize and enact our ideas. Armstrong's survey of birds in folklore and folk art demonstrates our propensity to use birds as symbols; in virtually every culture and place, birds show up in myths, rituals, song, and dance. Hybrid bird-human figures appear in art across the world from the paleolithic to the present, evidencing our urge to project ourselves onto or into birds. "The various forms of belief in which the human soul is thought to take the form of a bird, or persons are believed to become birds" are "ancient and widespread."[20] *Bird* then, is a potent and multivalent figure in the human psyche, so much so that it might be worthwhile to consider the possibility that *bird* is an archetype rather than a mere symbol of other archetypes.

---

15. Alexandra Fidyk, "'Gypsy' fate: Carriers of our collective shadow," Jung: The e-JournalKenneth M. Reeves, "Racism and projection of the shadow.," Psychotherapy: Theory, Research, Practice, Training 37, no. 1 (2000): 80-88.

16. Associated Press, "Staunton to try to scare away vultures," The Free-Lance Star, December 3, 2001.

17. Armstrong, Folklore of Birds, 1.

18. Genevieve Pullis La Rouche, Birding in the United States: A Demographic and Economic Analysis (Washington, DC: U.S. Fish and Wildlife Service, 2001).

19. Armstrong, Folklore of Birds, 24.

20. Ibid., 49

People certainly do use birds to symbolize archetypal ideas, sometimes going so far as to trick or force actual birds to enact our conceptions. This is especially evident in the realm of gender. We see female chickens as "mother hens" and "dumb clucks," often treating them in ways that reduce them to their reproductive functions and foster the dull-wittedness and passivity attributed to femininity. For example, as will be detailed below, hens in egg factories are deprived of cognitive stimulation and subjected to unrelenting trauma likely to produce learned helplessness.

Roosters, on the other hand, are celebrated as exemplars of masculinity, so much so that the word for male chickens does double-duty as a term for the penis in several languages.[21] As I have detailed elsewhere, cockfighting bouts are human-engineered spectacles of stylized masculinity.[22] Roosters used in cockfighting grow up in isolation and frustration, confined in cages or tethered to stakes. Prevented from learning the social signals by which roosters naturally resolve conflicts before they become deadly, fighting roosters are injected with testosterone and amphetamines, armed with steel knives lashed to their sawed-off spurs, and dropped into cacophonous combat rings from which the only escape is victory or death.[23] Proponents of cockfighting assert — and appear to sincerely believe — that the predictably deranged behavior of these unsocialized and terrified birds is both natural and emblematic of masculinit y.[24]

These are paradigmatic examples of what I call the social construction of gender via animals.[25] Social constructs are collective ideas that seem to be natural facts. Fighting roosters and other animals serve as unwitting tools of the social construction of gender through a three-part process wherein people project their ideas about gender onto animals, force or trick animals into acting out those ideas, and then read the consequent animal behavior as evidence that masculinity and femininity are natural correlates of maleness and femaleness. Sometimes the second stage is finessed by "reading" natural animal behavior

21. Clifford Geertz, "Deep Play: Notes on the Balinese Cockfight," Daedalus 134, no. 4 (2005): 56-87.

22. pattrice jones, "Roosters, hawks, and dawgs: Toward an inclusive, embodied eco/feminist psychology," Feminism & Psychology in press (2010).

23. Amir Efrati, "When Bad Chickens Come Home to Roost, Results Can Be Good," The Wall Street Journal, July 15, 2005.

24. Fred Hawley, "The Moral and Conceptual Universe of Cockfighters: Symbolism and Rationalization," Society & Animals 1, no. 2 (1993).

25. jones, "Roosters, hawks, and dawgs."

selectively, as when the primatologists of old "saw" male dominance among every variety of ape and monkey or when ethologists either didn't see or didn't record the same-sex sexual encounters we now know to be common among hundreds of species, including some 130 bird species.[26] The construction of birds as relentlessly heterosexual, mechanically fixated on reproduction, hinders our ability to see the spectrum of bird relationships and appreciate the degree to which relationships of all varieties are valuable to these social animals.

Birds and Brains

Hence, before we can begin to speak of bird psyches, we must clear away ideas about birds that reflect our fantasies rather than their realities. These include not only ideas rooted in our use of birds as symbols but also our more general fantasy of cognitive or spiritual superiority over other animals. In recent decades, findings in ethology and neurobiology have consistently undermined the notion that there is some special skill or capacity exclusive to humans or that, indeed, there is any biological reason to elevate or even separate *Homo sapiens* from all other animals.[27] Language, tool making, self-awareness: each of these and many other imagined reasons for human singularity have fallen before the onslaught of data concerning animal capabilities and comparative anatomy.

This is not to say that humans are in no way unique. Every kind of animal is special in some way. Furthermore, many animals possess capacities not shared by others. Giraffes can reach into the trees while standing on the ground. Whales send songs along miles of water. Bees use dance to convey precise navigational directions. Each of these is wondrous, as are many human abilities. But none stands as a reason to consider that animal as somehow apart from the rest of the natural world.

Birds not only use sound symbols and syntax to communicate as we do but also make and use tools. Like people, birds sometimes cooperate in the process of "cumulative technological evolution" by testing diverse designs, making cumulative changes to those designs, and dispersing new designs through social

---

26. Bruce Bagemihl, Biological Exuberance (New York: St. Martin's, 1999) 12.

27. Mario F. Wullimann and Grehard Roth, "Problems in the study of brain evolution and cognition," in Brain Evolution and Cognition, ed. Gerhard Roth and Mario F. Wulliman (New York: Wiley-Spektrum, 2001), 1-7.

networks.[28] Birds have also demonstrated evidence of episodic memory and theory of mind, two other cognitive capacities previously believed to be confined to humans.[29]

While emotional congruences between birds and people may be traced to the limbic system and other shared structures,[30] complementary cognitive capacities are most likely the result of convergent evolution, with birds sometimes achieving similar ends by different neurological means.[31] For both birds and mammals, the development of warm-bloodedness after branching off from reptiles "enhanced the potency of neural functioning" just as "flexible behavior became the key" to fitness.[32] For both birds and mammals, the brain growth encouraged by this combination of possibility and necessity promoted further brain plasticity and behavioral flexibility:

The divergent and complicated reproductive strategies of brooding and lactating emerged not least because of the need to release into independence offspring with brains too large to mature intrauterinely or intraov ally.... These strategies demanded differential parental care behaviors, for which these same brains had to evolve new capabilities. The accompanying birth or hatching at an early stage of embryological development caused the brains of the offspring to be exposed at an immature stage to an environment to which they had to match their behavior. This undoubtedly enhanced the role of neural plasticity in the adjustment of the behavioral repertoire of both avians and mammals and advanced the development of brain structures specialized for learning and memory.... This eventually converted the ecological niches in which birds and mammals operated into socioecologial niches that encouraged the evolution of capabilities for highly flexible social behaviors.[33]

---

28. Gavin R Hunt and Russell D Gray, "Diversification and cumulative evolution in New Caledonian crow tool manufacture.," Proceedings of the Royal Society B: Biological Sciences 270, no. 1517 (2003): 867.

29. Nathan J. Emery, "Cognitive ornithology: The evolution of avian intelligence," Philosophical Transactions of the Royal Society B: Biological Sciences 361, no. 1465 (2006): 23-43.

30. Jaak Panksepp, Affective Neuroscience: The Foundations of Human and Animal Emotions (New York: Oxford University Press US, 2004).

31. Erich D. Jarvis, "Avian brains and a new understanding of vertebrate brain evolution," Nature Reviews: Neuroscience 6, no. 2 (2005): 151-159.

32. Delius et al., "Cognitions of birds," 453.

33. Ibid.

In short, both birds and people have brains that evolved in an ecological context favoring behavioral flexibility and the maintenance of social relationships, both of which require the cognitive capabilities we call intelligence. This raises the question of consciousness, the complement of which is unconscious cognition, including the processes known in depth psychology as the collective unconscious.

Edelman writes:

"Since Descartes' dualistic proposal, consciousness has been considered by many to be outside the reach of physics, or to require strange physics, or even to be beyond human analysis. Over the last decade, however, there has been a heightened interest in attacking the problem of consciousness through scientific investigation. To succeed, such a program must take account of what is special about consciousness while rejecting any extraphysical assumptions."[34]

The same may be said of the collective unconscious. "Consciousness is not a thing but rather, as William James pointed out, a process that emerges from interactions of the brain, the body, and the environment."[35] Like consciousness, the archetypes said to reside in the collective unconscious[36] are likely to be processes rather than structures. Furthermore, archetypes, like the various processes collectively called consciousness, are means by which the organism organizes and responds to complex stimuli, including both incoming sensations and remembered experiences.

Consciousness, which arises from "a continual interplay of signals from the environment, the body, and the brain itself... confers an evolutionary advantage on individuals possessing it, for, by these means, richly structured events can be related adaptively to the past history of value-dependent learning events in an individual animal."[37] Birds are among the animals who enjoy the evolutionary

---

34. Gerald M. Edelman, "Naturalizing consciousness: A theoretical framework," Proceedings of the National Academy of Sciences of the United States of America 100, no. 9 (April 29, 2003): 5520.

35. Ibid.

36. C. G. Jung, "Archetypes of the collective unconscious," in Collected Works of C.G. Jung, vol. 9, 2nd ed. (Princeton, NJ: Princeton University Press, 1968).

37. Edelman, "Naturalizing consciousness," 5524.

advantages of consciousness.[38] (Unattached Footnote)[39] (Unattached Footnote)[40]

In[41] people, "consciousness is not a property of a single brain location or neuronal type, but rather is the result of dynamic interactions among widely distributed groups of neurons."[42] Similarly, consciousness in birds is likely to be "based on patterns of circuitry rather than on local architectural constrai nts."[43] However, "the neuroanatomical features of the forebrain common to both birds and mammals may be those that are crucial to the generation of both complex cognition and consciousness."[44] In other words, for both birds and people, consciousness is a widely distributed neurological process involving brain structures also associated with complex cognition.

Because of the constraints imposed by the relatively limited capacity of working memory, much of human cognition occurs below the threshold of consciousness. Given the parallels between human and avian brains, this is presumably true for birds as well. As unconscious schemas for recognizing and responding to salient patterns of external and internal stimulation, archetypes may be considered to be among the varieties of nonconscious cognition. Thus we can begin to see archetypes as natural processes likely to be shared by both birds and people. This has far-reaching implications for the concept of the collective unconscious.

Archetypes, Instincts, and the Collective Unconscious

---

38. Ann B. Butler and Rodney M. J. Cotterill, "Mammalian and avian neuroanatomy and the question of consciousness in birds," Biological Bulletin 211, no. 2 (October 1, 2006): 106-127.

39. Ann B Butler et al., "Evolution of the neural basis of consciousness: A bird-mammal comparison," BioEssays: News and Reviews in Molecular, Cellular and Developmental Biology 27, no. 9 (September 2005): 923-936.

40. David B Edelman, Bernard J Baars, and Anil K Seth, "Identifying hallmarks of consciousness in non-mammalian species," Consciousness and Cognition 14, no. 1 (March 2005): 169-187.

41. David B Edelman and Anil K Seth, "Animal consciousness: a synthetic approach," Trends in Neurosciences 32, no. 9 (September 2009): 476-484.

42. Edelman, "Naturalizing consciousness," 5520.

43. Butler and Cotterill, "Mammalian and avian neuroanatomy," 106.

44. Butler et al., "Evolution of the neural basis of consciousness," 923.

As Stevens notes, "the Jungian approach to the body has been one of neglect"[45] and this has tended to undercut the credibility of concepts like archetype and the collective unconscious outside of the field of depth psychology. In *Archetype Revisited: An Updated Natural History of the Self*, Stevens draws upon advances in neuropsychology to naturalize the concept of the archetype, thereby situating the collective unconscious within the nervous system.[46] Advances in comparative neurobiology allow us to go further than that, developing a more nuanced conception of archetypes as products of evolution and the collective unconscious as an ongoing and widely distributed interactive process.

Jung and subsequent depth psychologists hypothesized archetypes to be the human analogues of the instincts believed to determine animal behavior,[47] pointing specifically to the *innate releasing mechanisms* identified by Lorenz[48] and other ethologists as the avian equivalents of human archetypes. We now have a better understanding of biology, evolution, and ecology than was available to Jung or even early ethologists like Lorenz. We now know that that the seemingly innate and immutable patterns of perception and behavior we call instincts are (a) often more flexible than was previously believed, and always (b) the result of generations of *interactions* between organisms and environments that (c) are *ongoing*.

The implications of this understanding of instinct are profound for the concept of archetype. If archetypes are kinds of instincts, then they too must be rooted in generations of interactions between organisms and environments. In other words, as products of evolution, archetypes reflect the material and social circumstances in which our species evolved and is still evolving. Given that interactions between genetic endowment and environment begin before birth and that social learning begins at birth, Jung may have over-estimated our capacity to distinguish between innate cognitive or perceptual propensities (archetypes) and their culturally influenced manifestations (symbols). Just as it is impossible to disaggregate nature and nurture when speaking of intelligence,

---

45. Anthony Stevens, "Jungian psychology, the body, and the future.," The Journal of Analytical Psychology 40, no. 3 (July 1995): 353.

46. Anthony Stevens, Archetype Revisited: An Updated Natural History of the Self (Inner City Books, 2003), 17.

47. Ibid., 23-33.

48. Konrad Z. Lorenz, King Solomon's Ring: New Light on Animal Ways (New York: Thomas Y. Crowell Company, 1952), vii.

athletic ability, or even height, it may not be possible to confidently abstract archetypes from the situations in which they are expressed.

Furthermore, if archetypes are innate templates for perception and response rooted in interactions between psyche and the material environment, there may be many more of them than Jung identified. (*Bird* being one example.) In the current context of ecological crisis, it may be especially useful for us to understand those archetypes (and their common manifestations) that are not about ourselves or other people but rather about animals or what we have come to call nature.

Evolution is slow but ongoing. Whatever "instinctual" animal behavior we may consider, be it nest-building or migration or response to predation, we find that:

• The behavior evolved over the course of generations of interactions with environment.

• The behavior is itself an interaction with environment.

• Some environmental cue is generally needed to evoke the behavior.

• The tendency to engage in the behavior appears to be encoded in the genes and therefore can be said to reside within each bird's body.

• There is variation, across individuals, in how (and sometimes even whether) the behavior is performed; these variations may or may not affect the life chances of the individual or her offspring.

• Changes in environment may make the behavior, or particular variants of the behavior, more or less adaptive; over time, this may lead to changes in the "instinct" as observed in the population.

Consider migration. Already, we have seen change in this instinctive bird behavior as a result of global warming. Furthermore, these changes have been calibrated to place, with some birds hastening and others delaying departure dates.[49] Presumably, those birds displaying the most flexibility in their enactment of archetypal imperatives will have the most reproductive success, thereby continuing the evolutionary process by which birds developed the behavioral flexibility and brain plasticity associated with what we call intelligence.

Certainly, there is no evidence to suggest that our unconscious archetypes are more inflexible than the migration instinct. Thus, we must presume that archetypes are considerably less fixed than has been traditionally presumed within

---

49. Lukas Jenni and Marc Kéry, "Timing of autumn bird migration under climate change: Advances in long-distance migrants, delays in short-distance migrants.," Proceedings of the Royal Society B: Biological Sciences 270, no. 1523 (July 22, 2003): 1467-1471.

depth psychology. As our interactions with our ever-changing environments continue, our archetypes — like animal instincts — may change.

This way of understanding archetypes grounds psyche in the material not only in the sense of embodying mind but also in the sense of bringing the seemingly timeless back into history. Put another way, this way of looking at archetypes relocates them in place and time. Doing so may aid us in restoring humankind to a more realistic (and less dangerously estranged) relationship with place and time.

To do so, we will need a better understanding of the relational nature of the collective unconscious. Birds and mammals both are social animals. For both, the demands of sociality led to the evolution of emotional capacities such as empathy along with a wealth of intellectual capabilities. Social animals have social brains. Birds and people both are emotionally distressed and cognitively stunted by social isolation. This is because our brains evolved both *within* and *for* relationships.

The concept of the collective unconscious takes on new dimensions considered in the light of evolutionary neuroscience. Rather than a mythic realm of mysterious and possibly supernatural phenomena, the collective unconscious now may be seen as, simply, the subset of nonconscious cognitive processes that are both emotionally valent and rooted in the collective ecosocial history of our species. Since our species shares evolutionary history with birds as well as other mammals, including but not limited to those with whom our ancestors participated in coevolution, some of those nonconscious processes may be presumed to be shared with other animals, including birds.

Thus the collective unconscious becomes a significantly more lively location. First, as a product of evolution, which is ongoing, the collective unconscious no longer need be seen as a static site of archaic inclinations. Next, because even the most rigidly instinctive processes are differentially enacted in complex interaction with evocative environments, we are better able to see cultural influences as intrinsic rather than extrinsic elements of the collective unconscious. Finally, we can begin to see birds and other animals as fellow participants in the ongoing collective process that is the collective unconscious. Since many of them are more skilled than we at collective cognition,[50] perhaps this is cause for celebration. Certainly, this way of conceiving the collective unconscious mandates more cooperative relations with our avian kin. This may prove useful

50. Lain D. Couzin, "Collective cognition in animal groups.," Trends in Cognitive Sciences 13, no. 1 (2009): 36-43.

to all. It was, after all, a process of collective cognition inspired in part by observation of birds that led Rachel Carson to the conclusions published in *Silent Spring*.[51]

Avian Archetypes

Thinking of archetypes as instincts raises the possibility of thinking of instincts as archetypes, which might prove to be useful in understanding avian psyches. Certainly, birds do enact evidently instinctual patterns of perception and behavior, such as the alarmed Jackdaw response to anything resembling a predator carrying away a nestling.[52] And, indeed, these are the very phenomena to which some Jungian theorists have pointed as the nonhuman analogue of archetypes.[53] But let us go further than that, now that we know that birds are sentient, social, intelligent, and highly emotional beings who share many of the processes that we call psyche. As Bradshaw and Sapolsky note, "Historically, science has admitted inference from animals to humans but not the reverse,"[54] arguing that there is much to be learned from such a transposition. Analytic psychologists have considered how ethological concepts like *innate releasing mechanism* might apply to people; now, let's reverse the operation and consider how the the psychological concept of *archetype* might apply to birds. Since birds have brains that function similarly to ours, cognitive repertoires that overlap ours, and are conscious as we are, then perhaps they are also unconscious as we are. In other words, perhaps their inherited patterns of perception and reaction function in the same manner as do ours. In short, perhaps birds have archetypes. Jung himself did not discount this possibility, writing that "there is nothing to prevent us from assuming that certain archetypes exist even in animals, that they are grounded in the peculiarities of the living organism itself."[55]

51. Rachel Carson, Silent Spring (Greenwich, CT: Fawcett Crest, 1962), 97-119.

52. Lorenz, King Solomon's Ring, 43.

53. Stevens, Archetype Revisited, 44.

54. G.A. Bradshaw and Robert M. Sapolsky, "Mirror, Mirror," American Scientist, December 2006, 487.

55. Jolande Jacobi, Complex/archetype/symbol in the Psychology of C G Jung (New York: Routledge, 1999), 256.

If birds had archetypes, what might they be? A tentative list springs immediately to mind: *mother, safe place, offspring, predator, competitor, flock, sibling/cousin/age-mate*. The archetype of *partner* seems likely for birds who form lasting pair-bonds. An archetype of *elder* might be functional for birds, like chickens, who are raised primarily by their mothers but who receive both instruction and protection from other adult flock members. *Father* might be an archetype for those birds for whom the biological father plays an active and distinct role in the life of the young; for those birds among whom mothers and fathers play the same role, cooperatively feeding and protecting their young, it might be that both are perceived as *mother* or, simply, *parent*. Similarly, the term *offspring* is a close as I can come in English for juveniles in need of nurturing, who may or may not be (in species where sisters help to raise their sibling's offspring, juveniles stay to help raise their siblings, or other forms of cooperative care are practiced) one's son or daughter.

Birds also appear to have an archetype I call *friend* and by which I mean a helpful or otherwise friendly animal of another species. Perhaps this originates in the kinds of mutual aid observed by Kropotkin[56] wherein, for example, animals of different kinds sharing a watering hole might warn one another of the approach of a predator. Many birds appear to regard any animal who has not been flagged as a potential predator as a potential friend. At the sanctuary, I witnessed roosters huddling with barn cats for warmth on many a winter day. One dog, called Dandelion, was particularly adept at smelling out eggs left behind by hens. One group of hens became her regular entourage, trailing along after her in hopes of snatching the eggshells (a good source of calcium) once she had slurped out their contents. And, of course, birds like Heartbeat routinely slotted me and other people at the sanctuary into their schema of helpful-other-animal. This is, perhaps, the avian complement of our longstanding image of the helpful bird.

Like most mammals, most birds are deeply dependent on *mother* for some significant period during which both brain and body are growing rapidly. Hence, for birds as for people, the match (or lack thereof) between archetypal and actual mothering is likely to have long-lasting repercussions. Here we begin to see the assault on avian psyches implicit in captivity. Chickens and other captive birds birthed in hatcheries awaken to the world under the chilly warmth of electric lights rather than within the soft darkness of their mothers' wings.

56. Peter Kropotkin, Mutual Aid: A Factor of Evolution (Black Rose Books Ltd., 1989).

Like Harlow's poor monkeys clinging to cloth dolls for contact comfort,[57] birds deprived of mothers scan their environments for anybody or anything that might offer a semblance of mothering.

Like orphaned children, orphaned birds may attach themselves to each other, inanimate objects, or members of other species. I have seen birds raised together on factory farms, where chicks from hatcheries grow to slaughter weight among thousands of other birds of the same age and sex, clumsily alternate in seeking shelter under one another's wings. When chicks found their way to the sanctuary directly from hatcheries, we tried to place them with surrogate mothers but sometimes no hen was willing to enact that role. Hence, a tiny bantam rooster we called Mighty Mouse came to serve as surrogate mother for a succession of "broiler" chickens who quickly grew to many times his size but still fled to him for comfort and protection. Mighty Mouse never betrayed his young charges, but the surrogates to whom farmed and domesticated birds turn often do. Perhaps the experiences of abused and neglected children can help us to understand the psychic impact when *mother* kills your siblings before your eyes or cages or mutilates you.

These forms of psychic cleavage may be less obvious or acute than the extreme suffering inflicted by egg factories or cockfighting, but are no less real. Furthermore, archetypal betrayal tends to be perpetrated in tandem with these more obviously traumatic practices. It is, after all, a *friend* or surrogate *mother* who drops the fighting rooster into the combat ring to face an armed and terrified *predator*. And all hens in egg factories began life in hatcheries, where they are deprived of both *mother* and *flock*, interacting only with similarly deprived chicks.

Avian Psyches in Situ

No bird is an island. No bird psyche exists except in relationship to the surrounding ecosocial system. Unfortunately for birds, people have profoundly (mis)shaped the circumstances of virtually every avian species, often to disastrous effect. Our collective impact on bird populations — which includes not only hunting them and crowding them out of their habitats but also poisoning water, lessening the availability of food, spreading disease, and altering the climate — has led to a 20 to 25 percent decline in the number of individual

57. H. F. Harlow, R. O. Dodsworth, and M. K. Harlow, "Total social isolation in monkeys.," Proceedings of the National Academy of Sciences of the United States of America 54, no. 1 (1965): 90-97.

birds in the world since 1500; within the next hundred years, one in ten bird species will be extinct, with another 15 percent endangered.[58] Statistics like these are usually discussed without reference to the psyches of the survivors. What would it be like to be one of the comparatively few remaining members of an endangered species? What *is* it like to have one's home chopped down unexpectedly or to arrive at one's summer home after a long journey only to find that there's no food because the flowers haven't bloomed or have already bloomed and died due to climate change? We have the same sort of limbic system as a bird. Surely we can imagine the combination of heart-pounding fear and dispiriting helplessness that must arise in birds at such moments. That is psychic trauma. Some birds must, like people in war zones, live with the psychically catastrophic conjunction of chronic arousal and helplessness. How do they cope with this? If they survive the crisis, what impact will the cumulative trauma have on the psyches of future generations?

Birds have demonstrated remarkable resilience and creativity in adapting to changed circumstance. Many have literally changed their tunes, adjusting the frequencies of their songs in order to be heard over or under the din of our noisy urban environments.[59] Presumably, such adaptability is rooted in many generations of natural selection favoring brain plasticity and behavioral flexibility. Unfortunately, we have not allowed all birds to enjoy the benefits of such natural selection. Our interference with bird reproduction — which has included such tactics as segregation, selective sterilization, and forcible impregnation and has reached its apex in genetic engineering — has profoundly influenced not only the bodies but also the psyches of individual birds while altering the course of evolution for entire species. The effects of this on the bodies of birds such as "broiler" chickens is well documented[60] and increasingly well known. The effects of so-called domestication on bird brains has received less attention but is likely substantial and tragic. For example, "there are good grounds for believing that the artificial domesticating selection that has affected pigeons for several thousand generations might have tended to blunt their intelligence."[61]

---

58. Roddy Scheer, "Researchers Predict Massive Avian Decline," E - The Environmental Magazine, December 2004, http://www.emagazine.com/view/?2200.

59. David Luther and Luis Baptista, "Urban noise and the cultural evolution of bird songs," Proceedings of the Royal Society B: Biological Sciences 277, no. 1680 (2010): 469-473.

60. Peter Stevenson, Leg and Heart Problems in Broiler Chickens, Briefing (Surrey, UK: Compassion in World Farming, 2003).

61. Delius et al., "Cognitions of birds," 455.

Interference with reproduction is but one way people have degenerated bird brains and psyches. The suffering of caged birds can scarcely be imagined, except perhaps by reference to the voluminous literature on the effects of solitary confinement on people, which include not only emotional unrest but significant degradation of cognitive functioning.[62] Let us examine two examples: Parrots and other "pet" birds confined alone in cages and chickens crowded together in batteries of egg factory cages. In both instances, the constant frustration of the impulse for flight and other free movement is compounded by the absence of normal social relations. In the case of solitary caged birds, the extent of their loneliness is evident if not quite imaginable. Birds are *social* animals. Every aspect of their brain and behavior evolved to fit eco*social* environments within which *social* relationships were the the most salient and essential elements. Perhaps even more insistently than ours do, their emotions tell them to seek and maintain relationships with others of their kind. As William Blake poetically opined, "robin redbreast in a cage" does indeed "put all heaven in a rage" in the sense of perverting the natural order.

For hens crowded into egg factory caged, the interference with normal social relationships and other activities is different but no less acute. Hens often choose to sleep close together at night, but they forage widely all day, spreading out to do so. Although they often dust-bathe collectively, many prefer privacy for egg laying. Hens in egg factories spend all day every day crowded into barren cages with scarcely enough room to lie down or turn around, much less stretch their wings or walk away from one another. The cacophony of unanswered distress cries of thousands of hens is deafening. Choking ammonia fumes rise from the manure pits beneath the batteries of cages. Hence, normal social interactions are impossible. Age mates who might otherwise have been valued companions become *competitors* from whom it is impossible to escape. As I wrote in 2006:

Have you ever been bored? Frustrated? Uncomfortable? Cranky? Imagine yourself crowded into a cage, often thirsty and always a little hungry, with nothing to do other than jostle your cage-mates. They're not your friends — they're your competitors. There's never enough space and never enough food for everybody to feel satisfied. You can't ever get comfortable. There's no place to go to get away from each other. And there's never anything to do!

62. S. Grassian, "Psychopathological effects of solitary confinement," American Journal of Psychiatry 140, no. 11 (November 1, 1983): 1450-1454.

One of your cage-mates keeps screaming. She won't shut up! Another is slumped in a stupor. She won't move out of the way! Somebody else is dying. No — she's dead. Your eyes burn. Your feet throb. Your wings ache to open. You can't turn around or lie down. You wait.

Ten minutes. Five hours. Three weeks. Eight months. Two years. Two years you may wait for relief from the tedium and pain. Then the cage opens but you are not released. Instead you are trucked to a painful and terrifying death at a slaughter factory or, if no buyer has been found for your bedraggled body, simply buried alive in a landfill.[63]

Hens fortunate enough to go to sanctuaries rather than landfills or slaughterhouses often spend hours or days in a dazed huddle, evidently unable to comprehend that they may now move freely. Others careen confusedly, unable to gauge distances or control their nearly atrophied muscles. Some seem sunk in a state of learned helplessness while others respond with panicked flight to every surprising stimulus. Over time, most recover both physical and emotional equilibrium by observing and interacting with other sanctuary residents. They sun bathe, lay their eggs in nests, and roost in the branches of trees. However, some remain forever psychically scarred by early deprivation and trauma, never demonstrating quite the same courage and confidence consistently evinced by feral hens.

For the Birds

Like most "broiler" chickens, Heartbeat died too young. Chickens bred by the poultry industry suffer a host of health problems due to decades of genetic selection for rapid and excessive growth. On what would be his last morning, Heartbeat was very still and weak but seemed to appreciate the soymilk-vitamin concoction I fed him by hand. But then the liquid began dribbling from his mouth and I knew the end was near. I carried him to a quiet spot, holding his body to my heart and his drooping head in my hand. Crouching in the shade of a mulberry bush, I cradled him as he went into his death throes. As his body jerked, I cried out, "No, no, don't go, don't go!" but then I said, "Go, go with the wild birds," and, "You'll never be alone." He went with his eyes open. For a while after he died I thought he was still alive because his little chest still seemed to be moving up and down. But then I realized it was just my own heartbeat.

63. pattrice jones, "I know why the caged birds scream," Satya Magazine, February 2006.

Our habit of using birds as symbols has been and continues to be hurtful to their psyches and our own. Symbolism is a kind of objectification. Using imaginary birds as symbols makes us more likely to treat actual animals as if they, too, were mere objects to be manipulated in service of our fantasies. On the other hand, our evolved tendency to see birds as signals may turn out to be useful to both us and them. Birds are salient features of our environment; we appear to be primed to notice and attend them. If we can clear away the clutter of cultural symbolism in order to see birds and their psyches more clearly, we may become better able to use our own brain plasticity and behavioral flexibility to cooperate with them in salvaging the wreck we've made of our shared world.

Within clinical psychology, we rightly consider people who manipulate other people as if they were objects to be sociopathic. Similarly, the belief that other people are insensate robots without thoughts or feelings is rightly considered to be psychotic thinking. Birds and other animals are sentient fellow beings but are treated by most people as insensate objects to be manipulated without remorse. The statistical normalcy of this ought not deflect us from perceiving the sociopathic and indeed psychotic character of these patterns of thought and behavior. In our beliefs and behaviors concerning birds and other denizens of our ecosocial environments, we are profoundly disordered animals. Our maladaptive destruction of our own habitat is similarly rooted in reductive objectification and the refusal to act reciprocally within relationships.

Might we, by thinking about bird psyches, reshape our own? If so, we and other species might derive substantial benefits from the exercise. Even if that is not the case, thinking about bird psyches in relation to our own may allow us to apply the insights of psychology to birds whose psyches have been damaged by people. At the Eastern Shore Sanctuary, we adapted techniques used in the treatment of traumatized people to devise a rehabilitation program for roosters used in cockfighting.[64] In brief, this process provides these unsocialized and traumatized birds safe spaces within which to become less afraid of other birds and, most importantly, learn *from* other birds the social lessons essential to peaceful coexistence within flocks.[65] Similarly, techniques used in the treatment of PTSD in people have been applied to the treatment of traumatized parrots.[66]

---

64. Efrati, "Bad Chickens." A1.

65. jones, "Roosters, hawks, and dawgs."

66. Allison Milionis, "Birds of a Feather," Los Angeles CityBeat, June 7, 2007, http://www.lacitybeat.com/article.php?id=5632&IssueNum=209.

Given the varieties of psychic trauma suffered by birds at the hands of people, much more work remains to be done in the realm of extending psychological care to traumatized birds. Pigeons, parrots, and other birds in captivity have long been deprived of both freedom and normal social relations by psychological researchers. Psychologists of all varieties can act to end this ongoing trauma by pressing for changes in the guidelines for ethical research. Clinical psychologists might begin the process of offering reparations for the long history of animal abuse within the field by volunteering their expertise to animal sanctuaries.

In their own practices, clinical psychologists must resist the tendency to collude with sociopathic behavior and psychotic thinking in relation to birds and other nonhuman animals. If a patient dreams of birds, don't leap to the conclusion that they must symbolize *something else*. Inquire about the client's thoughts, feelings, and behavior toward birds. Does he or she watch birds? Hunt birds? Eat birds? If she dotes on bluebirds but makes soup of duckings, look for the dissociations and delusions that facilitate that discrepancy. How does she block or blunt her awareness of bird suffering? What else *isn't* she thinking about? If you fear you may be overstepping your boundaries with such inquiries, remember that the survival of your client and her offspring depend in part on our collective ability to reorient ourselves in relation to the biosphere and its other inhabitants.

Perhaps because so many of its theorists and practitioners are analytic psychologists, ecopsychology tends to share the Jungian neglect of the body. Given that the impact of human bodies on the body of the planet is or should be at the heart of ecopsychological concerns, the disembodied quality of ecopsychology theory and practice is both curious and dangerous. The ideas about archetypes and the collective unconscious put forward here remind us that these are *bodily* processes rooted in *material* history, which is *ongoing*. What we think and feel both reflects and is shaped by what we *do*, including what we do to other animals. At present, ecopsychology as a field is woefully incomplete due to its wholesale neglect of actual human-animal relations. Like other clinical psychologist, practicing ecopsychologists can begin to remedy this by by speaking with clients about birds and other animals *not* as symbols of the wished-for wild but as fellow beings whose own wishes must be recognized if we are to wrest ourselves out of ecologically destructive wishful thinking.

No animal sanctuary needs to be reminded that animals seeking refuge often arrive with psychic damage. The good news is that the psychic similarity of people and birds opens up new avenues of treatment for psychologically disturbed birds. The natural sociality and behavioral plasticity of birds, in conjunction with the remarkable ease with which they may view a member of another species as *mother* or *friend*, means that we often can extend psychologically reparative care to them. However, because birds are social animals with brains and bodies evolved for flock life, other birds must be part of the process of recovery. Full recovery can only be achieved within the context of relationships with other birds, ideally including integration into a pair bond or flock. At the Eastern Shore Sanctuary, people could help former fighting roosters become less afraid of other birds. But only other birds could model for them the social behavior through which roosters naturally mediate their relations.

Many birds at the sanctuary demonstrated both the desire and the ability to "rewild" themselves, shifting gradually from reliance on the sanctuary to living freely in self-selected flocks within which they raised successive generations of young, some of whom were never touched by human hands. Similarly, I have seen wild flocks of chickens (presumably the offspring of cockfighting industry escapees) living happily in a forest in Maui. While the norm for animal sanctuaries is to limit the reproduction of their residents, full psychological recovery — for individual and for species — cannot be achieved in the context of continued reproductive control. Hence, for birds at least, sanctuaries where space and circumstances make this feasible ought to restore reproductive freedom to their inhabitants, thereby returning to them the freedom to forge their own flocks and families.

One fine September afternoon, the founder of another sanctuary[67] *stopped by to pick up some brochures. She was distraught, having just come from euthanizing a bird at the animal hospital. People always ask her, she said, "How can you keep going without getting upset?" What they don't understand, she said, her voice rising, is that "I'm always upset!" Casting around for something, anything, to bring a little cheer into her day, I suddenly remembered: The feral chicks! Over the summer, the hen we called Minya had gone missing for so long we feared her dead. Suspecting she might be brooding eggs, we'd searched the underbrush for her with no luck. Just when we'd given up and begun to mourn her, Minya reappeared, trailing seven chicks in her wake. Thus we got our first chance to see chicks as the young birds they we meant to be. Minya encouraged them to forage rather than rely on the feed bowls. We watched as she showed them how to perch on higher and higher bushes. We gasped with wonder and trepidation one night*

67. This was United Poultry Concerns founder Karen Davis, who died as this volume was being prepared for publication. This chapter is dedicated to the memory of her steadfast dedication to chickens.

at twilight when Minya decided it was time to return to the trees. Jumping onto a low branch, she called to her chicks. All but one followed readily, and the straggler made it eventually. Minya then led them to successively higher branches until they roosted, the young birds arrayed on either side of their mother, and fell asleep far from the reach of any predator. Wanting to share the wonder of that moment with my friend, I dragged her into the backyard, where Minya and her chicks usually could be found foraging. They were so nimble and clever at fading into the shadows that we were only able to catch a glimpse of their tail feathers as they advanced into the woods.

3

Angry Emus

In December of 2018, I had the honor of delivering the opening keynote for the Animal Studies Network *Animaladies II* conference at the University of Wollongong in Australia. Just prior to the conference, one of the emus at VINE Sanctuary died. While she had been elderly, her death felt tragic to me because she had spent only a couple of years at the sanctuary after decades at a petting zoo and because, as I kept saying to myself, "emus don't belong in Vermont anyway!" And so one of the themes of the talk was the necessity of taking action in the face of almost certain failure when it is not at all clear what to do. I thought, and still think, that emus have something to teach us about that.

It seemed impossible to say everything I wanted to say but, with the help of gestures, movement, and the energy of other attendees, I managed to communicate much of what I'd hoped to convey at the conference. But then, when it came time to write the talk up for the *Animal Studies Journal*, I floundered again. It's hard for me to see anything other than my failures when I reread the piece. But, rather than rewriting yet again, I'm going to let it stand as an example of part of what I was trying to say: Do it anyway.

Derangement and Resistance

Reflections from Under the Glare of an Angry Emu

The situations of emus may illuminate the maladies of human societies. From the colonialism that led Europeans to tamper with Australian ecosystems through the militarism that mandated Great Emu War of 1932 to the consumer capitalism that sparked a global market for 'exotic' emus and their products, habits of belief and behavior that hurt humans have wreaked havoc on emus. Literally de-ranged, emus abroad today endure all of the estrangements of emigres in addition to the frustrations and sorrows of captivity. In Australia, free emus struggle to survive as climate change parches already diminished and polluted habitats. We have shot them with machine guns and plowed them down with motor cars. We have parched and poisoned their landscapes. But still they stride. Queer in every sense of the word, emus can remind us of the resilience of eros and instruct us on the praxis of resistance in catastrophic situations.

Under the Gaze of Emus

Five emus stalk the forested hills of VINE Sanctuary, an LGBTQ-led farmed animal refuge in the northeastern United States. There used to be six. One, called Louise, died shortly after I began researching this piece. Like all sanctuary folks, I have witnessed many deaths. Few have felt to me as tragic. Before coming to the sanctuary, Louise and her companion Thelma had spent more than 20 years in a small enclosure in a petting zoo. Her time with us was too short to recover from that trauma, if such a recovery would even be possible, and emus don't belong in Vermont anyway. The best that we could do for her was not good enough, and it is within that understanding of potential futility that I write today.

In Australia and around the world, wildfires rage as the slow-rolling emergency of climate change becomes ever more urgent despite decades of environmental activism. At the same time, persistent catastrophes such as war and poverty continue despite centuries of struggle for peace and equality. As I have argued previously concerning pigeons and capitalism, trying to see problems from animal standpoints can "change the question"[1] in ways that may lead to new insights. Bipeds who stand at about the height of humans, emus view the world from a vantage point that is simultaneously like and unlike our own. They have persisted for longer than humans have existed, and they continue to resist our hegemony while coping with the wreckage we've wreaked on their habitats. They may know us better than we know ourselves, and so it may be worthwhile to look at ourselves from their point of view.

I don't know whether you can imagine what it's like to walk along a wooded path with an emu on either side of you as you lug a jug of water down to the shelter that they refuse to use, no matter how cold or snowy it gets, except when the guys are sitting on eggs. They're about my height, so we are eye-to-eye, and I'm always aware that they could really hurt me if they wanted to. I'm pretty sure they're aware of that too.

The two who have walked side by side with me are called Tiki and Breeze, a father and son both born in captivity who came to the sanctuary in the wake of a tragedy. Along with Adele, who arrived some years later after being rescued from starvation at a roadside zoo, Tiki and Breeze conduct their affairs in what seems to be an approximation of the usual behavior of emus in their natural habitat. They have adapted themselves to the vagaries of their oddball environs ably, easily chasing off the sneaky sheep and rambunctious cows who like to steal snacks of emu food. (It's pretty funny to see thousand-pound cows chased by scrawny birds.) Overall, they have adjusted well to the social and environmental circumstances of the sanctuary, and this is reflected in their easygoing gaze as they walk alongside you on the path or approach you when you're filling water troughs on a hot day, indicating that they'd like a cooling shower from the hose you're holding.

That relaxed regard is very different than the angry glare of the emu in the title of this piece. Thelma arrived at the sanctuary a couple of years ago along with Louise, with whom she had been confined for two decades at a petting zoo. I feel fairly certain that Thelma is mad in both senses of the word. She has attacked both people and other emus. Her gaze is truly fearsome.

---

1. jones, "Property, Profit, and (Re)Production," 33.

I try not to flinch from it. I agree with Lori Gruen that "dignity is better understood as a relational concept"[2] that can be fostered, in a cross-species context, by being willing to be looked at by the animals upon whom one gazes. It can be difficult, though, to imagine what they think about what they see. When we think, our perceptions and ideas tend to be filtered and shaped by language, so much so that it can be hard to hang onto sensations and notions for which we don't have words. When we write, we arrange words into linear sentences and sentences into linear paragraphs, hoping that this process of compression and sequencing won't do too much damage to the holistic sense of what we are trying to say. This is always a fraught process, and becomes more so in this case, as emu perceptions do not necessarily conform to the boundaries of what human sound-signals can communicate, and emu cognition cannot be presumed to abide by our linear logics.

Thus, I find what I want to say after spending some months imagining myself into an emu point of view swirling in ways that resist efforts to conform them to the confines of an academic paper. For example, above I struggled vainly to come up with adequate synonyms for madness and mad-ness. Mad-ness is anger, that's easy. But our conceptions of the other kind of madness are inflected by our over-valuation of rationality, by which we falsely define the human. In this foundational human error, we both falsely fail to recognize the cognitions of other animals but also trick ourselves into mistaking the narrow slice of our cognition that is conscious thought for our very selves. Emus are not, so far as we know, deluded about themselves in that way. And so, when I speak of madness among emus I am talking about something analogous to when your body is flooded with feeling in a way that interferes with however you would usually navigate the word. You're panicked or enraged or otherwise jangled so much so that your perceptions or behaviors or communications or thoughts — or all of the above! — go astray. Like emus, we exist today in a world gone mad, in which the very climate has gone awry. Our bodies must know this, even as we continue to go about everyday life. We will need more of ourselves than our conscious minds to cope with that chronic emergency.

Please bear with me or — even better — join me by deliberately loosening your own associations and entering into an imaginary where you are just another animal to an emu, hoping to learn something from what they see about you or the situations created by others of your kind. Even though it may be difficult and disorienting, let us ask: How do emus themselves see their

2. Gruen, "Dignity, Captivity, and an Ethics of Sight," 232,

circumstances? How do they see us? How have they coped with both madness and mad-ness? Let's learn what we can from the living dinosaurs who dodge bullets, jump fences, know very well how dangerous humans can be, and have not yet conceded defeat. Let's begin by learning their history.

Feathered Dinosaurs

Our knowledge of emus can only be fractional because the span of human interactions with emus constitutes such a short segment of their much longer history. Even the fact of their much longer tenure must be surmised from fossilized fragments, to which human scientists have applied ever-changing methods of dating and analysis. Those fossils date back to the Miocene epoch (which ended more than five million years ago), from which there are remains of birds who differ only slightly from present-day emus; fossilized remains from the Pliocene epoch (which ended more than two million years ago) are "indistinguishable from the living emu."[3] By way of contrast, anatomically modern humans date back only about 160,000 years.

Therefore, emus knew each other, and other animals knew emus, long before any humans even existed to imagine the existence of such a bird. We can only dimly envisage the hundreds upon hundreds of thousands of years in which these flightless birds established and maintained their communities, transmitting habits and knowledge from each generation to the next. Therefore we must be modest in drawing conclusions based on our comparatively limited observations. We should also be aware that our perceptions may be skewed by biases. In the midst of The Great Emu war, which will be discussed below, a soldier spoke respectfully of the enemy, thus:

The emus have proved that they are not so stupid as they are usually considered to be. Each mob has its leader, always an enormous black-plumed bird standing fully six-feet high, who keeps watch while his fellows busy themselves with the wheat. At the first suspicious sign, he gives the signal, and dozens of heads stretch up out of the crop. A few birds will take fright, starting a headlong stampede for the scrub, the leader always remaining until his followers have reached safety.[4]

In point of fact, emu females tend to be larger than the males, so the enormous leaders seen by the soldier probably were female. And they probably

3. Patterson and Rich, "The Fossil History of the Emus," 85.

4. Crew, "The Great Emu War."

weren't leaders or even designated look-outs. Like many birds who graze in flocks, emus collaboratively alternate between eating and keeping watch while others eat. Here we can see how human ideas about gender and hierarchy can lead to 'observations' that confirm stereotypes.

Here's a fun fact: For a long time, the only emu sex that people had witnessed and recorded was homosexual sex,[5] so there was a period of time when, if all we had to go by was the observations of people, we would have to presume that male emus were exclusively homosexual and female emus somehow fertilized their own eggs. Which brings us to emu queerness. We can say that emus are 'queer' both in the sense of confounding our categories and in the sense that they are among the hundreds of species in which same-sex affection, parenting, and sex are common. Emus are birds who run rather than fly. The females are the fighters. The males hatch eggs and raise chicks, as single parents or in co-parenting relationships with other males; some male emus enjoy sexual relations with other males, and those relations tend to be marked by more gestures of affection than heterosexual matings.[6]

In these ways, emus are similar to other ratites, and thus we may safely presume that this has been an abiding feature of emu society. But what of the attacks by female emus on nesting males and unfledged juveniles that have sometimes been seen by people?[7] It's certainly possible that this has always been the case for emus, but it is also conceivable that such violence is a reaction to the traumatic circumstances in which emus have found themselves ever since humans happened upon their territories. As Bradshaw has ably demonstrated concerning elephants, hunting and habitat destruction by humans can not only traumatize individual animals but also, over time, their cultures.[8]

Everything changed for emus once they became the prey of mammals with weapons, and everything changed again when another wave of humans began clearing their habitat for farmland. As enduring as they have been, emus must be capable of changing their habits in response to changes in their environments. We cannot know which of their seemingly innate behaviors might be relatively recent responses to trauma. For example, here at the sanctuary as well as in the wild, emus tend to keep to themselves, mixing with other animals

---

5. Bagemihl, Biological Exuberance, 32.

6. Ibid., 622-623.

7. Ibid., 625.

8. Bradshaw, Elephants on the Edge.

less often than many other birds like to do. Has it always been this way, or did they become more insular in response to either or both of their near-extinction experiences?

Near-Death Experiences

As a person of European descent, I need to note that what follows does not in any way excuse or mitigate the later depredations visited upon both emus and indigenous people by Europeans, but if I am to tell the story from the emu point of view, then I must report that the arrival of the first humans to occupy the lands now called Australia was a calamity that led directly to their first brush with extinction.[9] Sixty thousand years ago, after millions of years of relative peace as animals with few predators, emus encountered an existential threat when the first humans to populate their habitats arrived with weapons, a taste for animal flesh, and the ability to start fires. When those humans discovered that oil made from the layer of fat that allows emus to tolerate both heat and cold could be used to treat various ailments, emus became an even more valuable target. We cannot imagine, although I think that we should at least try to imagine, what an earth-shattering surprise it must have been for individual emus to encounter beings unlike any they had seen before and to see their friends and family members ensnared or slain by objects they could not have imagined. Collectively, emus also faced an increasingly difficult quest for food as fires reduced forests and grasslands to scrub.[10]

Since our interest is in the emus' experience of this cataclysm, the ideas of their hunters, while important in other contexts, need not be visited in detail here. What mattered to emus was what happened to emus, and what happened was a catastrophe beyond imagining. Some species of emu did not survive the encounter, and evidence suggests that the surviving species came close to extinction. The first peoples of what is now Australia hunted emus with spears as well as with poisoned water and other forms of trickery. That last leads me to wonder whether emus, who to this day sometimes approach some people trustingly, used to be more sociable with humans and other animals. Here is where indigenous ideas about emus may be relevant to their story. As many hunters of many cultures have done historically and continue to do today, the

9. Carroll and Martine, "An Ecological and Cultural Review of the Emu," 78.

10. Miller et al., "Ecosystem Collapse in Pleistocene Australia and a Human Role in Megafaunal Extinction," 287.

first people to fortify their own lives by killing emus developed admiring ideas about their prey. Let us presume that hunters who professed reverence for emus really did feel great respect when approaching with a gift of poisoned fruit or a spear behind their back. Detecting that reverent energy, a bird who would otherwise run away or attack might allow such a person to come near, with fatal results. Any animal observing such a turnabout would be wise to become more wary. Sixty thousand years of such betrayals by people who approached as friends would be more than enough time for emus culture to adapt by adopting a less trusting attitude toward others.

That is speculation, but what is certainly true is that emus did not cede their inherent entitlement to peaceably occupy the lands in which they evolved. Again, caution is warranted. It's essential, when speaking of relations among humans, to recognize that the first humans to occupy these lands have not ceded their right — in the sense of agreements among humans about who will live where, how human relations within those territories will be governed, and how resources within those territories will be shared among humans — to those lands. But while speaking of nonhuman animals, and especially when trying to see things from their perspectives, then it is also important to remember that nonhuman animals have not consented to the conceptions of property implicit in human 'ownership' of any lands. Emus do not think of their homeland by any of the names that people call it, and they have not ceded to any humans the territory to which they are truly indigenous.

Perhaps through cultural changes such as becoming more wary, emus did adapt to the persistent threat of predation by humans, thereby surviving as a species even as individuals perished. I imagine that, if an emu historian were to divide time into epochs, there would be the multi-million year epoch of relative peace, a comparatively brief emergency period following the arrival of the first humans, a sixty thousand year era of vigilance following their adaptation to this new threat, and then another period of emergency beginning about 200 years upon the arrival of another group of humans. The emergency set off by that new wave of human immigration to emu lands led directly to their second near-extinction experience and continues to threaten their long-term survival even though emus are no longer considered at risk of immediate annihilation.

The new humans — who emus might or might not have noticed were different in coloration than the humans who came before — were much more numerous and much more lethal, sharply increasing the number of emus killed directly by humans while at the same time escalating the displacement of emus from their former lands and the despoliation of their remaining habitat. Again, this must have been such a surprise. By then, emus probably had an idea of the human based on the behavior of the humans they had watched warily for the past sixty thousand years. That idea did not include firearms or indiscriminate mass killing. These new humans even went so far as to explicitly wage war on emus.

Consider these headlines from Australian newspapers:

ELUSIVE EMUS (Canberra Times, 5 Nov 1932)

WAR ON EMUS: Machine Guns to be Withdrawn (Melbourne Argus, 10 Nov 1932)

REQUEST TO USE BOMBS TO KILL EMUS (Adelaide Mail, 3 Jul 1943)

New Strategy In a War On The Emu (Sydney Sunday Herald, 5 Jul 1953)

The term 'Great Emu War' refers to the battles of 1932-34 but, as the latter two headlines demonstrate, hostilities continued for decades. The battles of the 1930s began at the behest of farmers, many of whom were veterans of the first World War. Troops were sent out with machine guns, to mow down mobs of emus for the crime of refusing to recognise fields as private property belonging to humans. But the emus proved to be more able adversaries than anticipated, watching out while grazing and fleeing at the first sign of an assault, sometimes literally dodging bullets as they escaped. Hundreds were killed but thousands remained. Eventually, the government withdrew the troops but provided local citizens with ammunition, which the soldier-farmers used to kill more than 57,000 emus in the latter half of 1934.[11]

Imagine the devastation, to individuals and to social groups, of such massacres. Notice that, nonetheless, emus did not concede defeat. At no point, then or since, did emus signal consent for their former stomping grounds to be occupied, fenced, and despoiled by people. To the contrary! While emus do, wisely, tend to approach human habitations warily, they continue to disregard boundaries established by people. In Australia and around the world, local newspapers and television news programs regularly feature stories of wild or escaped emus going where they want to go regardless of where we humans think they ought to be.

Globalization

Around the world? Yes, some decades after the Great Emu War, descendants of its survivors would be subjected to new indignities, courtesy of capitalism. As had been the case with colonialism, the malignant growth of consumer

---

11. Crew, "The Great Emu War."

capitalism, with its incessant demand for new products and new markets, caused incalculable harm to emus and other nonhuman animals. Reduced to salable objects to be literally broken up into salable parts (flesh, feathers, eggs, skin), these formerly free birds now pace the confines of enclosures on every continent except Antarctica.

It's impossible to know whether this is something that emus have figured out about humans, but our own social nature makes us liable to fall for fads. Within capitalist cultures, 'get rich quick' schemes are particularly popular. Unfortunately for emus, they and their eggs have been shipped around the world to persons in search of easy profits. Most often, those dreams of riches have turned to ruin, with often gruesome outcomes for the unprofitable big birds. The only upside to this sad state of affairs is that it might, in the end, make it more likely for emus to survive the anthropocene.

The San Diego Zoo in the United States boasts of breeding and selling more than one thousand emus to other zoos in the years between 1948 and 1976. Whatever their intentions, they proved that emus could be bred in captivity. In the 1970s, the government of Australia allowed 300 emus to be captured as "a primary breeding stock for domestication."[12] By the 1980s, the idea that emus could be easily and profitably farmed began to be advertised outside Australia. This set off an emu boom in the United States, at the apex of which would-be emu ranchers paid each other exorbitant sums for breeding pairs.[13] When the boom went bust in the 1990s due to consumer indifference to emu meat, hundreds of thousands of birds were at the mercy of captors who often had no money to feed them. Some were left to starve in their pens, others let loose to fend for themselves. Some suffered extreme violence, such as being beaten to death by a baseball bat, at the hands of their frustrated former caregivers.

A similar situation has arisen recently in India, and again captive emus have been freed by the thousands as a result of "what began as a farming fad and turned into a Ponzi scheme."[14] As many as two million emus were concentrated on thousands of farms at the height of the craze just a few years ago. While some large scale ranches remain, nobody knows how many emus were let loose to fend for themselves after it became clear that the supply far exceeded the demand for emu products. Since the characteristics that allowed emus to survive for millions of years in Australia include the ability to tolerate drought,

---

12. Menon, Bennett, and Cheng, "Understanding the Behavior of Domestic Emus," 1.

13. Dallas Morning News, "Texans Unnerved by Roaming Emus Birds."

14. Upton, "The Emu Has Landed (in India)."

eat a wide array of plants and insects, survive extreme temperature shifts, and camouflage themselves in forests, it's possible that colonies of discarded emus could establish themselves there and elsewhere even as their habitat in Australia is devastated by climate change.

While such 'rewilding' is devoutly to be wished, let us keep in mind the fact that more emus are currently held in captivity elsewhere than Australia than are free anywhere. While some 700,000 emus stalk the grounds of Australia[15] (Birdlife International), this number is eclipsed by those held by hundreds of zoos (including both major zoological parks and roadside petting zoos) and thousands of ranches (ranging from industrial farms to small homesteads) around the world. Let us consider the impact of that captivity. Emus cannot be considered 'domesticated' birds. There have been no changes to their bodies or behavior as a result of a few decades of breeding in captivity. Like many other unfortunate prisoners of zoos, emus are wild animals who have not yet, if they ever would, evolved characteristics that might make captivity more tolerable to them. They are long-legged roamers whose bodies want to walk for most of every day. Hence, those who are not sunk into a state of depression tend to incessantly pace the perimeters of their enclosures.

Emus in captivity endure both invasions of privacy and interference with autonomy. On ranches, they are herded and handled in ways that assault both their dignity and their bodies. At zoos, they may be on display in ways that prevent them from disappearing into the foliage in the way that they usually would when confronted by humans who are strangers to them. At petting zoos, they may be held in tiny enclosures in order to make it possible for strangers to reach out and touch them. Whether on farms or at zoos, emus may be subject to forced breeding programs in which males are mauled for their sperm and then females held down and forcibly inseminated. The resulting eggs may be artificially incubated, so that hatchings enter the world alone rather than under the feathers of their fathers.

All of these things are done to emus in places that must feel profoundly alien to them, where the weather, the flora, the terrain, and even the skies differ from the environment their bodies come into the world ready to roam. This is true, to a lesser degree, even for emus in Australia, where human development, pollution, and climate change have rapidly reshaped landscapes in only a few decades. This is why I say that emus are literally de-ranged.

15. Birdlife International, "Common Emu (Dromaius Novaehollandiae) - BirdLife Species Factsheet."

Derangement

"They're like royalty from another planet... regal, but confused." Thus said duck rescuer Sarahjane Blum upon encountering emus in the woods of VINE Sanctuary. She had a point. The ecologies in which they evolved have been disrupted and despoiled; they have been displaced within Australia and transported around the world; and now climate change makes even familiar places dangerously strange.

Imagine the psychological impact of this. If emu minds, like ours and those of other social animals, are molded by interactions with conspecifics, what does it mean for them to grow up not within a small mob of other emus traversing forests filled with foraging opportunities but instead in unnaturally large and crowded aggregations on barren farms or, in the alternative, alone or among too few others of their kind at a petting zoo or as 'pets'? And what of the material environmental elements that shaped emu bodies, including emu brains, but from which they are now estranged? We humans are only just beginning to understand the complex interactions implicit in ecologies. It's not at all certain that our own brains are capable of glimpsing all of the factors that might be meaningful to emus, much less grasping the ways that the absence of some of these might madden them.

Starting from this baseline derangement, emus must cope with multitudinous crises and traumas engendered by human behavior. Imagine an escaped emu fleeing a California wildfire or a mob of Australian emus driven by thirst to approach a human settlement where water might be found. Or try, as I have done, to imagine the minds of a pair of emus confined for two decades in a small enclosure at a petting zoo until the facility downsizes and they are unceremoniously dumped in an unfamiliar place (which happens to be a sanctuary, but they cannot know this) where they suddenly encounter wide-open spaces and strangers of many species. Given all that we know about the fight-or-flight response to fright, it's no surprise that Louise sped off in a mad dash that ended in a snowdrift that first night nor that Thelma attacked sanctuary staff members so often over the next few months that we had to create a foraging yard for just the two of them, with a gate that could be closed when visitors were on site.

We can't know exactly what fear feels like to an emu, but birds and humans share the same basic limbic system responsible for emotion (as well as some of the same physical manifestations of fright, such as elevated heart rate and dilated pupils. I've spent enough time with roosters used in cockfighting to know that repeated extreme terror can lead to an avian equivalent of Post-Traumatic Stress Disorder, wherein a bird is more quick to feel fearful and more slow to return to a relaxed resting state than their peers.[16] Like songbirds, the ancestors of chickens evolved in ecological situations in which they were prey for many species. Perhaps as a consequence of this, such birds not only respond almost instantaneously to a threat such as a hawk or a fox but also seem able to calm down and return to normal foraging almost immediately. But emus evolved in different circumstances. Prior to the arrival of humans in their habitat, they had few predators. Perhaps this is why, at least in my observations, they remain on edge much longer than other birds after any sort of fright.

Both at liberty in Australia and in captivity abroad, emus today encounter far more frequent terrifying happenings than their bodies evolved to survive. At home, there are more wildfires, more motor cars, and more unpredictable human beings with their mystifying weapons. In captivity abroad, emus endure frights on top of the frustrations and indignities already discussed. To be herded and handled by mammals must be always alarming and even more terrifying when the handlers are deliberately hurtful or accidentally rough.

Breeze's mother, whose name we never knew, was one of those emus who turn up on the local news. She and Tiki had been purchased by a retired dairy farmer as pets for his grandchildren. They languished in a shockingly small yard for more than a decade, in the course of which Breeze was hatched and raised by Tiki. And then one day the female jumped the fence. For weeks, people called in sitings as she ambled from place to place, foraging and minding her own business. Then a would-be rescuer decided that she would be better off back in captivity and literally scared her to death (official cause of death: heart attack) while trying to capture her. That tragic turn of events motivated the retired farmer to allow the other two to be taken to a sanctuary. The people who transported them injured Breeze so badly that he couldn't stand, and it was only the extreme ingenuity of caregiver Cheryl Wylie, who devised a sling from old lawn furniture and then invented a physical therapy program for him, that he stalks the grounds of the sanctuary today.

It's a thin line between flight and fight, by which I mean fear and rage. Flight seems to be the default for most of us when faced with a dangerous situation. Only when escape seems impossible are animals likely to stand and fight. While they cannot fly, emus can run rapidly and — as evidenced during the Great Emu War, when they literally dodged bullets—seem to have excellent evasive reflexes. But they cannot run when they are confined in small enclosures, and they cannot run when they have been lassoed by human handlers, and they certainly

16. jones, "Roosters, Hawks and Dawgs," 369-370; jones, "Harbingers of (Silent) Spring," 205.

cannot run when held down to be forcibly ejaculated or impregnated. At such time their bodies may be telling them to fight, fight, fight. But, since emus fight most effectively by means of flying kicks launched from a run, they cannot do that either. People are most likely to develop PTSD when they are unable to escape, fight back, or take any other effective action in response to a horrifying event, and it seems probable to me that this is true for emus too. Thus, it seems safe to conclude— even without also considering indignity, frustration, grief, boredom, and other sorrows—that the preponderance of emus today exist within a perpetual state of derangement, the visceral experience of which we can only imagine. Nevertheless, they persist and resist, creating new pathways by walking.

Outlaws

Emus are outlaws on the planet of the apes, conducting their affairs without regard for regulations created by the hegemonic humans. Runaway emus hide themselves in forests, and mobs of emus descend on fields. As birds who have had war declared upon them by people and who continue to contest both captivity and human hegemony, emus illustrate the outlaw status of nonhuman animals, some of whom are protected by law from the most egregious abuses but none of whom are party to the agreements among humans that laws represent. While it can be easy for humans not to see the violence (armies, prisons, police) backing up even the most democratic of those agreements, emus are unlikely to forget that aggregations of humans always represent a threat.

From their vantage point, we may be the mob of deranged outlaws, endangering everybody by persistently flouting the rules of sensible behavior that most other animals seem to follow. When a subset of people collectively eschew the norms that make peaceful coexistence among people possible, the rest of us have to decide what to do to bring those folks back into the fold or protect ourselves from them. Do emus see human beings as a subset of animals who have gone wrong? I sometimes think that if there were some sort of parliament of fowls debating what to do about humans, emus would be arguing for the death penalty. I don't think we have to suicidally adopt that particular point of view, but perhaps we could think about what being allies of animals who see us as the problem really might mean. To do that, we will need to consider what emus may have learned about humans in the course of sixty thousand years of eying us warily.

Emu Perspectives on the Human

What might emus as a collectivity know about humans, based on their accumulated experiences? First, more so than we are generally comfortable admitting, emus understand that human beings often are dangerous and untrustworthy, so much so that the safest wager would be to presume danger and duplicity in the absence of other information. Emus know that humans are capable of the most depraved cruelty and cunning trickery. Emus probably don't know that the dishonesty goes as deep as it does, that we fool ourselves without knowing that we are doing so, but that may be what makes this exercise useful: Emus know what we do, not what we claim to be doing or think we are doing.

Emus know that much of what we do is nonsensical. Watching us polluting our own water supplies, cutting down forests upon which everyone depends, or accumulating thousands of birds only to let them go again, emus would be unlikely to share the assessment of homo sapiens as especially wise or uniquely rational. Attuned to our gestures, energy, and tone of voice rather than to the semantics of our sound-symbols, emus may be more aware than we of the role that emotion plays in determining our behavior.

Emus also know that humans are variable, capable not only of senseless violence but also of kindness. Despite all that humans have done to emus over the centuries, some emus still will initiate friendships with some humans. At times of crisis, such as droughts in Australia, some emus seek out humans who might share water with them. They do this because they know that it is at least possible that we will behave generously. They probably are also prepared to attack if we do not, but the fact that they tend to approach in peace suggests an awareness that some humans sometimes do the right thing.

What can we do with this information? First, focus on more on what people do and less on what people say and think. While the causal connections between what we think and what we do may be circuitous or counter-intuitive, altering behavior is sometimes as simple as making it easier to behave appropriately and harder to cause harm. If something as simple as large and visible recycling bins eclipsing tiny rubbish bins can change behavior—and it can—there must be many more ways we can nudge ourselves and each other to behave more responsibly. At present, the people promoting such measures tend to be technocrats implementing top-down solutions to state-identified problems or 'conscious capitalists' seeking to create change via consumerism, but there's no reason we could not, working from within an ecofeminist ethos that recognizes the power of place, engender grassroots efforts wherein people collectively agree to create circumstances that foster better human behavior. Or, taking a page from the guerrilla emu handbook, direct action of various kinds might make it harder to behave harmfully or easier to behave kindly.

Some may balk at such behavior-based approaches, which may seem to undermine human dignity. I wrestle as I write, wondering whether and how much we are obliged to honor a dignity that may be implicitly based in self-deceptive notions of the sagacity and rationality of humans. After nearly twenty years of trying to see situations from non-human points of view and more than forty years of trying, by various means, to stop humans from hurting each other, I have come to believe that speciesism contributes to our persistent inability to solve social problems. Speciesism confuses us not only about other animals but also about ourselves. Specifically, speciesism teaches us to vest our dignity in the ways that we allegedly differ from other animals, exaggerating the role that our vaunted reasoning actually plays in determining human behavior.

Most of our cognition occurs outside of conscious awareness. Our bodies often make choices ahead of our conscious minds, which then scramble to come up with ex post facto explanations. Why, then, do we persist in trying to solve the most difficult problems mostly by means of changing what people consciously think, know, feel, or believe? Only because we have devalued our bodies, our emotions, our non-conscious cognition, and our nonverbal ways of communicating. As the word-based world of social media cracks the very foundations of consensus reality, paving the way for demagogues who do not hesitate to harmfully manipulate humans by means of emotion, perhaps it is time for those on the side of peace and equality to set aside Enlightenment ideals of human rationality in order to honestly and whole-heartedly engage people as they are rather than as they imagine themselves to be. For too long, we have imagined rationality as a kind of check on human animality that mitigates our dangerousness to each other. But surely the time has come to see that our frontal lobes, like our thumbs, are value-neutral body parts, equally able to solve problems or wreak havoc. Perhaps it is time to bring the rest of our bodies, which are as much ourselves as the narrow range of perception and cognition of which we are aware, into the struggle.

Emus have seen the worst of us and then worse than that. Nonetheless, to this day, emus sometimes approach people with what can be called hope. They may or may not be aware of the complex confluence of choice and circumstance that determine whether any given person will behave kindly or cruelly on any given day, but they do know—and we should know too—that it is possible for us to behave less selfishly and violently than has been our unfortunate norm. It's up to us to adjust our own situations in order to enhance the likelihood of better behavior and thereby improve the situations of emus.

Eros

Tiki, Breeze, and Adele seem as content as it is possible for emus in such strange surrounds as a sanctuary in the northeastern United States to be. Louise did not attain that level of contentment before she died, and it seems unlikely that elderly Thelma will attain happiness before following her longtime companion into the grave. A more recent arrival, Earhart, spent we-don't-know-how-many years alone and has not yet figured out how to make friends with either the other emus or other sanctuary residents. He does seem to enjoy the woods, and perhaps he communes with wild birds in ways we don't recognize, but he may never enjoy the pleasure of communion with conspecifics and always will be far from his ancestral homelands.

The situation for emus seems unlikely to improve any time soon, and it seems unlikely that emus themselves feel anything resembling hope that human beings will collectively change our behavior. But: They do wish for that. When a drought-parched emu in Australia approaches a human habitation in search of water, it is with the wish that the people inside will behave kindly, or at least non-violently. They know they are taking a risk, but deep desire for what they need drives them to try.

Emus know that they are at war. This conflict simmered for sixty thousand years and has been raging for the past two hundred. Emus today may be unable to imagine any other way of being in the world other than perpetual battle with human beings. Nor may they be able to guess what a life less stressed by all of the harms engendered by humans might feel like. And still they stride.

Emus know, whether they think of it in these terms or not, that the environment is increasingly less habitable. They feel thirst and see wildfires. They know. And still they stride.

This suggests to me that we may be asking the wrong question when we wonder whether hope is warranted in the anthropocene. Emus walk and have kept on walking these 60,000 years since their first encounter with members of the species that would wreck their world again and again not because they have hope for a different future but because they have desire right now. That desire, which we might also call Eros, drives their persistence and their resistance.

Thus, the secret of emu survival isn't hope. It's desire. Emus want and so they act. They create paths by walking.

Relentless desire lives in us too. If we want is to be in better relationship to emus and other animals, then we will need to tap into that, resisting any urge to make it more rational or less queer because "Eros can't be hurried, ordered around, or expected to march in anything like a straight line."[17] If we can draw on our own deepest desires, maybe one day we will be able to stride alongside emus as trusted friends. It won't be easy, but wellsprings of emotion and imagination that have been dammed and diverted by the cults of rationality and consumption are there to help.

Stars in the sky have been burning since before there were people to see them. Among those stars are a cluster that the first people to see emus recognized as having the same shape as those big birds — the so-called Emu constellation.[18] It is maybe a measure of the human predilection for magical thinking that I find it soothing to imagine photons from those stars persistently finding their way to the feathers of emus as they persist despite what has now been a longer than sixty thousand year struggle to survive the human. I dare to dream that, whatever we do or don't do, they will continue to stride.

This essay is dedicated to the memory of Louise, to the fighting spirit of Thelma, and to the trees among whom Earhart feels most safe.

Works Cited

Bagemihl, Bruce. *Biological Exuberance: Animal Homosexuality and Natural Diversity*. St. Martin's Press, 1999.

Bhathal, Ragbir, and Terry Mason. "Aboriginal Astronomical Sites, Landscapes and Paintings." *Astronomy & Geophysics,* vol. 52, no. 4, Aug. 2011, pp. 4.12-4.16.

Birdlife International. Common Emu (Dromaius Novaehollandiae) - BirdLife Species Factsheet.

Bradshaw, G. A. *Elephants on the Edge: What Animals Teach Us about Humanity*. Yale University Press, 2009.

Carroll, Rory, and Christopher Martine. "An Ecological and Cultural Review of the Emu (Dromaius Novaehollandiae): Dreamtime - Present." *Scientia Discipulorum*, vol. 5, 2011, pp. 77–90.

Crew, Bec. "The Great Emu War: In Which Some Large, Flightless Birds Unwittingly Foiled the Australian Army." Scientific American Blog Network. Accessed 6 Dec. 2018.

Dallas Morning News. "Texans Unnerved by Roaming Emus Birds: Cowboys and Sheriff's Deputies Prefer Not to Corral the Big, Dim-Witted Animals, Which Can Be Dangerous When Cornered." *Baltimore Sun*, 15 Feb. 1998.

"ELUSIVE EMUS." *Canberra Times* (ACT : 1926 - 1995), 5 Nov. 1932, p. 4.

Gruen, Lori. "Dignity, Captivity, and an Ethics of Sight." *The Ethics of Captivity*, edited by Lori Gruen, Oxford University Press, 2014, pp. 231–47.

jones, pattrice. "Eros and the Mechanisms of Eco-Defense." *Ecofeminism: Feminist Intersections with Other Animals and the Earth*, edited by Carol J. Adams and Lori Gruen, Bloomsbury Academic, 2014.

---. "Harbingers of (Silent) Spring: Avian Archetypes in Myth and Reality." Spring: A Journal of Archetype and Culture, vol. 83, 2010, pp. 185–212.

---. "Property, Profit, and (Re)Production: A Bird's-Eye View." Animal Oppression and Capitalism, edited by David Nibert, vol. 2, Praeger, 2017, pp. 31–48.

---. "Roosters, Hawks and Dawgs: Toward an Inclusive, Embodied Eco/Feminist Psychology." Feminism & Psychology, vol. 20, no. 3, Aug. 2010, pp. 365–80.

Menon, Deepa G., et al. "Understanding the Behavior of Domestic Emus: A Means to Improve Their Management and Welfare—Major Behaviors and Activity Time Budgets of Adult Emus." *Journal of Animals*, 2014.

Miller, Gifford H., et al. "Ecosystem Collapse in Pleistocene Australia and a Human Role in Megafaunal Extinction." *Science* (New York, N.Y.), vol. 309, no. 5732, July 2005, pp. 287–90.

"New Strategy In A War On The Emu." *Sunday Herald* (Sydney, NSW : 1949 - 1953), 5 July 1953, p. 13.

Patterson, C., and P. V. Rich. "The Fossil History of the Emus, Dromaius (Aves: Dromaiinae)." *Records of the South Australian Museum*, vol. 21, 1987, pp. 85–117.

"REQUEST TO USE BOMBS TO KILL EMUS." *Mail* (Adelaide, SA : 1912 - 1954), 3 July 1943, p. 12.

Upton, John. "The Emu Has Landed (in India)." *Audubon*, Mar. 2014.

"WAR ON EMUS." *Argus* (Melbourne, Vic. : 1848 - 1957), 10 Nov. 1932, p. 8.

4

Mocking Birds

One morning at the sanctuary, I heard the most elaborate and lengthy birdsong I had ever encountered. It hardly seemed possible that a single bird could sing for so long. The song burbled on and on, ever-changing and yet coherent, like a melody from some foreign yet familiar culture. Enchanted, I tried to see who was singing but was unable to locate the source of the cheerful tune. Over the next few days, I heard variations on the theme—always different and yet somehow the same—and began to wonder whether somebody new had moved into the neighborhood.

Standing outside at dusk one day, I thrilled to the sound of the the baroque bird right above me. Peering upward through the foliage, I spotted... a common catbird. That hardly seemed possible, unless... yes! A little research confirmed that, while these birds most frequently call in ways that evoke the cries of cats to human ears, they also are among the improvisational musicians of the avian family, able to incorporate overheard sounds of all sorts into their songs. What I had mistaken for the routine song of some unknown-to-me group of birds from far away turned out to be the unique stylings of an individual whose creativity would be admired by any surrealist. Once I understood what I was hearing, I began to be better able to discern found sounds—such as the plop of a frog landing in the pond across the road—within the ever-evolving tune. I hope to never forget that lesson in ethnomusicology and humility.

This essay about our collective tendency toward similar errors was written for *Especismo y Lenguaje* (Plaza y Valdés, 2023). This is the first time it appears in English. Thanks are due to Catia Faria and Nuria Almirón at the Centre for Animal Ethics at Pompeu Fabra University for inviting me to write it and for editorial questions that prompted useful edits.

Mocking Birds

Mystery Symphonies and the Ableism of Speciesism

Like European starlings, catbirds of North America often incorporate the calls of other birds into their own songs. Like lyrebirds of Australia, catbirds also may mingle other kinds of sounds, such as those of insects or human machinery, into their compositions.

We humans cannot comprehend the resulting symphonies. Nor can we parse the songs of wrens, who may include more than a hundred notes into a five-second outburst of trills. Not only do the superfast muscles powering the syrinx (the voice organ in birds) produce sound variations too quickly for us to distinguish, but the birds may be listening to aspects of the song that seem unimportant to us, such as the lengths of the minute gaps between notes rather than the notes themselves.

Whatever they are saying to each other and other animals in their orbit, birds are capable of packing a lot of information into a brief message. That makes sense. Like humans, birds are social animals whose brains evolved to cope with the demands of collective life, which include communication in service of cooperation.

I am lucky to share a home with an African Grey parrot called Wiley, who reminds me every day of my comparatively impoverished cognitive and communicational abilities. In the absence of such an instructor, many humans make the mistake of presuming that any communication they cannot themselves understand must be meaningless. (For some humans, this is consistent with a habit of presuming that any language other than their own is literally non-sense.)

In English, "birdbrain" is an insult meaning silly and unintelligent. Similarly, the word "dodo" is used both to denote the large bird hunted to extinction by European colonizers of Mauritius and an especially foolish or stupid person. The demise of dodos contributed to a cascade of extinctions of endemic species, including the fruitful *tambalacoque* trees. And yet it is the dodos, rather than their clueless killers, who are remembered for their ostensible stupidity.

That sorry story is but one episode in a saga of human error dating back to antiquity. When it came time to name his own species, Swedish taxonomist Carolus Linnaeus chose *Homo sapiens*, which means *wise man*. The European habit of imagining humans to be especially intelligent dates back to Aristotle, who wrote that "man is the only *zōon logon echon*" or *rational living being*. There's some scholarly quibbling about whether Aristotle intended to *define* rather than merely *describe* humans in this way, but there's little doubt that, for the European men who made it their business to classify the world, intelligence was so prized—and the presumption of human intelligence so strong—that it seemed central to human identity.

And so it came to be that a self-serving claim of human cognitive supremacy became part of how many human beings see themselves and each other. This false claim then became a bedrock of both ableism and speciesism, by means of the following syllogism:

1. Only humans are rational/intelligent;
2. This superiority of human cognitive abilities reflects supreme worth;
3. Therefore humans may rightly treat nonhumans as objects, resources, or juniors.

Let's look at this argument closely, because there are errors and dangerous implications at every turn. First, the claim that only humans have a particular ability usually turns out to be false. Reasoning, memory, self-awareness, mathematics, and other cognitive capabilities falsely believed to be the sole province of our own species have, in fact, been observed in other species. Some other species have cognitive capacities that humans lack! This raises the question of what *intelligence* might be, if not the ability to solve species-specific problems in the contexts in which they arise. Definitions of *rationality* and *reasoning* are similarly murky in ways that favor the cognitive styles of the men who consider their own ways of thinking self-evidently superior.

Next, the idea that only humans are rational or intelligent can be interpreted to mean that persons who are not rational or intelligent are not fully human. And, indeed, humans who lack (or are perceived to lack) particular cognitive capabilities are often referred to by slurs that suggest they are subhuman. Laws authorizing practices such as sub-minimum wages for people with disabilities or sterilization without their consent rest upon the presumption that persons with particular disabilities do not deserve the rights reserved for humans.

But why should humans have rights not extended to others? This brings us to the claim that superior abilities reflect superior worth. The idea that human superiority justifies human supremacy is among the most commonplace rationales for speciesism. It's tempting to simply push back against the idea that humans *are* superior, but it's equally essential to contest the notion that ability equals worth, because that is the central thesis of ableism as well as this variant of speciesism.

I say "this variant of speciesism" because there are other rationales for human supremacy, such as the idea that a deity created animals for human use. Here too, there is a consonance: In many places, times, and faiths, disability has been seen as a sign of a deity's disfavor. However, the most common rationale for speciesism seems to be the combination of falsehood and ableism implicit in the demarcation and elevation of *human* by reference to particular cognitive capabilities.

Not surprisingly, given this conjunction of wrong-headed ideas, nonhuman animals and humans with cognitive disabilities or divergences have been subjected to many of the same violations excused by many of the same rationalizations. As is well known, animals are regularly incarcerated for life, made to work without compensation, experimented upon, and deprived of reproductive autonomy. People with cognitive and psychiatric disabilities also have been locked up for life, made to work for little or no pay, experimented upon, and deprived of reproductive freedom.

Persons with sensory disabilities or differences also have been subjected to such injuries and indignities. For example, in the United States, Deaf persons have been involuntarily sterilized, incarcerated in institutions, and prevented from using sign language, which the perpetrators of these abuses believed to be inferior to spoken words.

That makes a sad sort of sense. The *logos* of Aristotle meant both reasoning and word-using, and much of his writing displays a slippage between those two highly-valued capabilities. That slippage persists to this day in the attitudes of people who use terms like "dumb," which means both stupid and nonverbal in English.

Perhaps because many of our cognitive abilities evolved to facilitate communication, reasoning and language are closely linked. Following language acquisition, humans tend to think with words, so much so that it can be difficult to hold onto concepts for which there are no words. And so it is not surprising that language is among the exceptional cognitive abilities some have claimed to be the sole province of humans. In order to make this claim, it is necessary to discount quite obvious examples of complex vocal communications among other animals, such as songbirds.

Birds are not the only animals who communicate complexly with sound. For example, here are some of the ways alpacas communicate: Humming, clucking, snorting, grumbling, screeching. Chimpanzees augment their pant hoot vocalizations with drumming. Drumming is both gesture and sound, reminding us of the multiplicity of other ways of communicating. Humans use motions, facial expressions, and visual decorations. Bees do waggle dances to precisely communicate locations and what can be found there. Moths and many other insects communicate via scent. The fish called *mormyrids* signal to one another using electric fields. Cephalopods communicate with color.

Two concepts about communication from zoology are useful to remember: multimodal robustness and multimodal enhancement. As just described, animals use many different channels, or modes, of communication. Multimodal robustness is the idea that a message sent through more than one channel — such as a vocal warning also accompanied by a gesture or facial expression — will be more likely to be received and understood. Multimodal enhancement holds that the use of different channels can add more information to a message, such as when a facial expression signifies that the speaker is sad about the content of a spoken sentence. Both of these concepts highlight the value of communicating through multiple channels—a value that is undermined by the fallacious elevation of human-style language as the pinnacle of communicative efficacy.

I am particularly aware of the foolishness of that fallacy as I struggle to communicate what I aim to say using only the bare bones of written words, without the enhancements that speaking to you in person would afford. If only I could use gestures and tone of voice while simultaneously "reading" your posture and facial expressions to see if I needed to repeat myself or rephrase!

To summarize, rationality and language are two linked abilities, the real or imagined lack of either of which leads to exile from the vaunted status of "human" and thereby consignment to a lower status. This way of conceptualizing humanness not only harms those left out but also denigrates vital abilities, such as nonverbal communication.

In lieu of *Homo sapiens*, let me suggest another latin phrase to denote our species: *Errare est humanum*. Often said to remind humans not to expect god-like perfection from themselves or each other, this phrase might be more usefully adopted to remind us of not only the human propensity for making mistakes but also the errors built into the very concept of "human" as it is commonly understood within human supremacist culture.

Here are just a few of the errors built into the commonplace conception of human exceptionalism:

Dividing all animals into humans versus nonhumans makes no more logical sense than dividing animals into the categories of jellyfish versus non-jellyfish or dividing all plants into sunflowers vs non-sunflowers. The mental and linguistic habit of dividing the world in this way leads to a false sense of separation and, therefore, independence. In fact, humans are both embedded in and entirely dependent on the larger-than-human world. Without algae and trees making oxygen, we couldn't breathe. Without underground insects making soil from dead matter, we'd have nothing to eat.

Dependency is another feature falsely ascribed to both nonhuman animals and people with disabilities, as the obverse of the idea that humans are independent. Cultivating a more accurate image of everyone as always *interdependent* would not only help to bring humans back into right relationship with the larger-than-human world but would undercut one of the most pernicious elements of ableism.

Many humans experience an additional level of separation in the form of a conscious self that feels disembodied. This is a perceptual error rather than the sign of superiority that some people have claimed it to be. Various human fantasies created to explain this mythical self, such as religions in which a deity bequeaths souls to humans and only humans, have lead directly to wars of persecution against both nonhuman animals and humans who do not adore that particular deity.

Furthermore, many humans experience this seemingly disembodied self as their true self, saying "my body" rather than "me" — as if the body was an object owned by the conscious self. This way of thinking is associated with the habit of mind in which all of the material world is perceived as mere resource for human use. And *that* way of thinking, of course, had led directly to the climate emergency in which collectively find ourselves.

Humans have not yet collectively thought our way out of that crisis, perhaps because we value only a small part of our own cognitive capacities. The conscious self represents a tiny subset of human cognition, with hard-wired limitations in capacity. In contrast, non-conscious cognition is capable of much more complex problem solving. (Imagine if you had to consciously work out the physics of catching an item tossed to you — could you do the math in time?)

Similarly, words can say many things but can inhibit imagination by making it difficult to think about concepts for which there are no words. We recognize this by using numbers and other symbols in mathematical reasoning. Other ways of reasoning, such as drawing or dancing, might unearth even more possibilities for action if accorded more value.

When we assume that not only ourselves but *other people* are primarily rational animals who respond best to verbal communication, this leads to more error. In fact, humans are motivated by emotion more than reason and use many different communication channels. Action plans based on the presumption that humans are rational beings who will respond appropriately if only the right words can be found are likely to fail.

Therefore, over-valuation of conscious reasoning and word-based communication not only unfairly denigrates those who use other means of communicating and solving problems but also constricts our collective cognitive capacities and inhibits the effectiveness of interventions into emergencies like climate change and coronavirus.

What can we do with this information? First, those who advocate for nonhuman animals must be wary of arguments for animal rights that are implicitly ableist. It has become popular, particularly in the realm of animal law, to argue that one or another class of animal should be granted the status of person on the basis of their cognitive or communicative abilities. While such arguments may be tactically useful in the short term, they bolster ableist definitions of personhood.

Similarly, we who press for our own rights and dignity as people with disabilities also must avoid accidentally supporting the very ideas that disadvantage us. That can be difficult to do. For any human disadvantaged by systematic oppression, there can be a strong impulse to demand to be included in the category "human" as it is currently constructed rather than to demand that the category itself be reformulated or jettisoned. Due to past missteps on the part of prominent animal advocates, the disability rights movement may be especially unlikely to embrace antispeciesism as an element of liberation. Because Peter Singer and some of his acolytes have been explicitly ableist in some of their arguments, many disability rights activists energetically scorn and reject the very idea of animal liberation. In my view, the responsibility for correcting that sad state of affairs falls to animal advocates, who must be actively anti-ableist and consistently in solidarity with struggles for the self-determination and freedom of people with disabilities.

What else does the conjunction of ableism and speciesism in the definition of "human" by reference to cognitive or communicational capacities require us to do? Resist any urge to cast aspersions on the rationality of people with whom we disagree. In today's combative political arenas, people on both left and right seem to enjoy referring to the opposition as ignorant and/or unintelligent. What if, instead, we approached every debate with the presumption that nobody knows everything they need to know?

Seeing ourselves as more likely to err than not and being always aware of our own ignorance can be an antidote to the ableist and speciesist definition of human. Since there are many other reasons to reject that definition, such as its origins in explicitly racist science and its tendency to estrange humans from the larger-than-human world, anything we can do to demolish our own internalized "humanness" may be helpful.

Most importantly, we must find ways to access our own non-rational and non-verbal capabilities. Many of our current emergencies are crises of *imagination*. We will not rationally argue our way out of climate change, the quickening collapse of consensus reality, or the consequent surge in identitarian fascism. We urgently need to see our species more accurately and imagine new ways of solving our collective problems.

Perhaps other species have things to teach us about that. Here at VINE Sanctuary in the United States, members of our multispecies community use multiple means to communicate with one another, both within and across species, in the course of collective problem-solving. I recall Rocky the peacock jumping up in the air with his tail feathers outstretched in order to signal to an emu that he felt threatened by their nearness. The emu got the message and took a few steps back.

Peacocks communicate not only by means of visual signals but also with movement and two kinds of sound. In addition to vocalizations, peacocks can rap their outstretched feathers together to create a complex soundscape including both the percussive clicks of the hard stems against each other and a sound like rustling leaves in the wind caused by the softer parts of the features swishing. Many other birds also dance in ways that send both visual and audible signals.

The red-cheeked blue finches called *Uraeginthus bengalus* do a rapid tap dance as part of their courtship process. Because their sound-making movements are so fast that human eyes cannot see them and human ears cannot parse the sound, we didn't know about these remarkable feats of percussion until researchers filmed them with high-speed cameras and then slowed down the footage to watch.

What other reasoning and communication we might be missing? Only by setting aside ableist and speciesist definitions of ourselves can we hope to learn what we most urgently need to know and then cooperate with each other, and other animals, to foster a more sustainable and equitable state of affairs for everyone.

5

The Persistence of Pigeons

This piece was written for the forthcoming *Censored Landscapes* book of photographs by Isabella La Rocca González. Each photograph features a site of concentrated cruelty to animals, although usually the animals themselves cannot be seen. This piece was written in response to a photograph of an unremarkable building under an empty sky, which turns out to be a squab farm. Try to imagine it…

The Persistence of Pigeons

I can't not see the birds not flying in that sky.

Once so numerous that migrating flocks blocked out the sun, the passenger pigeons who had inhabited North America for 100,000 years were hunted to extinction within 300 years after European pilgrims landed on Plymouth Rock. Passenger pigeons roosted and foraged communally, traveling continuously except when they established temporary "cities" of as many as a million birds each, where they courted, built nests, hatched eggs, and tended the next generation until they were able to fly off with the community.

"Squab" is the inglorious word used by people to refer to the as-yet flightless offspring tended so carefully by pigeon parents. Hatched and nursed by both mother and father—who both produce a milk-like substance containing nutrients and antibodies—pigeon nestlings grow quickly, reaching adult size in about a month, at which point they begin to learn to fly. Squab sellers snatch those nestlings just before they fledge.

Flightlessness doomed dodos, ground pigeons who participated in the vibrant pre-human ecology of their island. About 3 feet high with large curved beaks, dodos foraged for fallen fruits and nuts, including the fruit of the tambalacoque or "dodo tree." Amazed by the ease with which these gentle birds could be captured, Dutch sailors soon snatched so many that their population plummeted. Dodos died out along with several other endemic species, including tambalacoque trees. Ourselves ignorant of almost everything about that destroyed ecosystem, humans added insult to injury by repurposing the word "dodo" as an ableist slur denoting stupidity.

People in the squab business dismissively refer to the doting parents upon whom all of their profits depend as "utility pigeons." Humans have used pigeons as tools in other ways, including as scientific instruments and weapons of war. People also use pigeons as toys, shooting captive birds for sport and relying upon the strong bond between mated pairs (and between parents and offspring) to compel birds bred for speed to race back home through unfamiliar terrain—risking their lives to storms or predation along the way—in the pastime known as pigeon racing.

It all began in the Levant. Neolithic peoples of the eastern Mediterranean built structures for native rock doves to nest, thereby making it easier for themselves to collect droppings to use as fertilizer. The birds who chose to roost in those structures gained access to agricultural spillage in addition to safe housing and were always free to leave. Thus, this might have become one of those mutually beneficial inter-species relationships so often found in nature. Instead, in several places around the region, people stole pigeons from nests to raise in captivity, manipulating their reproduction in order to favor desired features. Some people wanted plump birds to eat. Some wanted birds with feathers of specific colors to be sacrificed in religious rituals. Others valued birds with strong homing instincts and excellent navigational skills to be used for communications.

Successive imperialist empires spread these uses of pigeons around the world. The path from neolithic towers to this squat industrial squab farm runs through the Roman Empire, which spread dovecote culture through Europe. After killing off the native passenger pigeons, European settlers to North America imported pigeons for squab farming, the popularity of which has risen and fallen several times in the decades since.

Nobody knows how Mauritius blue pigeons lived. Nobody knows why all of the spotted green pigeons died. People sometimes think they have spotted a Choiseul pigeon, not seen since 1904, but it always turns out to be a crested cuckoo-dove.

None of us know pigeons, not really. The things about them that seem marvelous to us—such as their ability (unique among birds) to make "milk" for their babies or their aptitude for navigation—probably feel entirely unremarkable to them. Objects of endless experiments in countless psychology laboratories, pigeons have proven again and again that they are capable of not only constructing their own communities in a variety of habitats but also of solving artificial problems posed for them by apes in lab coats. But such tests tell us nothing about what pigeons themselves want, think, or wonder.

We can guess, from their behavior, what pigeons care about and what they enjoy. Pigeons value relationships. They mate for life. They protect, indulge, and instruct their young. They socialize constantly with their flock mates (coo

coo coo) and often organize exuberant collective aerial acrobatics. Judging from the evident joy that they take in those recreational flights, pigeons also value physical freedom and communal activity.

What are their other projects? We cannot know.

When ornithologist Johann Reinhold Forster spotted what turned out to be the last of the ground doves of Tanna, called "mahk" by the native people of that island, he shot her.

People are the primary predators of pigeons. They must know us better than we ever will know them. Since their views of people are undistorted by the rose-tinted spectacles of speciesism, they may know us better than we know ourselves.

What do pigeons know about people? Remember: In Pennsylvania, politicians raise money by staging events at which newly-fledged captive-bred pigeons are released for the first time—in order to be shot from the sky. Psychologists compel pigeons to solve problems by withholding food, sometimes deliberately mutilating their brains before playing such games. Pigeon fanciers proclaim their love for favored birds and then sell their offspring to the highest bidder.

What might we learn about ourselves or others by imagining pigeon perspectives? What do the preoccupations of people look like from those bird's-eye views? What might the 6,000 birds locked up in the buildings in that photo tell us that we urgently need to know?

While Rodrigues blue pigeons, Bonin wood pigeons, and Réunion pink pigeons are as extinct as passenger pigeons, dodos, spotted green pigeons, Choiseul pigeons, and Tanna ground doves, more than 300 species in the pigeon and dove family have survived the onslaught of the human, often exercising great ingenuity in so doing. They include wood pigeons, ground pigeons, mountain pigeons, and fruit doves as well as the rock doves who are the living ancestors of all of the human-engineered varieties of captive pigeons and doves. The colors of their feathers span the spectrum of the rainbow.

Pigeons persist. If a predator snatches their nestlings, they try again. And again. If their habitats are razed, they find ways to nest in new places. Those grey-and-black pigeons you see in cities? The ones who seem so pedestrian and are often perceived as pests? They're busy reclaiming the means of production, by which I mean their own bodies: These birds are the descendants of pigeons released from dovecotes by the thousands when squab farming became less profitable as well as escapees from this and other exploitive industries.

In Christchurch, New Zealand (where the wood pigeons called kererū are lauded for habit of getting drunk on fermented fallen fruit but the feral descendants of pigeons imported for squab production may be shot on sight), I have seen pigeons flying in and out of the homes they have made for themselves in the wreckage of buildings brought down by an earthquake.

In Rome, Italy (from whence the Roman Empire launched pigeons around the world) I have seen the self-possession of pigeons regarded by visitors as whimsical tourist attractions. Perhaps these indigenous mediterraneans, who are well-prepared to adapt themselves to whatever climate change may bring, know that they will be the inheritors of the future ruins of all of those fountains and cathedrals.

In Springfield, Vermont (where passenger pigeons used to soar), I see the re-wilded offspring of pigeons rescued from hunting, racing, and squab production swooping around the grounds of VINE Sanctuary every morning. Their descendants will survive me. I am heartened by their future feathers.

I can't not see the birds flying in that sky. But I know that nature abhors a vacuum, including the amorality and absence of empathy in the hearts of the owners and operators of that site of concentrated cruelty. Someday, one way or another, it will be gone. But pigeons will persist.

6

Beyond Despair

This brief piece, which shares one of the most important things I have learned from birds, was published in *Satya* magazine in June of 2007. *Satya* ceased publication shortly thereafter, but its former publisher maintains an online archive. Only a few of my articles and columns for that magazine are included here, but all can be freely accessed there.

Beyond Despair

It was a typical winter night at the Eastern Shore Sanctuary, meaning I was sitting on the couch brooding about big problems while dogs chewed carrot sticks on the carpet and catnip-fueled felines chased each other around around the chaotic kitchen. Some new piece of wretched information—probably something about polar bears—had punched me in the stomach. "Why aren't people doing more about global warming?" I muttered angrily. Elder dog Zami regarded me levelly until it hit me: I am people. Why aren't I doing more about global warming?

Feeling a bit abashed, I decided to really ask the question rather than rhetorically: Why aren't people doing more about global warming?

Since I am people, I asked myself first. I discovered that climate change didn't feel real to me, even though I knew it was happening. Only by making myself do so was I able to really feel the fear that ought to be associated with such a scary situation. Balanced against that fear were two unrealistic and opposing assumptions: 1) the environmentalists or scientists or somebody will take care of it; and 2) there's no use doing anything because we're doomed. Only by challenging those unconscious assumptions—which did not match my conscious beliefs—was I able to get past my own internal impasse.

Next I looked into the scholarly research on inaction concerning climate change. Many early studies found that people don't do anything about global warming because they don't understand it.

You might think that this is no longer a problem. But the college students in my classes still, more often than not, mention the hole in the ozone layer when talking about climate change. Asked what you can do about global warming, they tend to think for a moment and then suggest "maybe... recycle?"

Which brings us to the next reason people don't take action against climate change: They don't know what to do. Perhaps they don't understand the mechanics of climate change or maybe a planetary problem seems self-evidently too big for individual action to make a difference.

Which brings us to what may be the deepest reason for inaction: The feeling of futility. Research shows that many people won't make changes that cost them in any way—in money, time or lost pleasure—unless they believe that enough people also will be making the same sacrifice for it to be meaningful.

With these ideas in mind, I began to have conversations about climate change. I learned that even people who grasp the mechanics of climate change often have not thought through all of what they might do to reduce their own emissions of methane and carbon dioxide. They are often even less certain about what collective action against climate change might look like. Most importantly, many—perhaps even most—people believe that it simply will not be possible to get enough individuals/corporations/governments to make the changes necessary to save the world.

This is despair. Hopelessness forestalls action. Without action, there really is no hope.

From Cold War to Global Warming

We've faced a similar situation before, when very real fears about nuclear war left many people immobile in the face of a grave and mounting danger. When I was researching my book Aftershock I looked into the research about why people did or did not become involved in anti-nuclear activism during the years when the U.S.-USSR arms race made the prospect of nuclear annihilation even more likely than it is today.

One study concerned participation in the November 1, 1961 day of protest during which tens of thousands of women, many of whom had never before engaged in any sort of activism, took to the streets to demand an end to nuclear testing. It turned out that most of the participants in this action, which JFK cited as a determinant of U.S. participation in the Test Ban Treaty of 1963, got involved because a neighbor or friend asked them to do so.

Research related to nuclear activism also sheds light on the persistent problem of despair. In the 1980s, Psychologist Joanna Rogers Macy conducted "despair and empowerment" workshops in which participants directly confronted, rather than avoided talking about, their feelings of fear and hopelessness about the prospect of world wreckage due to nuclear technology. She found that talking about such feelings helped to lessen their paralyzing impact and promote action.

That makes sense. When despair remains unvoiced, we cannot argue against it. Meanwhile, the effort used to suppress the terror that springs from and feeds the despair deprives us of vital energy. Because flattening one feeling tends to dampen others, we become benumbed.

Getting Past Impasse

What, then, can we do to promote action on climate change? Whatever else we do, we have to talk about it with everybody we know. In order to do that effectively, we need to be prepared.

Taking the easiest tasks first, we all need to be good at explaining climate change so that everyone can understand. Practice explaining the mechanics of global warming in a few simple sentences. Be sure to include the fact that greenhouse gasses come not only from vehicles burning fossil fuels but also from power plants, manufacturing and animal agriculture.

Because denial is still a significant factor in inaction, memorize a few key facts proving that the problem is both real and urgent. I like to stress that polar ice is actually cracking, because this is easy to visualize. I also like to quote top climate change scientist Jim Hansen, who has said that we have less than ten years before the world becomes "a different planet" and to note that climate change turns out to be happening even faster than scientists have predicted.

Next, because most people don't know what they can do, get good at listing the full spectrum of ways that individuals can reduce their own emissions. These include reducing direct energy usage in both fuel and electricity; radically reducing consumption of new consumer goods by recycling, reusing and doing without; buying from local sources; and, of course, eliminating meat, dairy and eggs from the diet.

People also need to know what individual or collective actions might be taken to provoke institutional change by governments and corporations. Options range from lobbying for government controls on emissions to direct action aimed at raising the costs, or reducing the profits, of the industries responsible for carbon dioxide.

When beginning conversations, don't start with the facts and prescriptions. Remember the despair that must be voiced and dissipated. Start by saying, "I'm really worried about climate change. What about you?" Then, listen. Ask questions. Share your own feelings. Then, remembering that people are most likely to do something when invited to do so by someone they know and remembering that people need to believe that enough other people also will be acting, tell about what you've done, are doing, or plan to do.

Learning from Birds

Where can you find the hope to do this? You already have it in your muscles.

Here is what I learned from the birds: Hope is something you do. "Spent" hens arrive from egg factories in a state of abject shock, half-starved and barely able to walk. Nothing in their lives has taught them to expect anything other than constricted movement and misery. They huddle, shoulders slumped, in a corner of the barn. But then they take a step. And then they take another step. They discover freedom and their own abilities. They learn to use their wings.

Hope is something you do. We create hope by acting. As our actions create change, our hopes are realized. When it comes to climate change, action is our only hope.

How can we start? Follow the birds. Take a step. Then another step. Then...

II. ECOLOGICAL ANALYSES

Back in 1976, as red-white-and-blue fireworks burst into Bicentennial skies and Harold Melvin & the Blue Notes sang "Wake Up Everybody" on the radio, Richard Coe published an article entitled "Eco-Logic for the Composition Classroom" in *College Composition and Communication*. "Ecology" was in the air in those days. Rachel Carson's accessibly worded 1962 book, *Silent Spring*, had taught general readers the basic principles of ecology by explaining how household insecticides could end up poisoning songbirds. Gregory Bateson's 1972 *Steps to an Ecology of Mind* popularized ecological approaches to the social sciences. Ron Cobb's elegantly designed ecology symbol decorated t-shirts and flags at increasingly popular Earth Day events. Psychology, anthropology, and related departments at some colleges and universities combined themselves into new departments of "human ecology."

I came of age in that era, imbibing that ethos almost by osmosis. The word "intersectionality" hadn't been invented yet. None of us had read the 1977 *Combahee River Collective Statement*. Still, the Gay People's Alliance at my college in 1978 had two "co-coordinators," only one of whom could be white and only one of whom could be male, to ensure that we paid due attention to both gender and race. Ten years later, the ACTUP chapter in which I participated made a point of clearly spelling out how racism, sexism, classism, and ableism worked in combination with homophobia to create the AIDS crisis.

In the early 1990s, while working at a center for anti-racist education that centered its work on an awareness of the interconnections among different forms of oppression, I regularly set myself the challenge of identifying as many intersections as I could find for any given problem or type of oppression. For example, I might think about public schools and challenge myself to identify all of the ways that racism, sexism, classism, ableism, and homophobia might inhibit access to a high-quality education. Or I might think about a specific form of oppression and challenge myself to think about how other forms of oppression support it and vice versa. Later in that decade, I began incorporating speciesism and human supremacy into those analyses.

In the early 2000s, when Miriam Jones and I founded what was then the Eastern Shore Chicken Sanctuary and is now VINE Sanctuary, we immediately recognized the factory farms surrounding us as case examples of conjoined and compounded harm. Of course, the birds were the most numerous victims of the most substantial injury. But we also saw how the big corporations exploited the workers and even the farmers. We noticed the race and class stratification reflected in the poverty and injuries experienced by workers of color, who suffered much more than the comparatively privileged white land-owning farmers, even though they were in a form of debt servitude to the corporations. And, of course, we ourselves were among the people coping with the arsenic, campylobacter, and other pathogens poisoning the local environment due to the poultry industry.

When the sanctuary relocated to Vermont, we discovered a similar but different web of interconnected forms of oppression bolstering the local dairy industry. That was the subject of my book, *The Oxen at the Intersection*. It tells the story of two cows prevented from coming to the sanctuary by what we only belatedly understood to be a complex and profoundly local conjunction of sexism, racism, and speciesism. I have since made it a point to think of problems as situations in which identity, place, and history are likely causal factors.

The world comprises systems within systems in constant interaction with other systems. It's never possible to identify all of the factors active in any given problematic situation. But, whenever I have made a sincere effort to map out as many intersections as possible, I have always discovered potentially fruitful avenues of intervention. I encourage you to adopt the same habit of mind. I offer these essays, and those in the Queering Animal Liberation section that follows, as examples of what can come of such inquiries.

7

Free As a Bird

Like everyone, I was born an anarchist. Early experiences with irrational and injurious authority led me to remain that way long after most children accede to dominion by the powers that be. I came to adolescence at a time when queers like me were still outlaws, both in the sense of practicing sex acts that were themselves crimes and in the sense of being outside the protection of any laws against discrimination. I therefore remained unmoved by governmental claims of rightful rule.

All of this transpired in Baltimore, which at the time was blessed by a plethora of used bookstores, one of which functioned as a hub for anarchist publications. Thus did I come to discover not only books by anarchist luminaries such as Emma Goldman and Peter Kropotkin but also contemporary anarchist periodicals ranging from punkish magazines to quasi-scholarly journals.

In my late 20s, I finally stumbled upon anarcho-feminism, and I will always remember the embodied joy of first encountering those ideas. At about the same time, and for many years thereafter, my comrades in struggles against AIDS, for housing, against police racism, and for peace often included anarchists whose ideas entered my thinking. I suppose I should also mention that I was a dues-paying Wobbly[1] for many years and was lucky enough to live within walking distance of the headquarters of the Industrial Workers of the World when it was located in a storefront in Ypsilanti, Michigan.

And so *of course* after returning to Maryland, finding a chicken in a ditch, and cofounding the sanctuary that is now VINE Sanctuary, I began thinking about what we might learn from animals about solving the problems of collective living without needing to establish armed states. I also wondered whether and how our situation within the larger-than-human world might be taken into

1. Wobbly is the informal term used for members of the Industrial Workers of the World and was also the name of a nonbinary black cat who lived at the sanctuary for many years.

better account within anarchist theories. The essay that follows is the result some 20-odd years of musings in those directions.

Previous incarnations of some of the ideas (and even some of these paragraphs) that follow have appeared in in print in disparate places, including *Contemporary Anarchist Studies*[2] and the now defunct *Abolitionist Online* webzine based in Australia. Some were rehearsed at various events, including the 2021 Madrid Anarchist Bookfair, the 2013 Boston Anarchist Bookfair, and the 2007 New York City Anarchist Bookfair. I mention the latter two specifically, because attendees at those talks joined me in thinking collectively about the questions at hand, thereby contributing to the evolution of the ideas. Recognition is also due to Greta Gaard, who offered extensive comments on the 2009 version of this essay, and to the numerous Spanish and Italian anarchists who fed, sheltered, and conversed with me over the course of a 2014 speaking tour that took me through Barcelona, Florence, Rome, Bologna, Vicenza, Milan, and Bilbao. I remain grateful to you all! Special thanks to Lorikim Alexander, Sarahjane Blum, and Michelle Carrera for their generous and insightful comments on the latest iteration of this essay and to the future readers whose reactions surely will spark another revision someday.

2. pattrice jones, "Free as a Bird: Natural Anarchism in Action," in Contemporary Anarchist Studies: An Introductory Anthology of Anarchy in the Academy, ed. Randall Amster et al (Routledge, 2009).

Free As a Bird

Principles and Practices of Natural Anarchism

The Chicago Anarcho-Feminists warned us back in 1971, and now it's really true: "The world obviously cannot survive many more decades of rule by gangs of armed males calling themselves governments."[1] The violent partition of the planet into nations has brought us to the dangerous days of cracking ice caps, disappearing islands, and forest fires that burn up billions of animals[2] at a time. Relationships of all kinds are breaking down, from the vital bonds between plants and pollinators to the presumptions of good faith upon which human communities rely. In the midst of an insect apocalypse[3] during which authoritarianism gains more ground every day,[4] terror and despair may make meaningful action feel impossible or futile.

But hope, as Emily Dickenson wrote, is "the thing with feathers." Birds and other outlaws routinely disregard the authorities and boundaries established by people while working cooperatively with one another to co-create sustainable communities. This is anarchism in its purest form, and all of us who know the current state of affairs to be inherently injurious can learn from it, whether or not we think of ourselves as anarchists.

Working from within an ecofeminist understanding of the intersection of oppressions and the interconnection of all life, we can begin to restore the rela-

---

1. Chicago Anarcho-Feminists. "The Anarcho-Feminist Manifesto." Quiet Rumours: an Anarcha~Feminist anthology. London: Dark Star, undated. 4-5. [Article originally published in 1971 in Siren: A Journal of Anarcho-Feminism.]

2. "Australia's Fires 'Killed or Harmed Three Billion Animals,'" BBC News, July 28, 2020, sec. Australia.

3. Pedro Cardoso et al., "Scientists' Warning to Humanity on Insect Extinctions," Biological Conservation 242 (February 1, 2020): 108426.

4. Cara Daggett, "Petro-Masculinity: Fossil Fuels and Authoritarian Desire," Millennium 47, no. 1 (September 1, 2018): 25–44.

tionships that governments have torn asunder and then work within those relationships to build alternatives to armed states. Because more than rearrangement of power relations among people will be needed to rescue ourselves and our planet from man-made catastrophe, we will need to turn to plants and nonhuman animals as instructors and as allies in a shared struggle for peace and freedom for everybody. Luckily for us, they've been organizing their own affairs without governments for many more millennia than humans have existed.

Governments as Gadgets

Some 3.7 billion years ago, the pattern of organization we call life arose on the planet we call Earth. Nobody alive now knows how that happened. Some people think that the ancestors of our friends the blue-green algae (whose exhalations of oxygen set the stage for the evolution of plants and animals) were jolted by sunshine into the state we consider *alive*. Others imagine a similar underwater geothermal happening.

In considering such hypotheses, humans tend to center the organism rather than the energy. That makes sense, since we are organisms ourselves, but I invite you to join me in an exercise in eccentric thinking by switching your focus for a moment to energy itself. Every one of the billions of life forms on the planet today exists because energy finds it conductive.

What we call *life* is energy, organized. The organizations called organisms consist of relationships that cohere and persist. What this means is that relationships are at the heart of not only ecosystems and communities but life itself.

So is diversity. Energy radiates. There may be as many as a million species of algae and at least a billion species of microbes, all constantly evolving and intermixing. Back in the day, such transformations led to the emergence of vascular plants and multicellular animals. Now, none of the animals can survive without the plants, who join algae in converting sunshine into edibles, exhaling oxygen along the way.

Among the animals made possible by plants in the past 800 million years are the members of a comparatively young species of great ape with exceptional manual dexterity and a knack for using tools to solve problems. At the time of the appearance of this primate-come-lately in what is now called Africa, emus had stalked the forests of what is now called Australia for at least two million years. In what is now called North America, beavers had been busily contributing their labor to the construction of rich ecosystems for seven million years. Various members of the *Bovini* tribe—ancestors of the captives now called cows—grazed the mountains and grasslands of Eurasia, conducting their affairs as they saw fit.

All social animals confront the conundrum of maintaining cohesion despite the inevitable (and useful) diversity of personalities, interests, and opinions that arise within a group. All animals, social or not, also collectively face the fact of finite resources. All are entangled, whether they know it or not, within the complex webs of relationships that constitute ecosystems. Often, these require members of diverse species to figure out how to share territory and resources.

Different animals solve these problems in different ways. The closest living relatives of the newcomers, chimpanzees and bonobos, demonstrate how divergent those strategies can be. Essentially identical animals whose current morphological and social dissimilarities arose as a result of being separated by a wide river,[5] chimps and bonobos order their communities and resolve their conflicts very differently.

Similarly, subsets of *Homo Sapiens* developed diverse ways of solving the problems of living as they spread out of Africa and around the world. One of those ways, the taking and holding of territory by means of weaponry, led eventually to the evolution of states as we now know them: subdivisions of planet Earth, claimed as property by their human inhabitants and demarcated by borders defended by armies.

Weapons are tools, *arms* that extend the punching power of actual fists. Wielded by governments, weapons are always two-sided swords, simultaneously protecting and policing the state. Governments themselves are gadgets, haphazard implements grasped for purposes of solving problems.

Humans vary considerably in the degree to which they accept the authority of the governments that claim dominion over their homelands. However, at no point in time have the *other* inhabitants of the planet consented to be displaced, imprisoned, poisoned, controlled, sacrificed for or otherwise governed by a subset of primates. To the contrary, nonhuman have contested human hegemony at every turn and continue to resist. Therefore, insofar as they claim rightful rule over the larger-than-human world, governments of humans always have been and always will be illegitimate.

As the latest international summit on the worldwide fill-in-the-blank[6] emergency has demonstrated,[7] governments of humans also have failed to adequate-

5. Seth Borenstein, "The Bonobo, the Non-Murderous Version of the Chimpanzee, Gets Its Genome Mapped," Christian Science Monitor, June 13, 2012,

ly fulfill the function of problem-solving *for humans*. They have not ended hunger, despite the existence of more than enough food to feed everyone. They have not protected children from being conscripted into armies or trafficked into brothels. They are more likely to perpetrate than prevent genocide. And, of course, despite literally *decades* of negotiations, they have not even begun to respond adequately to a climate emergency that becomes more urgent with every passing day. Therefore, at present, all states are failed states.

States as Places

States are *places*. Aggregations of hominids calling themselves governments stake out the territory within which all will be compelled to cede to their rule. All national borders are battle scars. Many mark the actual sites of fights, and virtually all are defended by armed forces.

Borders are lacerations on living landscapes, often marked by ecologically disruptive constructions. Agreements among governments currently divide all of the land and much of the sea into dominions over which some subset of humans assert sovereignty. Most nations continue the process of division by splitting the geographic region under their control into sectors considered to be the property of particular people.

States are places claimed as *property*. The conversion of ecosystems and organisms into property requires a two-part process of denigration and alienation. First, the would-be property must be regarded as a mere object. Next, that object must be isolated from its envelopments, by force if necessary.

Because the nonsensical notion of property[8] has come to feel so normal to so many humans, we must take care not to forget the actual barbed wire and gunfire by which ownership is obtained and maintained. We also must work hard to remember all of those who have been disappeared into property, despite the turns of phrase and habits of mind that tend to make victims invisible. Just as *beef* obscures both the cow and the killing behind the hamburger,[9] *real estate* makes *parcels* of *property* seem like inert objects rather than vibrant places co-created by hosts of plants, animals, and microorganisms.

---

8. See "Property, Profit, and (Re)Production: A Bird's-Eye View" elsewhere in this volume for further thoughts on the human notion of property, which I have repeatedly tried and failed to conceptualize in a way that would make sense to other animals.

9. See Carol J. Adams, The Sexual Politics of Meat (New York: Bloomsbury, 2015) for an extended discussion of the problem of the absent referent.

The division of the earth into nations and the devolution of land into private property are linked acts of violence that rend the fabric of ecosystems, hurting their human and nonhuman inhabitants. Controversial border walls such as those currently under construction in the USA and Israel are merely extreme versions of the chain-link fences that demarcate suburban backyards. Even those who protest walls that obstruct the flow of people tend not to challenge, or even notice, the barriers that keep rabbits or dandelions from going where they want to go, although they may be just as destructive.

The things governments do change places. States bomb islands and authorize corporations to chop off mountain tops. States divert rivers and drench the earth with chemicals. Pollutants flow freely across borders, dispersing poisons across the planet, while police protect pipelines from protesters.

All places change over time, creating and delimiting possibilities for action. At present, we live on a substantially different planet than the one within which the modern state emerged. We have never been here before.

Nobody knows what happens next, but we do know that the practical and emotional havoc caused by environmental emergencies can upend everything. It may, therefore, become more possible to wobble the state. States may well collapse on their own. What happens then? Perhaps our kindred who have always managed their affairs without armories or other government apparatuses can teach us some of what we will need to know to ensure that something even worse does not arise from the floods and wildfires.

Animal Outlaws

Governments are groups of people. The groups of people calling themselves governments claim for themselves the rights of ownership and control over the ecosystems and animals within the borders policed by their armies.

Even those governments that purport to derive their authority from the consent of the governed do not even pretend to include nonhuman animals, much less fungi or forests, among those who must be consulted before decisions are made about their lives. While some governments concede some minimal rights to some animals, and a very few have granted the legal status of personhood to some small number of non-human entities, no government recognizes the sovereignty of other animals much less the superordinate position of the larger-than-human world in relation to the humans who depend on its networks for everything.

Legal systems codify agreements among people about how to divide up power and property among themselves. Governments enforce laws by various means up to and including lethal violence, thereby imposing those regulations not only upon those who agreed to them but also upon persons and other entities who were not party to them.

While the term "outlaw" has come to connote romanticized (and highly masculine) banditry in the popular imagination, the term originally referred to a kind of social execution in which the person so designated lost the protection of the law, thereafter having no rights others were bound to respect.

In United States history, enslaved Africans were outlaws in this sense of being beyond the protection of the law. Escaped slaves also were considered outlaws in the sense of having *stolen themselves* from their purported owners. Writing within the branch of legal thought known as Critical Race Theory, Monica J. Evans advances "outlaw culture" as a sustaining wellspring of resistance within African American communities.[10] Evans traces African American outlaw culture back to the so-called contrabands, "slaves who took it upon themselves — often with the aid of that most prominent of outlaw women, Harriet Tubman — to disrupt existing legal norms of property and to explode the boundaries of a destructive culture."[11]

Animals are outlaws in at least three ways, as beings who reside largely outside the protection of the law, as entities expected to endure governance to which they did not consent, and as persistent breakers of the rules made by such governments. From relentlessly trespassing raccoons to roadblocking baboons,[12] nonhuman animals demonstrate every day that their attitudes toward the law run the gamut from indifference to dissent. They are natural anarchists, sentient beings who neither recognize nor accede to the rules devised by human governments.

Evans expands the concept of outlaw to include not only those whose identities or activities locate them outside the law but also those "who are outsiders and whose stories lack the power to create fact."[13] The stories of such outlaws show us the dominant culture from a different standpoint. While Evans refers

---

10. Evans, Monica J. "Stealing Away: Black Women, Outlaw Culture and the Rhetoric of Rights." In Richard Delgado (Ed.), Critical Race Theory: The Cutting Edge. (Philadelphia: Temple University Press, 1995), 502-515.

11. Ibid.,. 504.

12. Abraham Odeke, "Angry Baboons Block Uganda Road," BBC News, April 30, 2003.

13. Evans. 506.

only to human beings such as women, youth, and people of color, it might be similarly fruitful to listen to the stories of animal outlaws with especial attention to those engaged in active struggle to salvage themselves or their habitats from human hegemony.

Organic Intellects

According to Antonio Gramsci, the organic intellectual emerges from within and helps to organize and articulate the consciousness of a social group. The organic intellectual is essentially a function of the social group, both evolving within and acting upon the group. Whether or not they have formal education, organic intellectuals learn and teach in the course of "active participation in practical life."[14] Within the context of class struggle, organic intellectuals articulate class perceptions and aspirations in the process of acting in the service of class interests. In his biography of civil rights and anti-poverty activist Ivory Perry, George Lipsitz notes that "organic intellectuals learn about the world by trying to change it, and they change the world by learning about it from the perspective of their social group.... Organic intellectuals generate and circulate oppositional ideas through social action."[15] From the outside in, organic intellectuals are those to whom allies ought to turn in order to learn about the aims and analyses of the social group.

Nonhuman social groups also have members who solve problems and communicate those solutions to the group. Even among plants, the function of the organic intellectual exists: Individual plants figure out how to beat a herbicide and then distribute that information to the next generation via their pollen. When we consider ecosystems as webs of relationships, we can see that entities fulfilling the functions of the organic intellectual can and probably do arise in the course of ecosystemic efforts to retain balance in the face of assaults from without or within.

In the context of inter-species class conflict and the struggle to survive in reduced and polluted ecosystems, problem-solving members of nonhuman social groups express the analyses and aspirations of their groups. Baboons who break into the apartment blocks that have encroached on their habitat, not

---

14. Gramsci, Antonio. Selections from the Prison Notebooks. (New York: International Publishers, 1971), p. 10.

15. Lipsitz, George. A Life in the Struggle: Ivory Perry and the Culture of Opposition. (Philadelphia: Temple University Press, 1988), p. 10.

only taking food but pausing to trash furnishings and urinate on closets full of clothing are saying: *This human settlement is hurtful to us. We want it gone.* When the elephant known as Nana, encircled by her protective herd, carefully undid the latches of a stockade in order to liberate antelopes who had been captured by people,[16] she not only freed those particular animals but sent a signal about her herd's views and values.

Direct Action

Natural anarchists vote with their feet, trunks, teeth, and tendrils. Vines clamber over and pull down fences. Elephants root up plantations of genetically modified crops. Sharks bite back.

When plants and nonhuman animals don't like something, they *do something* about it. In contrast, people tend to talk. And talk. The human propensity for language is encoded in our brains. This both helps and hinders us. The ability to communicate over distance and time has made possible the survival and spread of our species, but the highly symbolized nature of our language and thought helps to abstract us from ourselves and our environments.

Humans sometimes confuse words for their meanings. We see this slippage in action when activists mistake verbal dissent for material resistance. Marchers in weekend peace parades shout "Not in our name!" and feel that they have done something when, in fact, their vocalizations did not in any way impede the war machine funded by the taxes they continue to pay. In contrast, Ugandan baboons protesting a dangerous highway stage *their* sit-ins on the road itself, throwing stones at passing cars.[17] South African baboons protesting suburban sprawl break into the new houses and trash them.[18]

I use the term *direct action* to refer to any effort that seeks to directly intervene in a problem rather than indirectly solve the problem by means of intermediary steps such as persuasion, voting, or education. Two forms of direct action, *propaganda of the deed* and *mutual aid*, may be particularly potent in the context of current emergencies.

From the sayings of Saint Francis of Assisi, who called upon people to show love by works rather than words, to the drumbeats of Max Roach, whose album

16. "Elephant unlatches gate to save South African antelopes," Agence France-Presse, 8 April 2003; "Elephants on a rescue mission," South African Press Association, 9 April 2003.

17. "Baboons protest road killings." New Internationist, June 2003.

18. "Baboons on rampage in South African town," Agence France-Presse, 16 June 2004.

"Deeds, Not Words" provided an energizing backbeat to countless civil rights activists, the notion that action speaks louder than words spans centuries and cultures. As it arose within anarchism, the term "propaganda of the deed" adds a strategic twist, favoring actions that simultaneously intervene in problems *and* inspire others to do the same.

Propaganda of the deed is direct action that speaks. When artist Yvette Watt and her comrades floated a barge on a Tasmanian lake to dance a flamboyant routine as a recording of Swan Lake blared from stereo speakers, they simultaneously saved the lives of countless birds by disrupting duck hunting on that day *and* drew public attention to their campaign to abolish the 'sport' of shooting birds out of the sky. That they interfered with this traditional expression of the most toxic of masculinities while tweaking gender norms—dancing in pink tutus, hard hats, and work boots—added a deliciously subversive communicative spin to their successful stoppage of the killings that otherwise would have happened that day.

Propaganda of the deed in the widest sense of the phrase — *making a point by doing something* — satisfies the mandate to take action in the midst of emergency while also fulfilling the human need for symbolism and the strategic imperatives of communication and persuasion. The kinds of direct action that can be deployed as anarchist propaganda include property damage; salvage (rescue of plants, animals, and places from those who would exploit them as well as creative reuse of the detritus of industrial consumer culture); radical noncooperation; and — on the upside — creation and propagation of highly visible nongovernmental projects that do the things government purports to do (e.g., keep the peace, feed the people, etc.)

All of these forms of direct action are practiced by nonhuman animals, albeit usually without the communicative elements that would make them true propaganda of the deed. Nonhuman animals routinely and deliberately destroy walls and other structures erected by people; "steal" themselves and other animals away from human possession; and refuse to accede to human authority, hegemony, or boundaries. Birds, insects, and other social animals often organize themselves to fulfill collective purposes by nonhierarchical and non-coercive means and thus offer models of alternatives to governments.

Both within and across species, many animals practice the sharing of resources and responsibilities that Petr Kropotkin called *mutual aid*. Kropotkin called mutual aid "a factor in evolution,"[19] arguing that such cooperation

---

19. Petr Kropotkin, Mutual Aid: A Factor of Evolution (1914 Edition) (Boston: Porter Sargent, 1976).

enhances the long-term well-being of communities. Often wrongly dismissed as an anarchist fairy-tale rather than serious science,[20] Kropotkin's outlook was in fact rooted in his own observations as a naturalist. His emphasis on collective rather than individual struggle has since been affirmed by fascinating findings in realms such as plant cooperation,[21] fungi communication,[22] and evolution by association.[23]

Even if we don't delve into the molecular details[24] of this scientific saga, we still can be mindful of its political implications. European men were in the habit of conceptualizing social life as a constant struggle of each against all. This unexamined assumption led prominent theorists to tell the story of evolution as a chronicle of individuals in competition with each other. In so doing, they entirely erased the vital role of often quite queer[25] associations in the evolution of both organisms[26] and ecosystems.

The same biases undergird conventional thinking about politics, which also takes the imaginary independent individual as the starting point and presumes competition to be the most natural attitude of those individuals toward each other. In fact, humans are often internally motivated to cooperate with each other, and this impulse makes mutual aid one of the most promising forms of anarchist direct action.

As Michelle Carrera explains it, mutual aid among humans is as simple as asking "what can we do from where we are with what we have?"[27] Mutual aid requires no special training, no knowledge of political theory, and no particular

---

20. Gould, Stephen Jay. "Kropotkin was no crackpot." Natural History 97, no. 7 (1988): 12-21.

21. Susan A Dudley, "Plant Cooperation," AoB PLANTS 7 (January 1, 2015): plv113.

22. Andrew Adamatzky, "Language of Fungi Derived from Their Electrical Spiking Activity," Royal Society Open Science 9, no. 4 (April 6, 2022): 211926.

23. Jan Sapp, Evolution by Association: A History of Symbiosis (Oxford, New York: Oxford University Press, 1994).

24. Dorion Sagan, "Metametazoa: Biology and Multiplicity," in Incorporations, ed. Jonathan Crary and Sanford Kwinter (New York, NY: Zone Books, 1992).

25. Myra J. Hird, "Naturally Queer," Feminist Theory 5 (2004): 85–89.

26. Scott F. Gilbert, Jan Sapp, and Alfred I. Tauber, "A Symbiotic View of Life: We Have Never Been Individuals," The Quarterly Review of Biology 87, no. 4 (December 2012): 325–41,

27. In Context: Mutual Aid with Michelle Carrera, 2022, https://www.youtube.com/watch?v=ZGdzroo-YZE.

attitude toward government. Moreover, people *enjoy* participating in networks of care that generate tangible positive outcomes they can see for themselves.

Such networks are the building blocks of communities that can solve their own problems without recourse to armed agents of the state. In combination with other forms of direct action, mutual aid can be the heartbeat of a decentralized strategy in which natural anarchists simultaneously interfere with the machinations of profit, undermine the notion that states are necessary, and build the alternative social structures that will make governments irrelevant.

Natural Anarchism

Many people think of "anarchy" as synonymous with chaos and "anarchism" as an inexplicable devotion to the same. In fact, *anarchism* refers to a diverse array of political theories and practices that share a commitment to solving the problems of collective living without relying upon the always two-sided sword of the state. Like all humans, anarchists disagree with each other regularly and vociferously and enjoy devising monikers for their favored flavors. Here are just a few of the varieties of anarchism: anarcho-syndicalism, anarcha-feminism, mutualism, social anarchism, and, inevitably, "anarchism without adjectives."

Why so many? Because, once we set aside the presumption that governments as they are currently constituted are necessary, a wide world of possible ways of organizing human communities becomes imaginable. Suddenly, we have many questions to answer, not only about what kinds of communities we would prefer but also about how to bring them into being. Self-described anarchists vary considerably in the degree to which they believe that some sort of mechanisms for collective problem-solving are necessary, the kinds of mechanisms (if any) they propose, and whether it is preferable to challenge the state directly or to simply build alternatives from the ground up, making the state irrelevant.

In proposing the following axioms of "Natural Anarchism," my aim is to clarify our thinking about such questions by grounding them in the context of the larger-than-human world—a world in which anarchism already exists and is, indeed, the norm. From the perspective of other animals and the planet itself, governments are strange and dangerous contraptions devised by hapless humans who haven't yet figured out other ways to maintain peace and solve collective problems. In order to avoid being equally hapless anarchists, those of us who hope to summon up non-state solutions to the persistent problems that arise among humans might be well-advised to take the following propositions into account:

A. Natural Anarchism is Actual Anarchism

Natural anarchism is a real process rather than an abstraction. For anarchism to be realized among humans, we have to *be real*, both in the sense of sincerely seeking that outcome and in the sense of facing facts. Relevant facts include not only the persistence of anarchism in the larger-than-human world but also the perseverative power of states and psyches as they are currently constituted. Both states of mind and police states tend to perpetuate themselves unless actively interrupted. We cannot wish away the effects of generations of violence. Fantasies of all kinds, including the myths about human beings embedded in the ideology of human supremacy, must be rejected in favor of an unflinching assessment of the foibles and follies to which members of our species are susceptible. Only in this way can we hope to help ourselves achieve the equity and harmony that seems to come more easily to other species.

B. Natural Anarchism is Situated Anarchism

Nothing happens in a vacuum. Everything has a context. Because people are physical beings living in ecosystems and because states are places carved out of the biosphere, efforts by people to abolish or reconfigure governments always are physical actions—*movements*—occurring at particular points in space and time. The efficacy of those movements will depend in part upon whether or not they are well-matched to their circumstances.

C. Natural Anarchism Evolves

Situated anarchism is located in the here *and now*. Here is a polluted planet upon which more people than ever jostle with each other for diminishing resources in the midst of ever-more erratic weather. *Now* for you will be some weeks, months, or years after I type these words today. What seems most salient to me right now—the conjoined triple crisis of a collapse in consensus reality, a worldwide upsurge in fascism, and a climate emergency that becomes more catastrophic every day. Natural anarchists look around at the facts on the ground and ask, "what do we do now?" Not in some romanticized past or imagined future, but *now*. In this way, natural anarchism evolves in response to changing circumstances, just like the so-called 'superweeds' that survive and thrive to continually plague agribusiness.

C. Natural Anarchism Is Social Anarchism

Human beings are social animals. Unlike precocial animals who can function independently shortly after birth or hatching, all members of our altricial species reach maturity only after an extended period of dependence during which estrangement from the group would mean death. Even after maturity, virtually all humans live with or near other humans, depending upon networks of other humans for access to the necessities of living. Therefore, solidarity rather than individualism is the only realistic anarchist ethos.

D. Natural Anarchism is Ecological

Solidarity must extend beyond the human. To remain alive, every human being must breathe. Oxygen exists within the biosphere only due to the existence of algae and plants. To remain alive, every human must eat. Edible calories exist on the planet only due to the same photosynthetic processes that create oxygen. Most of the plants that convert sunshine to edible calories themselves exist only due to complex interactions among fungi, microbes, and other entities that collaborate to create soil. Since no group of humans can exist outside of the biosphere or apart from ecosystems that make eating possible, any realistic anarchism must take such ecological factors into account.

E. Natural Anarchism is Nonlinear

Ecosystems are *systems*—complex networks of relationships. Human beings also are systems —who organize systems among themselves! Every aggregation of humans is a complex and ever-changing system that is interconnected with other systems. Governments are systems. Neighborhoods are systems. Non-governmental organizations are systems. Therefore, anarchist strategies always must be *eco-logical*[28] in the sense of working within an understanding of how systems operate and interact.

For humans schooled in the style of problem-solving wherein a single variable is isolated and scrutinized, it can be daunting to begin to think in terms

28. Shout out to Richard M. Coe, whose 1975 article "Eco-Logic for the Composition Classroom" (College Composition and Communication 26, no. 3: 232–37) inspired me to adopt "eco-logical" as a catchphrase for systems thinking of all kinds.

of systems with all of their constantly moving parts and unpredictable interactions. But one need not learn the details of complex systems analysis to develop the habit of analyzing problems as *situations* in which multiple social and material factors play a role. Practices like collective brainstorming, system mapping, and role-playing can all help to identify elements of the situation and avenues for intervention.

X. Natural Anarchism is Larger-Than-Human

Plants, animals, and ecosystems push back against capitalist exploitation and state control every day. What can we learn from a study of their strategies? Their successes and failures? How can we join their ongoing rebellions, as allies rather than self-appointed leaders?

Y. Natural Anarchism Must Be Multifaceted

By asking such questions, we can begin to imagine some of the things we need to do. We don't have to agree to do the same things. Given the multitude of emergencies and chronic crises currently facing us, not to mention the diversity of projects that will be necessary in order to make states as they are currently constituted irrelevant, the realization of natural anarchism among humans will require a multiplicity of people using a multiplicity of tactics. While many anarchists are already comfortable working within an ethos of tactical diversity, others will need to regularly remind ourselves not to slip into the all-too-human habit of seeking consensus when more might be gained by divergence.

Here are just a few of the many things we need to do: Restore or repair relationships severed or made toxic by states. Organize local, regional, and global projects capable of doing the things people currently count on states to do. Help humans become better able to experience empathy, enact solidarity, and imagine otherwise. Make it less profitable to behave exploitatively and more rewarding to participate in mutual aid. Learn and teach the things we need to know to do these things.

We can do these things *together*, even when we are far apart and focused on different aspects of the struggle, by keeping the principles of Natural Anarchism in mind and extending mutual aid to each other whenever opportunities arise.

Z. Natural Anarchism Will Be Queerer Than We Can Suppose[29]

Nobody can predict what will happen next. That's always the case, but particularly true right now, as cascading systemic collapses of various kinds surprise experts and laity alike. Collapses of state functionalities in the ensuing emergencies may make anarchism *necessary* in order to avert anarchy. Given the widespread availability of weapons, malicious or merely mercenary non-state actors may seek to supplant government rule with their own. At the same time, the willingness of extant governments to use force against both other states and their 'own' people may escalate.

Meanwhile, algae will continue to evolve, fungi will facilitate communion among trees, and microbes will keep on turning dead bodies into living soil. New ecosystems will organize themselves from the novel configurations of living matter that arise. We cannot know what forms these will take, but we can prepare ourselves to participate more generously and mindfully than humans historically have done.

Liberation as Connection

As earthbound apes, humans always have been fascinated by birds. Virtually everywhere in the world, images, stories, and imitations of birds date back to antiquity. "Free as a bird," we say, trying to imagine what it might be like to soar *and* to be free of other constraints that limit us.

But few birds are loners, and all birds — like us — depend upon others to make their own lives possible. Some co-evolved with particular plants that depend on them for pollination even as they depend on the plants for food. For such birds, mutual aid is literally built into their bodies.

Imagine a migratory bird arriving at her springtime stomping grounds only to discover that it feels like summer and the flowers she depends upon have already bloomed and withered. According to Christiaan Both et al., "mistiming as a result of climate change is probably a widespread phenomenon."[30] Such uncouplings do not make birds more free.

---

29. Knowing nod to the late great biologist JBS Haldane, whose oft-quoted remark that "the Universe is not only queerer than we suppose but queerer than we can suppose" brings comfort to me every day.

30. Christiaan Both et al., "Climate Change and Population Declines in a Long-Distance Migratory Bird," Nature 441, no. 7089 (May 2006): 81–83.

In cultures defined by the masculine ideal of individualism, *liberation* can seem to mean not only freedom from unjust or unnatural restraints but also freedom from all constraints, including legitimate social and natural limits on action. In this way of conceptualizing freedom, liberation is separation. However, as our feathered friends could tell us, a more ecological outlook leads to the conclusion that liberty can only be realized in the context of connection.

States sever connections by chopping ecosystems into property and warping the wish for connection into weaponized emotions such as patriotism and nationalistic pride. Capitalism continues the process of disassembly by alienating workers from the fruits of their labor and by forcing workers into competition with each other. Late consumer capitalism[31] carries that sorry story to its inevitably absurd conclusion: the Ram truck, an expensive avatar of petromasculinity[32] named after purportedly macho animals whose actual behavior unsettles human notions about gender and sexuality.[33]

Those bighorn sheep, simultaneously living their lives without regard for human schemes *and* menaced by the incursion of humans and our effluents into their homelands and the very air they breathe, both need us to leave them alone *and* require our solidarity. They also know things we don't know and may be able to see things we can't see. It may yet be possible to find common ground in a resistance to authority and property that does not depend on the subjugation of anybody. This could lead to a new conspiracy of thieves taking nonviolent direct action against property and the governments that protect it.

For birds and bighorn sheep alike, liberation from human hegemony will require the reconstruction of ecosystemic relationships that humans and their states have torn asunder. Similarly, the liberation of humans from the strictures and trickeries of states will require the repair of relationships that have been severed or skewed by governments.

Thus the ultimate aim of natural anarchism is the restoration of relationships. We can do that by building and bolstering healthy relationships among humans and between humans and the larger-than-human world. In natural anarchism, the ends and the means are the same.

---

31. See "Property, Profit, and (Re)Production: A Bird's-Eye View" elsewhere in this volume for a reflection on the impact of late consumer capitalism on our ways of being in the world.

32. Cara Daggett, "Petro-Masculinity: Fossil Fuels and Authoritarian Desire," Millennium 47, no. 1 (September 1, 2018): 25–44.

33. Stacy Alaimo, "Eluding Capture: The Science, Culture, and Pleasure of 'Queer' Animals," in Queer Ecologies: Sex, Nature, Politics, Desire, ed. Catriona Mortimer-Sandilands and Bruce Erickson (Bloomington, IN, USA: Indiana University Press, 2010), 51–72.

Flux

No emu or turkey could have predicted the calamities that would visit their species upon the arrival of humans to the forests in which they had evolved. If world history teaches us anything, it's that the unimaginable can happen.

Life is energy, organized. When circumstances are suitable, energy flows. Every participant in every system helps to co-construct the state-of-affairs that is that system, and every system is always in flux.

Natural anarchists know: All we can do is organize, watch what happens, and then organize again from within an altered situation. Along the way, relationships grow. We cannot predict what will happen, but we always know that those relationships, in and of themselves, are vital, meaningful, and consequential.

Whatever we do or don't do, energy will continue to radiate and anarchists of all species will continue to commune in ever-changing ecosystems until the day comes when there are no more days on this planet because its sun has imploded, exploded, or exhausted itself. In the interim, what we do or don't do matters because we are part of the mix.

Tune into all of the mixes in which you participate, including both social systems and ecosystems. Where are some relationships in need of repair? What do you have, whether it be matter or energy, that might help? Start there.

8

KIWI SURREALISM

"I'm interplanetary, my insect movements vary."[1] Those words by the Digable Planets rang through my house, along with various interplanetary tunes by Sun Ra, as I prepared for a talk based on this abstract:

Val Plumwood called for a "thorough rethink"[2] of the logic of domination that has authorized both colonialism and the exploitation of animals. But this mandate creates a conundrum: That logic elevates mind over matter and cognition over emotion. If Audre Lorde was right that "the master's tools will never dismantle the master's house,"[3] then we are unlikely to succeed in undermining that logic by rethinking it. We need practices that will expose the tedious nonsensicality of human supremacy while simultaneously awakening our capacities for empathy, imagination, and full-bodied ecological reasoning. Plumwood noted the power of poetry, but nonverbal methods of cognition and communication such as music, dance, and visual art may be even more vital to the struggle to think truly differently. Underground currents of art and activism including dada, tropicália, Afrofuturism, and surrealisms from around the world may offer both instructive and cautionary lessons. Kiwis and other category-defying animals, whose minds are very different than our own but whose ideas may be legible through their ways of being in the world, may be especially important instructors in the praxis of eco-logic.

Aptly, at the 2019 *Decolonizing Animals* conference of the Australasian Animal Studies Association, a projection of an oversized insect shone behind me as I delivered the talk. This was the "Val Plumwood Memorial Lecture" for

1. Ishmael Butler, Mariana Vieira, and Craig Irving, "Where I'm From," Reachin' (A New Refutation of Time and Space), Pendulum/Elektra, 1993.

2. Plumwood, "Nature in the Active Voice," 113.

3. Lorde, Sister Outsider: Essays and Speeches, 110.

that conference, and I took seriously the implicit remit to both draw on and carry forward the work of Val Plumwood, who was an important ecofeminist philosopher from Australia, in the talk. The result was a conversation of sorts among ecofeminists, surrealists, and others who have endeavored to provoke people to break free from mental constrictions in order to bring themselves and each other into less violent and more creative relationships with each other and the wider world.

In preparing this chapter from that talk, I have to *reduce* to words what was a much more embodied experience for me and attendees at an event at which each day's work began and ended with song. At the same time, I have *added* some ideas that have occurred to me subsequently. Thus, this is a substantially different work than that talk. Luckily, the talk was recorded and can be accessed via the YouTube pages of both VINE Sanctuary and the Australasian Animal Studies Association. Check it out if you're curious or just want to experience the vibe.

Ever since giving the lecture for which this essay was prepared, I have tried to apply Plumwood's precepts to my own art and activism. I find it extremely useful to ask myself whether and how any project I am planning will do one or more of the things Plumwood felt would help human beings to decenter ourselves. I think that you might find it useful to do the same. If so, let me know how it goes!

Birds Beyond Words

Fantastic Animals and Other Flights of Imagination

One morning at the small chicken sanctuary that would grow into VINE Sanctuary, I wobbled into the yards at sunrise and then stopped in my tracks. Rubbing my eyes, I considered the possibility that I was having my first close encounter with extra-terrestrial life. The cartoon creature before me had a tubby body, no neck, and a comically long beak. None of the parts seemed to match the others. It was as if she or he had been drawn by surrealists playing the exquisite corpse game.

After a moment, the being levitated, making an eerie whirring sound before disappearing over the fence and into the marshy woods. Not entirely trusting my own eyes, yet still quite ready to believe I had glimpsed something other-worldly, I returned to my morning chores, filling food and water bowls and then opening coop doors, ducking to avoid being hit on the head by egg factory survivors swooping from their perches to explore the new day.

Consulting a field guide after finishing my rounds, I learned that I had seen neither ET nor a kiwi but a common American woodcock. Like kiwis, whom scholars have called the "most aberrant"[1] of the always anomalous flightless birds, woodcocks confound our categories. Woodcocks are the shorebirds of the forest, combining the long, thin beak of a sandpiper or oystercatcher with the mottled black-and-brown plumage of other shy denizens of the woods. That mysterious noise I heard wasn't a vocalization but rather the sound of air whistling through the whirring feathers of a bird lifting off vertically, like a helicopter, as male woodcocks often do on their *singing grounds*[2] during mating season.

1. Reid and Williams, "The Kiwi," 301.

2. Dwyer, McAuley, and Derleth, "Woodcock Singing-Ground Counts and Habitat Changes in the Northeastern United States."

Now, this might not seem like much of a story: pattrice once saw a bird who happened to look a bit like a kiwi, and that bird turned out to have some fascinating features. But listen: At that moment, something about the combination of my surprise at seeing such a strange creature and my quasi-dreamlike state led me to be entirely open to the possibility that things might be otherwise than I had believed, that things I couldn't have even imagined might yet be true.

That disorientation, that *dépaysement*, that readiness to rethink *everything* that you thought you knew—that's the state we will need to induce—and be willing to enter ourselves!—in order to participate in the "thorough rethink"[3] of rationalism that Val Plumwood believed we need. Because of the entanglement of language and logic, I think we will need to go beyond words to do so, drawing upon all of our other ways of reasoning and expressing ourselves, many of which may be rusty from disuse. Noticing, admiring, encountering, and learning from nonhuman animals may help us awaken those capacities within ourselves while at the same time giving us practice in the vital work of de-centering and deconstructing 'the human.'

The Plumwood Problem

Val Plumwood was a philosopher—a thinker—who challenged the centrality of rationality to human identity and also enumerated several of the ways that rationalism leads to harmful social and environmental outcomes. In so doing, Plumwood enumerated five characteristics of thinking that underlie Eurocentrism, androcentrism, *and* anthropocentrism: radical exclusion, homogenization and associated stereotyping, denial or backgrounding, incorporation, and instrumentalism[4] (each of which I will discuss below). If we can unsettle those ways of thinking, Plumwood believed, we can undermine the shared structure of several ostensibly different forms of oppression.

Therefore, Plumwood called for a "thorough rethink"[5] of rationalism and associated centrist ways of thinking. She knew this would be difficult, saying that "the big question is: Can we think differently? Can what has been stripped

3. Plumwood, "Nature in the Active Voice," 113.

4. Plumwood, Environmental Culture. See pages 92-122 for her analyses of these elements of centrist thinking.

5. Plumwood, "Nature in the Active Voice," 113.

out of our conception of the material world be put back?"[6] I will discuss some artists and activists who have tried to do this over the past hundred years, often motivated by analyses striking similar to those of Plumwood. My hope is that doing so will motivate us to go beyond words ordered rationally, because I doubt very much that we will be able to *think* our way out of rationality.

Which brings me to what I call the *mind-ass problem*. Every day, on my way to graduate school, I used to walk past a mural of the Funkadelic album entitled "Free Your Mind... and Your Ass Will Follow," which includes a song of the same title. That would remind me of a different Funkadelic song, "One Nation Under a Groove," which suggests that we "dance our way out of our constrictions,"[7] thereby freeing our minds by way of our asses. And so I would continue on to classes in clinical psychology, wondering which tactic might work best.

As usual when confronted by either/or binaries, I concluded it was both. I still believe that. And so, in order to free our minds in the ways that Plumwood wanted, we may need to free ourselves *from* our minds. In other words, in order to do a truly thorough rethink, we will need to rethink thinking.

Rethinking Thinking

The rational reasoning that, for many people, forms the very basis of both humanity and individual identity is but a subset of a subset. Rational reasoning represents a small subset of conscious thought, which itself represents a small subset of cognition.

Let's dispense first with the Aristotelian and Linnaean notion that reasoning defines the human species. While most of us *can* sometimes engage in the kinds of conscious calculations known as rationality, this is but one of many cognitive capabilities common to members of our species. Furthermore, members of many other species also are capable of reasoning. To define the human by means of a capability that is neither confined to humans nor possessed by all humans is both ableist and speciesist.[8]

The descriptor of humans attributed to Aristotle, *zōon logon ekhon*, is typically translated to mean *the living being having logic* but is also sometimes

6. Ibid, 124.

7. George Clinton, Walter Morrison, Garry Shider, "One Nation Under a Groove," Funkadelic: One Nation Under a Groove, Warner Bros., 1978.

8. jones, "Especismo y Capacitismo."

understood to mean *the living being having language.*[9] If language rather than reason is the claim for exceptionality, the same problems remain: The claim is both false and injurious, harming all who communicate by different yet equally complex expressive methods.

These are well-established points that I and others have elaborated elsewhere. My interest here is on the harm done to those who *do* both use and define themselves by reason and/or language. Just as conscious reasoning is but one kind of cognition, communicating by means of sound symbols strung in logical sequences is but one of many means of communication of which we may be capable. Over-reliance on either may stunt our ability to collectively solve problems—including the climate emergency that threatens us all.

Here are some of the consequences of the elevation of rationality and its associated means of communication to the status of hallmarks of humanness:

Over-estimation of our rational capabilities. Humans often fail to follow the rules of logic, even when we believe we are doing so.[10] When we falsely believe our own intuitions to be the results of pure reason, we may take useless or counterproductive actions. When we falsely believe *others* to be capable of pure reason, this can lead to over-reliance upon syllogisms when other forms of persuasion might be more useful.

Over-estimation of the role of rational thought in making choices. Humans often choose based on non-conscious beliefs or inclinations and then generate ex post facto rationalizations for those choices. "We are multiplicities, pursuing disparate goals that are obscured from consciousness."[11] When we mistakenly believe our own rationalizations, we lie to ourselves. Believing other people to be rational actors leads to follies such as economic theories that presume that "economic agents are omniscient about their own preference orders, their budget constraints and the attainable set of outcomes."[12]

Over-estimation of the role of conscious thought in determining behavior. People vary considerably in the degree to which their behaviors reflect their conscious choices. While the mismatch known as *cognitive dissonance*—a perceived divergence in beliefs vs. behavior—does tend to trouble people, rationalization

---

9. Doxtader, "Zōon Logon Ekhon," 453.

10. See Gilovich, Griffin, and Kahneman, Heuristics and Biases for numerous examples of the kinds of logical errors toward which human cognition tends to trend.

11. Levy, "Choices Without Choosers: Toward a Neuropsychologically Plausible Existentialism," 119

12. Rosenberg, "The Metaphysics of Microeconomics," 361.

and other cognitive stratagems tend to be less effortful than changing behavior and are therefore frequently the favored response to such discomfort. While some people can and do change their behavior after being alerted to discrepancies between their stated values and actual behavior, others do not. Thus, even when rational argumentation leads to changed opinions, this may not lead to changed behavior. When we rely exclusively on argumentation to change minds, assuming this will change behavior, we may miss other opportunities to motivate change.

Existential confusion about who we are. The misidentification of the human as supremely rational not only denigrates the capabilities of other animals but also confuses us about ourselves. This confusion often goes much deeper than the errors described above. Many people are in the habit of considering the subset of cognitive processes of which they are aware to be their very selves, thereby inadvertently relegating the rest of themselves to the category of other. Given that these self-declared selves are not only partial but also prone to confabulation, this represents a substantial error that can lead directly to delusion.

Subordination of other aspects of the organism. In addition to falsely claiming the mantle of *self* for only themselves, our conscious selves tend to treat our larger-than-conscious selves in much the same way that humans treat the larger-than-human world. They imagine themselves to be independent and in charge when in fact they are dependent and woefully ignorant. They see themselves as the heroes of their self-told tales, treating muscles and sensations as mere tools or backgrounds. Because they are minds that cannot apprehend the material processes from which they arise, they value mind over matter.

Undervaluation of other capabilities. As they aggrandize themselves, our conscious selves valorize their own cognitive and expressive capabilities, denigrating or ignoring other ways of thinking and communicating.

Atrophy of other capabilities. Because our conscious selves do, in fact, exercise *some* control over the behavior of the organism, their disdain for other ways of thinking and communicating can lead to neglect of those potential methods of problem-solving. Lack of practice can lead to atrophy.

Can we think differently? Yes, but we will need to forge new neural pathways while strengthening others that have been dormant. I mean that literally—to think differently we will need to *think* differently. We won't be able to argue ourselves into it. Other methods will be necessary. Luckily, artists are already offering alternative avenues and have been doing so for centuries—often in response to the same problems Plumwood wrote about. So, let's take a quick spin through art history for instruction and inspiration.

Pacific Surrealisms

"Logic is a complication. Logic is always false. It draws the superficial threads of concepts and words towards illusory conclusions and centres." No, that wasn't Plumwood writing in the early twenty-first century; that was Tristan Tzara in the 1918 howl of outrage known as the *DADA Manifesto*.[13]

World War I dislocated the bodies and minds of the Europeans who were its perpetrators and primary victims. Tanks, airplanes, and machine guns mechanized warfare as never before: 40 million people killed or wounded in four short years. Surviving soldiers shadowed the streets of European cities, their make-shift masks mimicking eyes and noses melted by poison gas, crude wooden arms and legs replacing those blown off by bombs.

Out of the carnage came Dada, a movement of artists, writers, and musicians dedicated to unmasking European civilization. Dadaists staged disturbing cabaret shows, recited poems of senseless syllables, composed disorienting collages of words and images, caricatured militaristic nationalism, and painted vividly surreal depictions of everyday life in a world made mad by madness.

Although primarily remembered as a progenitor of surrealism, Dada was not an aesthetic movement. "Dada is a protest with the fists of its whole being engaged in destructive action,"[14] said Tristan Tzara, the Romanian poet who composed the Dada Manifesto, and he meant it. Many Dadaists staged protest events and contributed words and images to the dissident publications of their day. All aimed to disrupt complacency in the face of atrocity.

In retrospect, Dada's provocations may seem tame or quaint, but they were deadly serious. They'd been undone by war and—unlike most people today—they *knew* it. They knew that returning to normal could only lead to more of the same. They were desperate to interrupt the rationalized non-sense that led directly to mechanized killing.

They failed. Europe lurched inexorably into another world war marked by mechanized killing. Concentration camps. Atomic bombs.

"Like everything in life, Dada is useless," said Tristan Tzara in 1922.[15] In general, presumptions of futility tend to become self-fulfilling prophecies.

---

13. Tzara, Dada Manifesto 1918.

14. Ibid.

15. Tzara, "Lecture on Dada."

My guess is that Dada's uncanny replication of nightmarish nonsensicality expressed the helpless anguish of wartime all too well, leaving people even less likely to imagine a way out. As Robin D.G. Kelley has noted, truly revolutionary artistic practices "compel us to relive horrors and, most importantly, enable us to imagine a new society."[16]

And yet. Somehow, their howls echoed around the world, merging, harmonizing, and standing in atonal counterpoint with those of other artists whose works would have more material political impact, such as Caribbean Surrealists and Brazilian Cannibalists. As Elisa Veini writes, "More interesting than to ask who was influencing whom and where the whole avant-gardist lot originated, I think, is to view the Brazilian Cannibalist modernism and the European Surrealist and Dadaist avant-gardes as twin movements or parallel streams that were each developing in their own particular context, while ideas — and artists — traveled back and forth between Europe and Latin America."[17]

Poet and novelist Jayne Cortez refers to surrealism as a tool,[18] and nowhere has that tool been deployed more effectively than in the Caribbean. In the introduction to his collection of surrealist writings from the Caribbean, Michael Richardson refers to surrealism in the region as "a generalized revolt against the very foundations of Western civilization."[19] That meant rethinking thinking. "Aristotle's logic? A practice of things and corpses," wrote surrealist Réne Ménil from Martinique in 1945, "Thought is bio-logical or not at all."[20] In 1943, feminist and anti-colonial writer and activist Suzanne Césaire wrote that "The most urgent task was to liberate the mind from the shackles of absurd logic and so-called reason."[21]

This project included a reorientation to the larger-than-human world. "You have encircled the globe," wrote Aimé Césaire in 1944, "You have yet to embrace it. Warmly."[22] Suzanne Césaire wrote that we "can only guess at the

---

16. Kelley, Freedom Dreams, 9.

17. Veini, "Cannibals, Crabs, and Carmen Miranda," 232.

18. Kelley, Freedom Dreams, 187.

19. Richardson, Refusal of the Shadow, 3.

20. Ibid., 150.

21. Ibid., 124.

22. Ibid., 119.

uncomplicated loves of the fishes."[23] In 1945, Réne Ménil said something that I have heard so many modern-day ecofeminists and animal advocates say: "If only we could awaken, if only we would awaken suddenly, as the sleeper does, to what is all around us."[24]

This was a *political* project with real, material aims. In a 1933 article on the "antifascist significance of surrealism," Pierre Yoyotte argued that leftists have "failed to understand... the political importance of collective emotions."[25] The potential political impact of surrealism was demonstrated in Haiti in 1945, when a lecture by a visiting surrealist ignited a series of events that ultimately led to the fall of the government.[26]

At around the same time in the United States, a musician by the name of Herman Blount moved to Chicago (a hotbed of surrealism) and began recording music that, like the interventions of the Caribbean surrealists, was intended to enable new kinds of collective emotions. Better known as Sun Ra, this innovative composer and bandleader would perform and record until his death in 1993.

Comparing his own works to more standard compositions, Sun Ra said: "It was always about human emotions that everybody could feel, but it was just a repeat thing. It wasn't bringing people any new emotions, you see, although they got a wide range of emotions that they never used, a lot of feelings they never felt."[27]

A vegetarian who said "I am a little afraid of normal people. Their greatest desire in life seems to be to maim and destroy either themselves or others,"[28] Sun Ra consistently and repeatedly said "I'm not a human."[29] His project of reshaping humanity by using nonverbal means to enable new ways of thinking and feeling was entirely consistent with what Plumwood prescribed and exemplifies what I am arguing we need urgently to do today. And it works!

23. Ibid., 157.

24. Ibid., 162.

25. Rosemont and Kelley, Black, Brown, & Beige, 42.

26. Richardson, Refusal of the Shadow, 20. See Depestre, "André Breton in Port-Au-Prince" and Laraque, "André Breton in Haiti" for extended reportage of that remarkable series of events.

27. Szwed, Space Is the Place, Chapter Three.

28. Ibid., Chapter Two.

29. Ibid., Chapter One.

While I cannot confirm or deny new feelings, I can report that I am indeed able to think differently when certain Sun Ra recordings are cued up on repeat. I imagine that his performances, which were happenings including dance, lights, and chants, were even more powerful. Certainly, "Sun Ra and his Arkestra inspired other Afrofuturists"[30] whose own work in numerous artistic realms continues to provoke people to imagine otherwise.[31]

Inspired in part by Dada and surrealism as well as by innovative jazz musicians such as John Coltrane (who himself was influenced by Sun Ra), members of the Situationist International of the 1960s devised *détournement*, in which artifacts of the dominant culture are detoured to make them expose their own lies. Like artist George Grosz, who pasted Dada phrases on Berlin shop windows, making himself an enemy of the Nazi state, Situationists scrawled slogans in surprising places, hoping to catch passersby unawares. But, unlike the defeatist catch-phrases favored by Dadaists, Situationist slogans voiced the unspoken desires that underly despair: "Under the paving stones — the beach!"[32]

In his book *The Revolution of Everyday Life*, Situationist Raoul Vaneigem described the 'situations' he and his comrades sought to create in terms that echoed both Sun Ra and earlier Caribbean surrealists. Like jazz, Vaneigem said, situations were improvisations in which new ways of thinking and feeling might arise.[33]

"Our ideas," the Situationists believed, "are on everybody's mind."[34] Maybe they were right. Certainly, their sentiments helped to inspire the Parisian worker-student uprising of May 1968, which had both immediate and long-lasting impact in France.

At the same time in Brazil, artists and musicians associated with the *Tropicalismo* or *Tropicália* movement were practicing a different kind of détournement. According to musician Caetano Veloso, "We took what was kitsch — what was considered bad taste — and we placed it in a more sophisticated repertoire."[35]

---

30. Kelley, Freedom Dreams, 31.

31. See, e.g., Ko, "Creating New Conceptual Architecture: On Afrofuturism, Animality, and Unlearning/Rewriting Ourselves."

32. See Knabb, Situationist International Anthology, for more examples of Situationist tactics and slogans.

33. Vaneigem, The Revolution of Everyday Life, 195.

34. Wark, The Beach Beneath the Street, 156.

35. Veloso and Dunn, "The Tropicalista Rebellion," 121.

In response, the military dictatorship imprisoned, tortured, exiled, or locked them up in psychiatric institutions.

What was so subversive about Caetano Veloso, backed by the rock band *Os Mutantes* (The Mutants) singing "É Prohibido Prohibir" (It is Forbidden to Forbid) while swishing his hips? Did the authorities know that was a Situationist slogan? Did Veloso's long hair and girlish movements threaten the masculinity upon which family and nation depended? Or was there something more?

At first, the Tropicalists were opposed by the left as well as the right because they looked like US hippies and played electric guitars.[36] But Tropicália was not another example of US pop culture eating the world. Quite the contrary! The founders of Tropicália self-consciously enacted *Antropófago* (cannibalism) as outlined by Brazilian poet Oswald de Andrade in 1928. Inspired both by stories of triumphant native Americans eating invading Europeans and by the Dada journal, *Cannibale*, Andrade promoted Antropófago as a process by which dispossessed people become stronger by taking in the products of more powerful cultures and making them their own.[37] Tropicalists went a step further, incorporating not only the products of the powerful but also those of other oppressed peoples and then blending all of that with indigenous Brazilian artistic, literary, and musical forms. They did so with an energy that made people feel free, winning over those who had booed them for their electric guitars. Their hybrid glee mocked the rigid cultural nationalism of the dictatorship even when their lyrics were about Carmen Miranda. This was a revolution people could dance to. It had to be shut down. Brazil's military dictatorship weathered hurricane Tropicália but was ultimately unable to hold its ground against the sea change signaled by that tropical storm. Tropicálist Gilberto Gil became Brazil's Minister of Culture in 2003.

Introducing the Plumwood 5+2

And so, I introduce to you the Plumwood 5+2, which sounds like an old-school hip-hop combo but is just my spin on five of Plumwood's precepts plus two of my own. In her book subtitled *The Ecological Crisis of Reason*, Plumwood both critiqued centrist logics and showed the many ways that they lead to injurious, and therefore irrational, outcomes. Importantly, she also offered potential an-

---

36. See Dunn, Brutality Garden, for a full history of Tropicália.

37. de Andrade, Manifesto Antropofago.

tidotes, which we all can use today in whatever forms our work might take. However, these might not be enough. Hence, my two addenda.

The five elements of centrist thinking that Plumwood elaborated in *Environmental Culture: The Ecological Crisis of Reason* are: radical exclusion, homogenization and associated stereotyping, denial or backgrounding, incorporation, and instrumentalism.[38] She also had ideas about how these might be undermined. Let's now imagine how we could draw upon the spirit and praxes of the movements just discussed for that task. I also think that we need to undermine the hegemony of rationality itself and that we won't be able to do any of this unless we expand our own other-than-rational capacities, so I will offer some ideas about those two aims as well.

1. Radical Exclusion results from drawing a bright line between humans and other animals (and between culture and nature). To counter radical exclusion, Plumwood called for "emphasizing human continuity"[39] with the other-than-human world in order to "challenge or disrupt human conceptions of identity."[40] This might be done in any number of ways in verbal, visual, or performance arts, as well as in creative activist tactics.

2. Homogenization and Stereotyping occur when humans lump the multitudinous and diverse elements of the larger-than-human world together as 'the environment' or reduce all animals to automatons motivated only by instinctive imperatives. Noting that "terms like 'nature' lump seals and elephants along with mountains and clouds,"[41] Plumwood suggested emphasizing "nature's amazing diversity"[42] to counteract homogenization and stereotyping. Again, this might be done in any number of ways in verbal, visual, or performance arts as well as in creative activist tactics.

3. Denial and Backgrounding occur when people perceive the larger-than-human world as mere background to the endeavors of humans, simultaneously denying our dependence on plants and other animals for oxygen, calories, and other essential elements of our very existence. In order to counter the denial and backgrounding, Plumwood felt it would be necessary

38. Plumwood, Environmental Culture. See pages 92-122 for her analyses of these elements of centrist thinking.

39. Ibid., 111.

40. Ibid., 112.

41. Ibid.

42. Ibid.

to "puncture the Illusion of Disembeddedness."[43] This is surprisingly easy to do, merely by encouraging an audience to take a deep breath while reminding them that they are imbibing the exhalations of algae and trees. That tends to create a pleasant feeling of being held by the larger-than-human world, but I can imagine other interventions that might provoke a more distressing recognition of human frailties.

4. In order to challenge **Incorporation**, a key element of which is the definition of the Other by way of reference to the allegedly both normal and superior One, Plumwood felt it would be necessary to "displace the deeply rooted traditional view of non-human difference as lack."[44] Again, there are so many ways that reminders of the utility and delight of difference might be incorporated into verbal, visual, or performance arts, as well as creative activist tactics.

5. In order to counter **Instrumentalism**, in which elements of the larger-than-human world are reduced to mere resources or tools for human use, Plumwood called for more attention to "nature's own creativity and agency."[45] "Forget the passive machine model," she said, "and tell us more about the self-inventive and self-elaborative capacity of nature, about the intentionality of the non-human world."[46] Such stories might be easily woven into scholarly, artistic, and activist endeavors of all kinds.

Please note that all of these elements of centrist thinking are active not only in anthropocentrism but also in ethnocentrism, androcentrism, and similarly oppressive logics. Thus, similar antidotes might be used to help undermine racism, sexism, ableism, and other forms of bias among humans.

6. Even Plumwood, who critiqued rationalism, seemed to believe that thinking would be our primary tool for undoing the hegemony of **Rationality**. I suggest that we had better augment her prescriptions with tactics drawn from the history of counter-logical activist/artistic movements discussed above. Recall that 'surreal' means *more* real. As Plumwood noted, "our human-centredness weaves a dangerous set of illusions about the human condition right

---

43. Ibid.

44. Ibid.

45. Ibid., 113.

46. Plumwood, "Nature in the Active Voice," 124.

into the logic of our basic conceptual structures."[47] What better way to help humans set aside such illusions than a turn toward the more real?

7. Ourselves. It's not just that conscious, rational thought is inherently limited in what it can conceive. It's also that our capacities for imagination and our ability to reason in other ways must be presumed to be stunted. It's one thing to say, "Yes, we should think differently!" It's another to become able to do so. You may find that some of the exercises used by surrealists, such as automatic writing or drawing, loosen your associations sufficiently to allow new ideas and emotions to emerge. You may find that listening to Sun Ra does, as he had hoped, produce in you altogether new emotions. Because some poets take words apart and put them back together again differently, reading (or writing!) experimental poetry might, counterintuitively, help to loosen the stranglehold of words on your cognition. Drawing rather than describing your thoughts can also be useful in bringing new insights to light.[48]

Many of these practices can and should be collective rather than individual. I'm imagining an animal liberation movement and associated animal studies associations where, instead of demonstrating their capacity for self-sacrifice by enduring decades-long dreary meetings, activists — *and* scholars! — analyze problems by drawing and devise strategies by dancing.

Bringing ourselves into heartfelt and awestruck relationships with fantastic animals might also help to spark our imaginations while dampening our hubris.

Fantastic Animals

As Plumwood said, animals and other elements of the larger-than-human world are "presences to be encountered on their own terms."[49] This can be difficult to do when the presumption of human supremacy patterns your perceptions. At the same time, those humdrum human misconceptions mean that most people are walking around ready to be wowed.

Of course, flamboyantly non-categorical animals like kiwis or emus can prompt people to rethink what they thought they knew.[50] Similarly, animals with unique capabilities such as sonar, echolocation, or underwater engineer-

47. Ibid., 114.

48. Kantrowitz, Drawing Thought.

49. Plumwood, Environmental Culture, 112.

50. jones, "Derangement and Resistance."

ing can prompt awe. Octopi and other shape-shifters can leave people agape, as can any other animals whose ways of being in the world feel alien to humans.

But we need not turn to breathtaking examples to alert people to the wonders they encounter every day. Fantastic animals aren't always elsewhere: They live in our neighborhoods. Pigeons can detect the magnetic field of the Earth.[51] Bees teach their offspring to waltz.[52] Snails are mollusks of the earth, devouring detritus and leaving behind frass rich in nitrogen, phosphorus, and potassium as they aerate the soil they help to create.

In the co-creation of habitats and communities, other animals and their floral friends are always 'thinking' ecologically, in the sense that their perceptions and cognitions are attuned to the world beyond their bodies. Attuning ourselves to their multitudinous methods of solving problems might help us to become better able to think eco-logically, in the sense of using all of ourselves to perceive and respond to systems, whether they be ecosystems or our own interconnected systems of injustice.

Beneath the Paving Stones—The Beach!

The self-constituting creativity of ecosystems surrounds everyone, if only we would notice. Every modicum of earth contains multitudes, all interacting in ways that make our own lives possible.[53] Perhaps the persistent underground river of in some way surrealist art and activism might offer some avenues for making this underground more visible. The Situationists did, after all, inspire Parisians by reminding them of the pleasures smothered by concrete constru ctions.[54]

Some animal advocates are already working along these lines. I think of lynn mowson's powerful evocation of the voice of a cow[55] and the fabulous Duck Lake intervention of Yvette Watt and her colleagues, who blared Tchaikovsky from a boombox while flamboyantly dancing on a floating platform on a lake

51. Hopkin, "Homing Pigeons Reveal True Magnetism."

52. Grandoni, "Bees Teach Their Babies How to Dance."

53. Nardi, Life in the Soil, 47-236.

54. See Marcus, Lipstick Traces: A Secret History of the Twentieth Century for examples of delightfully subversive Situationist tactics.

55. mowson, "Bloodlines." Watch the talk about this and other projects at https://youtu.be/Xe4uiM QkHc4 to begin to imagine the full effect.

at sunrise on the first day of duck hunting season in Tasmania, simultaneously saving the lives of ducks that day and drawing media attention to their opposition to the hunt.[56] I recall the activists in the United States who did something similar, using paddleboats rigged out to look like giant bathtub rubber duckies.[57] More recently, I've seen news of business-suited men suckling from life-sized fiberglass cows and hoped that city-dwellers happening upon such activist-art installations experience the same sort of mind-opening surprise I felt when I saw the woodcock.

Just thinking of such interventions makes me feel more alive. My memories of similar actions in which I have participated are especially vivid. Even when the action was the equivalent of an aside or one-off amidst an allegedly more substantial campaign, the impact was palpable.

People want to feel more alive. That wish for vividness might be our way in. If there is a defining feature of our species, it may be the behavioral plasticity that allowed us to colonize so many different habitats, devising so many different ways of eating, clothing, and housing ourselves as well as so many different kinds of artistry in the process of forging so many diverse cultures. If so, it is at least possible that people, collectively, can become otherwise than the currently dominant modes of being-in-the-world. And, if the Caribbean surrealists were right that those modes are deadening, people would want a way out, if they knew that other ways of being were possible.

"Our ideas are on everyone's minds." That situationist slogan might apply to us, too. Just as they aimed to activate already-existing dissatisfaction with capitalism and tap into longing for less alienated relationships with other people, those of us who advocate for animals can call to already-existing wishes for fuller and better relationships with the larger-than-human world. It's lonely at the top! We can help people step off of their self-constructed pedestals, thereby becoming better able to enter into more equitable and satisfying relationships with each other and other animals.

When speaking of VINE Sanctuary to civic organizations in our small North American town, I try to remember to mention the wonders of local flora and fauna along with the happenings among sanctuary residents. For example, I often mention that turkeys co-created these forests in cooperation with beavers long before our species of great ape evolved on another continent. I wish I could convey to you the evident awe and delight with which audiences of everyday

---

56. Gallasch, "Duck Lake Performance a Protest against Hunting."

57. Chorush, Fowl Gestures - Cutting Edge Adventures in Animal Activism.

people greet such news. I'll sometimes mention some small thing I noticed that day, such as how vivid the lichens on the trees have become due to recent rains, in the hope that my own evident delight will spark attendees to be more attentive to such wonders themselves.

These are just a couple of examples of how easily anybody can incorporate Val Plumwood's suggestions into their ongoing academic, artistic, or activist work. As she wrote, "There are many ways we can challenge anthropocentric culture, and all of them are urgent."[58] I hope that anyone who is inspired by these words to do so in the spirit of surrealism will do me the favor of sending me news of how it goes.

Works Cited

Andrade, Oswald de. *Manifesto Antropofago*. 1928. .

Chorush, Bob. *Fowl Gestures - Cutting Edge Adventures in Animal Activism*. FriesenPress, 2013.

Depestre, René. "André Breton in Port-Au-Prince." In *Refusal of the Shadow: Surrealism and the Caribbean*, edited by Michael Richardson, 229–33. New York: Verso, 1996.

Doxtader, Erik. "Zōon Logon Ekhon: (Dis)Possessing an Echo of Barbarism." *Philosophy & Rhetoric* 50, no. 4 (November 15, 2017): 452–72.

Dunn, Christopher. *Brutality Garden: Tropicalia and the Emergence of a Brazilian Counterculture*, 2001.

Dwyer, Thomas J., Daniel G. McAuley, and Eric L. Derleth. "Woodcock Singing-Ground Counts and Habitat Changes in the Northeastern United States." *The Journal of Wildlife Management* 47, no. 3 (1983): 772–79.

Gallasch, Rosita. "Duck Lake Performance a Protest against Hunting." *Hawkesbury Gazette*, March 5, 2016, sec. Regional Focus.

Gilovich, Thomas, Dale Griffin, and Daniel Kahneman. *Heuristics and Biases: The Psychology of Intuitive Judgment*. Cambridge University Press, 2002.

Grandoni, Dino. "Bees Teach Their Babies How to Dance." *Washington Post*, March 9, 2023.

Hopkin, Michael. "Homing Pigeons Reveal True Magnetism." *Nature*, November 24, 2004.

jones, pattrice. "Derangement and Resistance: Reflections from Under the Glare of an Angry Emu." *Animal Studies Journal* 8, no. 1 (January 1, 2019): 1–20.

———. "Especismo y Capacitismo." In *Especismo y Lenguaje*, edited by Catia Faria and Nuria Almirón. Madrid: Plaza y Valdés, 2023.

Kantrowitz, Andrea. *Drawing Thought: How Drawing Helps Us Observe, Discover, and Invent*. MIT Press, 2022.

Kelley, Robin D. G. *Freedom Dreams: The Black Radical Imagination*. Boston: Beacon Press, 2002.

Kietzmann, Christian. "Aristotle on the Definition of What It Is to Be Human." In *Aristotle's Anthropology*, edited by Geert Keil and Nora Kreft, 25–43. Cambridge: Cambridge University Press, 2019.

Knabb, Ken, ed. *Situationist International Anthology*. Bureau of Public Secrets, 1981.

Ko, Aph. "Creating New Conceptual Architecture: On Afrofuturism, Animality, and Unlearning/Rewriting Ourselves." In *Aphro-Ism: Essays on Pop Culture, Feminism, and Black Veganism from Two Sisters*, edited by Aph Ko and Syl Ko. New York: Lantern Books, 2017.

Laraque, Paul. "André Breton in Haiti." In *Refusal of the Shadow: Surrealism and the Caribbean*, edited by Michael Richardson, 217–28. New York: Verso, 1996.

Levy, Neil. "Choices Without Choosers: Toward a Neuropsychologically Plausible Existentialism." In *Neuroexistentialism: Meaning, Morals, and Purpose in the Age of Neuroscience*, edited by Gregg D. Caruso and Owen J. Flanagan, 111–25. Oxford University Press, 2018.

Lorde, Audre. *Sister Outsider: Essays and Speeches.* Berkeley, CA: Crossing Press, 1984.

Marcus, Greil. *Lipstick Traces: A Secret History of the Twentieth Century.* Cambridge, MA, USA: Harvard University Press, 1989.

mowson, lynn. "Bloodlines." Presented at the Decolonizing Animals, Christchurch, NZ, July 4, 2019. .

Nardi, James B. *Life in the Soil: A Guide for Naturalists and Gardeners.* University of Chicago Press, 2009.

Plumwood, Val. *Environmental Culture: The Ecological Crisis of Reason.* New York; London: Routledge, 2002.

———. "Nature in the Active Voice." *Australian Humanities Review*, no. 46 (May 2009): 113–29.

Reid, Brian, and G. R. Williams. "The Kiwi." In *Biogeography and Ecology in New Zealand*, edited by G. Kuschel, 301–30. Monographiae Biologicae. Dordrecht: Springer Netherlands, 1975.

Richardson, Michael, ed. *Refusal of the Shadow: Surrealism and the Caribbean.* New York: Verso, 1996.

Rosemont, Franklin, and Robin D. G. Kelley, eds. *Black, Brown, & Beige: Surrealist Writings from Africa and the Diaspora.* Austin: University of Texas Press, 2009.

Rosenberg, Alex. "The Metaphysics of Microeconomics." *The Monist* 78, no. 3 (1995): 352–67.

Szwed, John. *Space Is the Place: The Lives and Times of Sun Ra.* Knopf Doubleday Publishing Group, 2012.

Tzara, Tristan. *Dada Manifesto 1918.* 1918. .

———. "Lecture on Dada." 1922. .

Vaneigem, Raoul. *The Revolution of Everyday Life.* Rebel Press, 1994.

Veini, Elisa. "Cannibals, Crabs, and Carmen Miranda: How Brazilian Modernists Keep On Unsettling Modernity." *Third Text* 18, no. 3 (May 1, 2004): 229–38.

Veloso, Caetano, and Christopher Dunn. "The Tropicalista Rebellion." *Transition*, no. 70 (1996): 116–38.

Wark, McKenzie. *The Beach Beneath the Street: The Everyday Life and Glorious Times of the Situationist International*. Verso Books, 2015.

9

Fighting Cocks

This essay was originally published in *Sister Species: Women, Animals, and Social Justice*, which was edited by Lisa Kemmerer and published by University of Illinois Press in 2011. This collection features reflections by a diverse array of animal advocates and is well worth your attention. I used my own contribution not only to elaborate the ideas about social construction of gender via animals that had arisen from my work with roosters but also to delve into my own psyche in order to try to answer a question that vexes many animal advocates: How is it that so many feminists withhold their solidarity from animals despite the deep linkages between speciesism and sexism?

Fighting Cocks

Ecofeminism Versus Sexualized Violence

I'm sitting in a low lawn chair, wearing boxer shorts and a t-shirt that says "Feminists for Animal Rights." My legs are streaked with mud and there's a bright yellow patch on one ankle that can only be dried egg yolk. My forearms are dotted with abrasions encircled by bruises. It's sunny and hot.

From under the brim of a floppy hat, I've got one eye on a Penguin paperback and the other on a multicolored rooster who might or might not start a fight. My hat sports the colors of the Brazilian flag, but ought to be UN blue, because I'm a peace-keeper today. At any moment, I might be forced to place myself between combatants. In the interim, I wait. And wait.

Welcome to the exciting yet enervating world of rooster rehabilitation. At the Eastern Shore Sanctuary, we help roosters who have formerly been used in cockfighting to live peacefully with other birds. Although illegal in many countries, and in most of the United States, cockfighting persists in parts of Asia, on some Pacific Islands, in parts of South and Central America, and in the southern United States. In this cruel "sport," roosters are socialized to view other roosters as predators, provoked by injections of testosterone and methamphetamines, armed with steel blades attached to the stumps of their sawed-off spurs, and then matched in bloody battles from which the only escape is death. In between events, they are typically isolated in small cages or tethered to stakes adjacent to A-frame shelters.

Because cockfights are inevitably the site of illegal gambling, authorities are quicker to intervene in cockfighting than in other forms of animal cruelty. Unfortunately, their interventions usually do not aid the true victims of the crime —roosters. Most often, birds confiscated from cockfighting operations are euthanized. We are able to rescue and rehabilitate only a handful of the hundreds of former fighting cocks who are confiscated every year. For each rooster we are able to save, our sanctuary means everything. Because chickens are very close genetically to the wild jungle fowl (the living ancestors of modern chickens), many former fighters choose a feral lifestyle, sleeping in trees and wandering the woods all day. Others move into the coops, joining former egg factory inmates and big "broiler" chickens, in a more sedate lifestyle. It's their choice, as it should be.

How did a lesbian-feminist from Baltimore end up rehabbing roosters in a rural chicken yard? Just like the old joke, it all started with a chicken crossing a road. Shortly after unknowingly moving to an epicenter of industrial poultry production, my former partner Miriam Jones and I rescued a chicken from the roadside. I'd always admired birds from afar, but was surprised to find myself growing emotionally close to this ungainly creature, who sometimes looked so much like a reptile that I knew scientists were right about birds being dinosaurs. I also noticed that she had my grandmother's eyes (as well as her stubborn charm) and that her feet were amazingly similar to human hands. I'd always felt so earthbound, but here was the evidence: People are related to birds! I was excited by this discovery, and very touched by this particular bird's growing attachment to me.

One day, Mosselle (as we called her, after my grandmother) made a new sound that seemed some kind of announcement. "Maybe she laid an egg!" I thought. I ran around looking for where she might have hidden her prize. A few days later, early in the morning, she gargled like she was choking, and I worried that she might be sick. Luckily, somebody with some sense commented, "That bird's a rooster." I had misunderstood an adolescent rooster's first attempts at crowing!

I struggled with the realization that my beloved friend was a rooster, rather than a hen. Even though he hadn't changed, it was hard not to see him differently. I struggled not to let all of the things I had heard about arrogant, posturing, aggressive roosters change the way I saw this dear young bird, who had come to count on me. This was my first inkling of the ways that gendered preconceptions alter our perceptions of chickens and other nonhuman animals.

That insight was a long time coming. "*What was I thinking?!?*" That's what I wonder every time I remember the years I spent as a vegetarian-but-not-vegan lesbian/feminist/anti-racist/pro-peace/anti-poverty activist who insisted that *everything* — racism, sexism, homophobia, capitalism, militarism, etc., etc. — was connected . . . but somehow managed to leave nonhuman animals out of the equation. For me, the question is not "what led me to include other animals in my activism?" but, rather, "what took me so long to include other animals in my activism?" It is a question worth answering. After we make a radical change in thought or behavior, we have a tendency to distance our new selves from our previous selves. That's understandable, but not useful. If we can't remember —

much less have empathy with — our former ways of thinking and feeling, how can we make meaningful contact with those who still think and feel as we used to do? And, if we can't make contact, how can we prompt others to rethink what feel to them like intensely personal choices?

So, as much as it makes me feel queasy to do so, I'm going to try to actually answer the question of why an altruistic, animal-loving, vegetarian feminist activist, who insisted that all forms of oppression were linked, took so damn long to go vegan.

I quit eating meat in 1976, the same year I turned 15, came out, and went to my first gay rights rally (not in that order). When I say that I "came out," I mean that I resolved to never lie about my love for women, never deliberately pass for straight, and never deny a lover by calling her "him." To do so, I felt, would be to betray not only the women I desired, but my deepest self.My decision to quit meat was equally simple. Somehow, through the confluence of mid-seventies influences, I knew that vegetarianism was a particularly healthy way to eat. One day, quite suddenly, I realized: If I didn't need to eat meat to stay alive, then eating meat was killing for pleasure. I couldn't live with myself, wouldn't be the nonviolent person I believed myself to be, if I killed other beings — beings who had their own desires — merely to satisfy *my* desire for the taste of their flesh.

Looking back, I see that both decisions, coming out and quitting meat, are about the interplay of desire and integrity. Sometimes integrity means being true to your desires, and sometimes integrity requires you to refuse your desires. I also notice that both decisions were about bodies and consent. A primary tenet of gay liberation is that what consenting people do with each other's bodies is nobody else's business. And, of course, eating meat is something you do to somebody else's body without their consent. Since both of these ethical decisions were about bodies, I don't want to leave out their visceral dimensions. These were full-bodied decisions. I didn't just *think,* "I'm going to quit meat," and "I'm not going to lie about my sexuality." Once I had thought through the questions, my body recoiled at the *notion* of eating a cow or pretending to be straight. I remember very clearly the feeling of revulsion that arose whenever I summoned up the mental image of a cow, and imagined eating her, which is particularly interesting in light of what I'm going to tell you a little later.When I look back on that earnest teenager making those two seemingly unrelated decisions, it seems to me now that in both instances she was decisively rejecting patriarchal control of her body. I know now that homophobia is what Suzanne Pharr calls "a weapon of sexism," one of many means of coercing people into patriarchal families. And I know now that patriarchy (male rule) and pastoralism (herding farmed animals) co-evolved, the ideas and practices of each commingling with and compounding the other.

But I didn't know any of this back in 1976. Or 1986. Or even 1996, although then I was on the brink of an emotional and intellectual breakthrough that would lead me to go vegan and become an animal advocate.

Meanwhile, I was vegetarian, not vegan. Not even reliably vegetarian. I held out well enough while I was living rough, as a teenager, supporting myself at an urban fast food restaurant. All of us relied on free food from the restaurant to augment salaries that didn't cover rent and groceries. Sometimes, when I was really hungry and couldn't bring myself to stomach one more meal of salad and french fries, I'd break down and resentfully eat a burger or piece of chicken. I have a very clear memory of me, at about 17, sitting in a cheap molded plastic chair, looking out the grimy window at a grey day, choking down chicken flesh thinking, "this is so wrong!"Those were raw years for me, with the wounds of a troubled childhood still oozing anger and pain that anybody could see. Maybe that's why it was so easy for me to hold onto the bodily empathy in which my vegetarianism was most deeply rooted. But then I entered a period of years wherein I walled off feelings in order to focus on pulling myself out of the dangerous lifestyle into which I had drifted. I got a good job. I started night school. And I forgot about nonhuman animals.

In the early and mid 80s, I lived with lovers who ate meat and I also occasionally ate, or even prepared, meat. But when those relationships ended, I went back to being steadily vegetarian at home, and happily so. But if I had a really strong urge for a hamburger or a pepperoni pizza, I sometimes gave in, rationalizing that compromise would maintain a vegetarian diet in the long run better than rigidity.

Somehow, the ethical clarity of my original decision to be vegetarian had become muddied and muddled. I knew very well that I tended to want to eat meat when I felt angry. I knew very well that eating that hamburger would be displacing my aggression onto an innocent nonhuman. And yet I did eat that hamburger every once in a while. More often than I want to admit.

Those murderous "lapses" were mentally and morally tolerable to me, leaving me feeling only slightly more guilty than I already felt, because nonhuman animals had gone missing from my emotional landscape. Those occasional hamburgers were just "meat" to me rather than the remains of dead nonhumans with whom I actively empathized.

All of that stopped, thanks to Alice Walker. In her essay, "Am I Blue?" Walker describes going out for a celebratory steak dinner only to have the thought, "I am eating misery" interrupt her pleasure. That phrase must have stealthily planted itself in my brain, because the next time I tried to give into a craving for meat, I had no sooner taken a bite than the words "I am eating misery" echoed in my head. My stomach reeled. I spit out the half-chewed flesh and have never been tempted again.

So, for me at least, the ethical mandate had to be full-bodied — a matter of heart and gut as well as mind — in order to be truly sustainable. I suspect that's true for many people. Abstract rules are easily broken. People often do things they know they ought not to do, if they can get away with it, especially if they can tell themselves that it doesn't hurt anybody.

Which brings us to the next lesson we can learn from my past misdeeds: We must keep the real repercussions of our actions (or inaction) *on actual nonhuman animals* always in mind. That's true, I think, not only for would-be vegans but also for those who purport to be advocates for nonhuman animals.

The question remains: Why did I think of the decision whether or not to eat meat as an apolitical personal choice rather than a political decision (like every other decision)? The ardent activism of my teens returned with a vengeance in my late twenties, once the chore of working my way through college was behind me, and I was safely ensconced in graduate school. I involved myself in local struggles for fair housing and against police brutality and in national struggles against AIDS and for peace. I marched and chanted, led workshops, organized sit-ins and kiss-ins, distributed condoms and clean needles, and sat through endless hours of tedious meetings. Whenever I had a little extra money (which wasn't often), I gave it to PETA (the only animal organization I knew about). And yet, when one of the students in the social change class that I was teaching asked me why our line-up of social change movements didn't include the animal rights movement, I incoherently responded that I supported animal rights, but that this issue was tangential to the linked oppressions (racism, sexism, etc.) that were the focus of our scrutiny.

What was I thinking?!? As a feminist, I was well-versed in the theory behind the slogan, "the personal is political," which simply means that everything we choose to do (or not do) *matters.* What in the world led me to believe that every decision in life — including decisions about how to conduct one's most intimate relations — was a political decision *except* the decision whether or not to eat meat? I can't even say "except what we eat," since I was boycotting grapes (farm workers) and Coca-Cola (apartheid) at the time. I also believed in, although couldn't always afford to support, organic agriculture. I recognized that many food decisions were political decisions.

This very strange notion that the decision whether or not to eat nonhuman animals is a purely personal decision, uniquely exempt from the ethical and political considerations that ought to inform every other decision, is quite common and worthy of our attention. When I interrogate this notion, I find that, for me, declaring vegetarianism a political decision would have been tantamount to mandating vegetarianism for everybody, and that there were two reasons I hesitated to do this: excessive deference to religion and a misplaced application of the right to bodily self-determination.

Like many people raised to respect "freedom of religion," I used to shy away from analyzing the implications of the political ideologies that call themselves religions. Even though I was an atheist, I never challenged anybody about their religious beliefs. And though I had not yet had the pleasure of hearing Christians shout "God made chickens for us to eat!" I knew that most Christians view the eating of meat as a literally God-given right. Since I saw religion as a sacrosanct personal decision, I felt that I had no right to challenge this religious understanding. Only when I quit thinking of religious ideologies as uniquely exempt from ethical scrutiny was I free to directly challenge the human hubris implicit in most of the belief systems that men have constructed to explain the world and claim dominion over nonhuman animals.

I say "men" rather than "people" because it *was* men, and also because those same stories have been and continue to be used to assert male dominion over women and girls. So, it's not surprising that an association between animal advocacy and feminism dates back to those hunger-striking vegetarian suffragists who were force-fed meat in a vain effort to get them to swallow male domination. Of course, control of female bodies is precisely the point of patriarchy. Maybe that's why — in spite of the fact that women have made up the majority of animal advocates from the earliest days of anti-vivisection agitation to the current era of open rescues — many women feel oppressed when somebody tells them they ought not to eat farmed animals. The mandate to "go vegan" can *feel* to some women like one more instance of others telling you what you must or cannot do with your own body. That's because, as was the case for me during my lapses from vegetarianism, the nonhuman animals are absent from the mental equation. Only if other animals enter the picture is it possible to see that eating meat is doing something to *somebody else's* body.

Women make most food purchases and preparation decisions. If women are going to *both* go vegan *and* withstand the demands of male family members for meat, then women must be emboldened to resist their own subordination and *at the same time* reject the oppression of nonhuman individuals. In other words, animal advocates must balance the demand that women *give up their power* over nonhuman animals by encouraging them to *seize their power* among human animals. This sounds tricky, but comes easy once you see that sexism and speciesism, having grown up together across the centuries, are co-dependent siblings of dysfunctional patriarchal families.

But before I illustrate this assertion, I have one more question for my former self: Why did it take me so long to extend my personal ban on meat to include dairy and eggs?

Here are some of my predictable and common answers to "*What was I thinking*?": I didn't know about battery cages and forced pregnancies. I didn't think about what happened to cows and hens after their bodies stopped producing economically profitable quantities of milk and eggs. I had been seduced by Elsie the Cloverland cow and other fictions designed to deceive us into believing that happy hens and placid cows live on spacious farms and are not at all inconvenienced by the friendly farmers who collect their eggs and relieve them of excess milk.

My former partner, Miriam Jones burst my bubble a couple of years before we moved to the country and found that first chicken. We jiggled our checkbook, and I was able to donate a lot more money than I had ever been able to donate before. Soon the newsletters of the animal rights organizations, farmed animal sanctuaries, and anti-vivisection societies began flooding our mailbox, and we learned more than we ever wanted to know. Thanks to an early childhood trauma involving a flood of blood, I have a hard time with gory images, so Miriam screened the brochures, telling me the relevant facts and showing me the photos she felt I really needed to see. One picture I really needed to see was of hens in battery cages. I quit eggs. Dairy was more difficult. I had a really hard time believing what Miriam was reading to me. Something about the whole issue was deeply destabilizing, so much so that I half-believed that animal advocates were trying to trick me, even though I knew that was an absurd idea. *What was I thinking?!?* Perhaps the more apt question would be: *What wasn't I thinking and why wasn't I thinking it?*

To answer this question, we need to explore an incident years earlier. I really don't want to tell you about this; I had forgotten all about it until I started writing this essay. Indeed, my wish not to speak of this incident was so strong that I was even more belated in meeting this essay's writing deadline than I usually am. I repeatedly stopped right at this point in the essay, set my work aside, and forgot about it for days or even weeks. What I kept wanting to forget, what I don't want you to know, is that I *did* know that something was very wrong with dairy. I *did* see, felt uncomfortable, then promptly forgot that cows were hurt in the process of producing milk and cheese.

Here's what happened: I went to visit my sister in Vermont, where she was living while finishing her undergraduate degree. I was in my mid twenties, just starting graduate school, and the demands of working my way through college and getting myself into graduate school had precluded any substantial attention to activism for several years. Soon I would again be the fierce fire-breathing activist I had been in my late teens, but at that moment I was disoriented, coming up for air after years of scholarly submersion to find myself living in a university milieu so substantially different than the streets of my teens that it might have been a different planet.

My younger sister was my only family connection, though she was living far from our hometown of Baltimore. Maybe that's why I was so hesitant to challenge her when she assured me that those mean-looking milk machines didn't hurt the cows. Maybe it was my overall sense of dislocation that led me to feel so dizzy as I looked down the row of milking stalls.

Or maybe there's some other reason that I can't even remember whether or not there were cows in those stalls as I stood there feeling silly and silenced and angry and ashamed all at the same time. Maybe it's significant that *I can't even tell you whether or not I saw a cow at all.* All I know for sure is that my sister took me to a local, probably small, maybe organic, dairy farm; I felt uneasy and we argued briefly, and then the incident disappeared from my memory along with the cows, leaving me free to continue to consume dairy products without even a twinge of bad conscience.

It would be years before cows reappeared in my consciousness, before Farm Sanctuary newsletters would combine with my own scholarly musings about daughters and dairy cows as property of husbands to finally lead me to the cows themselves, what they wanted, how they felt, how terribly unfair it was for them to be ensnared not only by our ideas about nonhuman animals but also by our ideas about femaleness. And even then it took me more than a year to get what I now call "the demon dairy" all the way out of my life, actively wrestling with what now seem to be inane rationalizations all the way.Understand: I do not forgive myself for this; I am just reporting what happened. Nor do I seek to expiate my wrongs by confessing. No. What I want to know—what I think we need to know—is *why*. Why was that dairy farm visit so profoundly upsetting that I immediately repressed it, and my recollection of it now, years later, has all the hallmarks of a traumatic memory? Why, once I brought the issue back into consciousness, did I so strongly resist remembering what I knew, and doing what I needed to do?

I can't explain from the inside. From the outside the response is easy: "she didn't want to give up that sharp Vermont cheddar, so she put it out of her mind." But since the forgetting was not a conscious choice, I doubt that's how it happened. Perhaps, more than the loss of favored dairy products, I dreaded the sickening feeling of complicity that emerged when I finally confronted, and rejected, dairy.

I'll never know for sure why the queasy uneasiness I felt at the dairy farm slithered out of sight so easily. What I do know for sure is that this kind of shifty slippage probably helps to explain why the altruistic, animal-loving, feminist friend who sat next to me sobbing as we watched the documentary "Peaceable Kingdom" is still eating meat. Animal advocates need to understand this response more clearly so that we can understand why efforts to force people to confront their complicity in cruelty rarely lead to behavior changes.

The ease with which we forget facilitates animal abuse and all other atrocities that tend to make us sputter and reach for the word "unspeakable": child abuse, nukes, poverty in the midst of plenty. We need to learn how to speak of such things in a way that keeps them uncomfortably conscious. This requires us to see and think about the sexual and perversely sexualized exploitation of female farmed animals *that is the norm* in animal agriculture.

When I look closely at dairy, I see the hurtful exploitation of specifically female bodies so that some people can enjoy sensual pleasures of consumption while others enjoy the psychological pleasure of collecting profits from the exertions of somebody else's body. Cows are forcibly impregnated, dispossessed of their children, and then painfully robbed of the milk produced by their bodies for those children. No wonder I didn't want to see my complicity! Most women don't consciously perceive the everyday violence against girls and women that permeates and structures our society. How much harder it is, then, to see the gendered violence against nonhuman animals behind the everyday items on the grocery store shelf. When we, as women, partake of that violence, we participate in sexism even as we enjoy the illusory benefits of speciesism. No wonder a glimpse of the sexist violence behind my breakfast cereal left me dizzy.

If we're going to make any headway on dairy and eggs, we've got to confront this directly. We've got to start talking to women about the sexist exploitation of female reproductive capacities to produce consumer goods that hurt women and children. We' must talk about this explicitly, knowing that one in three women has herself been raped or battered, and may thus have strong or seemingly strange reactions to the facts. We need to confront the sickening collision of sex and violence by which nonhuman animals are electroejaculated and forcibly impregnated for human pleasures. We have to be able to look at *all* of the complicated and uncomfortable dynamics that drive and derive from this sexualized exploitation. Similar conflagrations of gender, violence, and pleasure smolder at the source of cultural products and activities as seemingly disparate as pornography, interrogatory torture, and cockfighting.

Which brings us back to chickens. Roosters are both the victims and the unwitting agents of human sexism. One of the most damaging aspects of sexism is the confusion between sex (maleness or femaleness) and gender (masculinity or femininity). Some people are more assertive while others are more yielding. Some are brave; some are nurturing. Sexism assigns such characteristics to gender and then asserts that gender is a natural expression of sex. Thus, girls who are assertive and boys who are nurturing are led to believe that there is something unnatural about them. While sex is a physical fact, gender is what social scientists call a "social construct." Social constructs feel real but are, in truth, just ideas made up and maintained by members of a social group. People use other animals to make gender seem as real as sex, pointing to nonhuman animals as "proof" that certain kinds of behavior are typically male or typically female. Not surprisingly, given the wide range of animal behavior in nature, they always find what they're seeking. For many years, male field researchers studying primates explained away, refused to record, or simply failed to perceive behaviors that were inconsistent with their preconceived dominance hierarchies. (Similar biases and blind spots led scientists to miss or dismiss observations of homosexuality in hundreds of species.)

People also force or trick nonhuman animals into acting out sexist stereotypes, then point to those same beings as evidence that the stereotypes reflect a "natural order". This is nowhere more clear than with fighting cocks, who are subjected to an array of abuses designed to trick them into murderous aggression.

Roosters have long been seen as embodiments of masculinity. That's how the word "cock" came to be used as slang for a human penis. International studies of cock-fighters show that men and boys see fighting roosters as expressions of their own masculinity, and they feel shame if one of "their" roosters behaves normally, fleeing from an aggressor or declining to attack a retreating bird. In contrast, unnaturally aggressive birds are accorded an almost totemic respect. Cockfighters have very strong ideas about what they believe to be natural behavior for roosters, and they fail to recognize how their interventions create unnatural fights where roosters kill one another.In nature, roosters are the sentinels and protectors of the flock. They constantly scan the skies and the horizon for predators, while joining the hens to look for food.

In contrast to the myth of male stoicism, roosters tend to be more emotional than hens, probably because they need to be more sensitive to potential threats. Of course there is much overlap between the characteristics of roosters and the characteristics of hens, as well as much variation among roosters and among hens. A rooster will risk his life protecting the flock from a predator. A hen will often take the same risk protecting her chicks. Some roosters are very nurturing toward chicks; others simply ignore their offspring. Some roosters spend all of their time with hens. Others prefer the company of other roosters, or stay to themselves. Neither wild jungle fowl nor feral roosters risk their survival in death matches with other roosters. Roosters sometimes struggle for dominance and territory, but the fights are short and rarely lead to serious injury. Certainly, fights such as are seen in cockfighting spectacles, where the victorious bird continues to attack until the loser is dead, do not occur. When a rooster has been bested, he assumes a submissive posture or runs away. The victor then postures or crows, signaling, "I've won!" Breeders and trainers of fighting cocks prohibit roosters from learning the social signals of conflict resolution. Isolated in cages or tethered to stakes, fed less than they would choose to eat, and kept apart from hens, these roosters are in a constant state of frustrated excitation. Add the stress of transport, the confusing sights and sounds of a busy event, and the injection of drugs or hormones, and it's easy to see how terrified roosters can be brought to fight to the death when faced with a similarly terrified bird armed with steel talons. This is the secret that cockfighters can't face, and don't want you to know: Roosters fight from fear, not aggression.

That's the secret of our rooster rehabilitation program, too. We rehabilitate fighting cocks by teaching them that they don't have to be afraid of other birds, using the same principles that a psychotherapist might use to help patients overcome phobias or post-traumatic stress. At first, they simply need to be soothed and given time to see and be near other birds without fear. Then, during supervised free periods, such as the one that began this essay, a former fighter is allowed to roam freely until he starts a fight, at which time he is placed back in his spacious rehabilitation cage, from which he can see and interact with, but not hurt or be hurt by, the other birds. Over time, a rooster is able to be free for longer and longer periods (hence the boredom for us), until he can be trusted to mingle peacefully with the other birds all day long. The rehabilitation process takes anywhere from a few days to several weeks. Some birds "get it" very quickly, and seem palpably relieved to be out of harm's way. Others take longer to relax. While personality clashes sometimes have required us to shift birds from yard to yard, we've never had a fighting cock so incorrigible that we couldn't find a place for him to be free. Fighting unto death is not their natural behavior.

People need safety to find freedom, too. More than we realize, we all lead lives structured and constricted by lies and fear. That's why I've tried so hard to tell the truth in this essay, because none of us can be truly free in the context of violent duplicity.

10

Animale

I wrote this piece for a special issue of the Italian journal *Liberazioni* published in the Spring of 2020. For their 40th issue, 40 writers and activists reflected on the word "animal" or "animal." This piece was translated into Italian before publication, so this is the first time it appears in English. Many thanks to Gorgo Losi for that translation and to my comrades at *Liberazioni* for their efforts to foster truly radical animal activism in Italy.

Animale

Plants are more rational than you.

If a tree learns, through scent signals, that insects are eating nearby trees, it will immediately release chemicals to make its own leaves less palatable.

If you learn that you are endangered, you might take similarly effective action. But you also might freeze or do something nonsensical.

That's because you're an animal, and animals have emotions.

Emozione and *movimento* both descend from the Latin *movere.* That's apt because emotion evolved to motivate motion.

Emotions are natural processes arising in animal bodies, including our own. In addition to prompting action at times of danger, emotions motivate us us to value and preserve meaningful relationships.

Emotions are our most powerful renewable resource, but they also can lead us astray, particularly if they are overwhelming or have been warped by trauma. Most humans today, whether or not they have been personally victimized, have emotions that have been shaped in some way by the violence that divides the whole world into pieces of private property policed by armies. All are now faced with the terrifying crisis of climate change. We are, in short, injured animals faced with a crisis of our own creation that is, nonetheless, beyond our comprehension.

Luckily, we are not the only animals on the planet. While we all have emotions, each species is unique in some way. Stop for a moment to recall all of the different animals you've ever heard about. Bats. Octopuses. Elephants. Ducks. Imagine how many things they can perceive that you cannot, how many things they may know that you don't know. Remember: Some species existed for millions of years before humans evolved.

I write these words as Australia burns. Billions of animals have perished in wildfires made more ferocious by human-engendered climate change. Many species may be gone forever.

In that country, men in power continue to defend fossil fuels and to deny climate change. These are the same men who have set up detention centers for asylum seekers. All over the world, we see the same pattern of racist anti-immigrant policies enacted by parties that deny reality. Masses of people fanatically support fascistic strongmen who tell them fantastical lies. Many of those who oppose such cruelty and falsity seem stunned into immobility. Others seem not able to imagine any responses other than those that have so-far failed to prevent the crisis.

Meanwhile, dialogue falters as consensus reality crumbles. We cannot seem to agree on the facts, or even whether such a thing as a fact exists, which is not surprising, since we are not truth-seeking creatures. We are problem-solvers who have reached the limit of their collective abilities. We are social animals whose bodies tell us to seek the safety of the group when in danger. So long as our groups are defined by supremacist ideologies—including the belief in human supremacy that underlies all other claims of superiority—we will collectively continue to respond to the climate emergency in ways that endanger ourselves and other animals.

We need new groups, based upon empathy rather than illusory identities, from within which to feel safe-enough to try new ways of solving problems. We need new stories, new narratives within which to construct ourselves and our communities. Remember: Nonhuman animals have been resisting human supremacy for as long as humans have been behaving badly. So, other animals must be part of our stories and communities—as neighbors and comrades, not objects or symbols.

How can we begin?

Prima: Recognize emotion—including desire, in all its queerness—as the primary driver of animal behavior, including our own.

Seconda: Recognize the webs of relationships—including both social and material ecologies—in which we all operate.

Terza: Learn to think differently. I mean this literally: We must become able to think in different neural patterns, to envision truly new ways of being in the context of a climate that is itself different than animals like us have ever experienced before. We may also need new emotions, by which I mean new patterns of responding with our bodies to our physical and social circumstances.

Nobody knows how to do this, not yet. I do have three ideas: (1) work locally, being attentive to place; and (2) learn from the larger-than-human world.

We will need to rebuild our communities from the ground up. So, begin where you are: Consider the plants and animals, including human beings, who share your habitat, whether this be household, neighborhood, or city. What can be done to make this a more peaceful, equitable, and habitable place for everyone? How can you personally strengthen your relationships within this habitat?

Notice especially the ways that other animals—whether insects, birds, or mammals—resist or ignore rules made by humans. Also notice the ways that trees and other plants anchor everything. Remember that without their ability to turn sunshine into calories none of us would have anything to eat or any oxygen to breathe. We depend entirely upon them.

Plants are more rational than you. Birds and bees can see colors you can't see. Trees and fungi can communicate in ways that you cannot sense or understand. The world swirls with life forms, including but not limited to other animals, from whom we can learn and to whom we can extend solidarity as we struggle together against the hegemony of the "human."

11

Queer Eye on the EA Guys

In recent years, the theory of Effective Altruism has gained increasing traction within animal advocacy, influencing both donors and the organizations who seek their support. Published by Oxford University Press in 2023, *The Good It Promises, the Harm It Does: Critical Essays on Effective Altruism* collects essays by critics of EA ranging from professional philosophers to grassroots activists. This was my contribution to that volume, the whole of which I hope you will read, especially if you or someone you know has been swayed by the promises and claims of EA.

QUEER EYE ON THE EA GUYS

Imagine this: You live in an enchanted forest, but the forest is on fire. You have to decide what to do. As thickening smoke makes it harder and harder to see, your own rising panic makes it harder to think clearly. All around you, other animals are in similar predicaments. Flee? Where and with whom? Fight the fire? How and with what? The questions become even more befuddling when you try to take the interests of others into account rather than thinking only about your own skin and kin. Alarm cries and howls of pain surround you.

Out of the din and smog steps a hero with a shining sword. He once saved a whole village by giving them mosquito nets! Surely, he will know what to do.

He does know what to do, he assures you: It's merely a matter of using the magic sword to slice away superfluities and sentimentality in order to avoid wasting resources on anything other than what will bring the maximum benefit per unit of energy expended. You must be ruthless, he says. Pay no attention to the squirrel screaming in that tree! Stopping to save her will only detract you from what you need to do, which is to save the lives of five future squirrels by preventing future fires.

"You know how to do that?" you ask. "Yes!" he says confidently, but you notice that he mumbles the explanation and that nonhuman animals seem unmoved by his boasts. You feel uncertain too: In the midst of an emergency caused, in part, by the failure to think ecologically and respond multidimensionally, could there really be one best thing to do.?

I asked you to imagine all of that, but in fact it's all true: You really do live in an enchanted forest: Life thrums all around you, whether or not you happen to be tuned into it. Your very life depends on trees, who converse with one another via underground networks of fungi as insects and other underground animals convert dead matter into life-giving soil nearby. The forest really is on fire, both literally and figuratively, as climate change sparks wildfires, floods, and other death-dealing catastrophes.

You really do need to decide what to do. With so many competing emergencies — did I mention the slow-moving collapse of consensus reality and the consequent upsurge in neofascism? — it can be hard to figure out how to expend your own finite time, energy, and other resources. And here comes our hero, calling himself Effective Altruism, to show you the way — if only you will agree to use his sword to slash anything and anyone he considers to be superfluous.

I want to encourage you not to follow him, even as I understand how emergencies can lead people to embrace decisive men offering simple solutions (*see neofascism above*). I too long for clear answers that might be found by means of easy assessments. Alas, it is not so. Solutions that are at once frugal and significantly useful are vanishingly rare when solving even the most simple problems. The likelihood of decisively identifying such solutions for complex problems tends to zero.

I said that you need to decide what to do, but I do too. When I jumped into activism as a queer teen in the 1970s, I already had an inkling that I was choosing to do what I was best suited and situated to do. Since the 1990s, when juggling urgent work on the AIDS emergency with long-term projects to undermine the structural inequalities that led that crisis to fall hardest upon people already disadvantaged by homophobia, racism, poverty, and disability, I have been urgently aware of an internal imperative to strategically make the most of my finite energies.

My own ways of reckoning are rather more queer than those of EA. I believe that effective activism begins with an accurate analysis of the problem to be solved, including the relationships among its causes as well as its relationship to other problems. Every problem is a *situation*, by which I mean a set of circumstances at a particular time and place. So, let's begin our assessment of EA by being sure to situate *ourselves* accurately, as great apes in the midst of unprecedented emergencies who urgently need to figure out what to do.

Here We Are

Here we are, on planet Earth, at the present moment. Of course, I can't know what will happen in the interval between the day I type these words and the day you read them, but what's happening as I write is that humans are coping with—or, rather, failing to adequately cope with—three interrelated emergencies: (1) the climate emergency, which becomes more catastrophic with each passing day; (2) a worldwide pandemic; and (3) cascading collapses in consensus reality, which make solving the other two problems seem impossible.

Who is this "we" of whom I speak? A species of great ape who, by virtue of exceptional behavioral plasticity, have dispersed across the planet, often wreaking wreckage along the way. Their ability to solve discrete problems via technology can be remarkable, but social and ecological problems tend to vex them. They fight with each other a lot, often over the sound symbols they call words and other metaphorical matters.

Within their social groups, problems such as inequality or violence can persist for decades or even centuries despite steady efforts at amelioration. Until they ran out of planet, ecological problems tended to be solved by going elsewhere or sending some subset of the population elsewhere.

At present, despite decades of concerted effort by many of the most knowledgeable and politically powerful among them, they have collectively failed to make any substantial progress in confronting the escalating emergency of climate change—itself a result of lack of foresight among many of the most knowledgeable among them in past decades. Now in the midst of a pandemic that has killed millions, their experts are unable to convince enough people to take even the most self-evidently useful measures to protect themselves and their offspring. Of course, they cannot agree about what might be the cause of the breakdown of the social processes by which they used to be better able to agree about what reality might be.

Like all animals, humans are less rational than plants. Emotion, which evolved to motivate motion, infuses all of their cognitive processes. Jolted by fight-flight-freeze reactions, they can become confused. Driven by desire, they reach for happiness, safety, and each other.

A Question of Methods

We reach for each other. Because we are animals, we have wishes. We *want* to live and to be happy. Because we are social animals, we want and need to do this in the company of others, who also wish to live and to be happy. Our feeling good depends, in part, on the wellbeing of the social groups in which we participate. As social animals, we are physically predisposed not only to want to feel good but also to *be* good (or at least be *seen* as good), and that means we have to make some methodological decisions, whether or not we recognize them as such.

First, we must decide what we mean by "good." Next, we must decide how we will assess ourselves against that standard. So, in order to determine whether EA will be helpful to humans in the current context, we have a series of questions to answer: First, since EA is rooted in utilitarianism, we have to decide whether utilitarianism is the method of moral reckoning we want to use. If so, then we also need to decide whether EA's methods of assessing efficacy really do add up.

Methods of Moral Reasoning

I've had a number of conversations with young acolytes of EA, and those dialogues always seem to founder upon the same shoals. The problem turns out to be rooted in their presumption that the common-sense utilitarian precept of "the greatest good for the greatest number" is self-evidently the best goal of both moral and practical decision-making. Indeed, some seem not to realize that there are competing methods of moral decision-making nor be able to imagine that there might be equally—or more!—valid ways of thinking about efficacy. In dialogue, this leads to mutual frustration: The EA acolyte cannot understand why I so stubbornly resist what seems self-evidently true to them. Meanwhile, I feel increasingly exasperated by what feels to me like discussing comparative theology with a fundamentalist.

So, let's avoid that impasse by making sure that we are working with the same facts about the diversity of ways of thinking about ethics. While we all do begin from the same place at birth, as squalling bundles of sensation and emotion who feel good or bad in the physical sense and are highly motivated to win the favor of the adults upon whom we depend for survival, people can and do develop different ways of thinking about good and bad in the moral sense. Utilitarianism as it is popularly understood is one of those methods. It's popular because it is simple to understand, but that simplicity is also its downfall as it falters in situations of ambiguity and grinds to a halt when encountering the unquantifiable.

Understanding more about how moral reasoning develops may help us to situate utilitarianism as one among many options for deciding what to do. Moral reasoning develops over time. We all begin as infants, who feel good or feel bad. Being scolded or punished feels bad. In contrast, being praised or rewarded feels good. And so begins the process of association between *feeling* good or bad and *being* good or bad.

Notice that we use the same words—good, bad—for both physical sensations and moral evaluations. This association often carries over into adulthood, regardless of whether or not we consciously believe that riches are the result of virtue. You know what I mean, probably, because you've felt it yourself.

Perhaps you have emerged from an aquatic workout refreshed and energized, your body brimming with endorphins, and felt not only physically well but somehow virtuous. This can go horribly wrong when people are shamed for ill-health or disability, so it's worth being aware of what seems to be a built-in bias.

Luckily, our bodies also seem to be primed to feel good when we do good. Presumably, that's because, for social animals like us, helpfulness, generosity, and even self-sacrificing altruism tend to maximize the survival of the group—and survival of the group is necessary for survival of individuals. Whether or not I am right in that presumption, the fact remains that human toddlers appear to be predisposed to try to help those in need, and very young humans also consistently tend to both recognize and reject inequality.

Over time, through the process of socialization, these building blocks evolve into adult methods of moral reasoning. Developmental psychologist Lawrence Kohlberg broke that process down into six stages ranging from the most infantile (being good to avoid being punished or to get a reward) through the conventional (doing good so as to be seen as a good person or following the rules simply because they are the rules) to the ostensibly superior realm of self-chosen universal principles. Within that system, utilitarianism comes in at level 5—mature but falling short of what he considered to be ideal.

I don't share Kohlberg's Eurocentric esteem for abstract principles, but I do find it useful to reflect on the process by which embodied infantile experiences evolve into what often feel like purely cognitive processes of moral reasoning. Students of developmental psychology often find it enlightening to reflect on the factors that played a role in their own moral development, and I would encourage adherents of EA to do the same.

One of those factors is gender. Kohlberg did his initial research using only male subjects. Later, when his typology began to be used to assess the maturity of the moral development of individuals, girls and women consistently fell short. Carol Gilligan then performed a close analysis of the kinds of answers that were leading girls and women to be judged as immature in comparison to boys and men. She found that, probably due to the effects of socialization, girls and women tended to reason differently than boys and men, often trying to find a solution that made sure everyone's needs were met rather than focusing on abstract ideas about justice. In Kohlberg's reckoning, this practical ethos of care was considered to be inferior to adherence to abstract principles without regard for actual consequences.

Like modern-day adherents of EA who do not *intend* for their prescriptions to disadvantage projects led by women, people of color, and people with disabilities, Kohlberg did not intend to disadvantage girls and women. Bias was built into his methods of data collection, analysis, and interpretation. At this late date in social science history, the potential for such biases to creep into research results by way of careless methodologies is well known. And so, if we do choose utilitarianism as our preferred method of moral reasoning, we still will need to be very careful in selecting methods of measuring "greatest," "good," and "number."

Methods of Measurement

I can't count the number of times I have stood at the back of an auditorium listening with escalating alarm as an animal advocate—sometimes a conman, sometimes a friend—spins numbers to "prove" that promoting veganism is *the* most effective way to help animals. Sometimes the numbers literally spin, in dramatic visual displays behind the speaker. The point is that farmed animals represent *the greatest number* of animals harmed by humans. But what about the billions harmed by climate change? Sometimes a word or phrase such as "captive" or "under human control" erases them from consideration without explanation. More often they are simply ignored. Also unremarked is the reason why all farmed animals are lumped together. Even if we are only considering captive animals, it would be just as valid to break out the numbers by species, in which case we would learn that the number of rats used in animal experimentation is greater than the number of cows used in dairying. My point is not to suggest that those of us who work for cows ought to drop everything in order to focus on rats in labs or insects menaced by climate change, but rather to make clear the lack of transparency behind the numbers most often used by EA within animal advocacy.

It gets murkier. In presenting raw numbers of animals harmed as the reason why activists ought to focus all of their energy (and donors all of their their money) on promoting veganism, EA adherents typically fail to offer any argument at all in favor of drawing that conclusion from the numbers. This is where my conversations with EA adherents have tended to go haywire, because it seems self-evident to them that of course promoting veganism will bring the *greatest good* to those large numbers. But it would be equally valid to use the same numbers to argue that the thing to do is to devote all time and energy to directly rescuing the animals *currently* captive—thereby surely ending their suffering—rather than focusing on suffering that hasn't happened yet.

But that would be impossible, you might be thinking, and that leads us to another way of imagining how to do the most for the billions of animals currently suffering in some way at the hands of humans: The theory of low-hanging fruit. Here, the argument is that it will be most effective to focus your energy on the things that you are most likely to succeed in doing. So many people tell me that they have not yet succeeded in convincing a single person to go vegan. Almost all animal advocates report extreme frustration at how hard it is to convince even the people they should be most able to persuade—friends, family, and neighbors sharing similar circumstances, identities, and world views—to go vegan. Multiply that difficulty by billions of people, factor in the resistance of the millions whose livelihoods depend on animal agriculture, and you've got an uphill struggle, to say the least.

In contrast, it's comparatively easy to convince people to forgo fur, circuses, and non-medical products tested on animals. So, some activists have argued that it would be most effective to organize the people (including not-yet-vegan people) who oppose those forms of cruelty in order to decisively end them. According to the kind of social psychology studies EA activists like to cite, it's easier to get people to make a big change after you've convinced them to make a small change. So, in addition to ending the suffering of all of the animals exploited in those ways (which in the case of product testing is considerable), this might make it easier to tackle animal agriculture going forward. From that point of view, the turn toward promoting veganism has been profoundly *ineffective* because it drew activists and donors away from efforts to reduce suffering that were more likely to succeed.

Another way to think about doing the most with your finite resources is to think about intensity or urgency of suffering. Of course, it is often impossible to make fine comparisons among varieties of suffering within even one species yet alone across several. Nonetheless, it is possible to imagine which animals might be experiencing the most intense suffering. This is a different way to conceptualize *greatest good* than counting numbers of animals.

I'm not arguing for either of these ways of thinking as a method of deciding how to expend one's resources (although I wouldn't be mad at anyone who chose to use them to guide their own choices about their own activities). I mention them merely as examples of the *many* different ways one might parse the well-known utilitarian precept. Different methods lead to different conclusions. It's simply not possible to say that this or that course of action will reduce the most suffering. And so the promise made by EA—we can show you how to most effectively expend your resources—is factually false.

The Fact of Fallibility

"To err is human," we say, but we don't really mean it. Even those of us who have consciously rejected human supremacy tend to see human irrationality and propensity for catastrophe as glitches rather than features of our profoundly fallible species. I have had experiences that have allowed me to glimpse myself from the vantage points of other animals, and these have tended to mute my own human hubris.

Once, while weeding my vegetable garden, I viscerally experienced myself as nearby insects might have experienced me: a giant lumbering lummox who might ruin everything at any moment. More than once, at the sanctuary I cofounded and currently direct, I have noticed ducks talking smack about me, clearly unimpressed. Once, when I was having a hard time convincing newly rescued turkeys to go inside for the night, a giant cow called Thunder all but rolled his eyes at my incompetence while gently showing me what I needed to do.

Such experiences have led me to adopt a stance toward myself and other humans that presumes we are more likely to be errant than otherwise. I also believe that we can learn from failure. So, I offer the following list of some of the many failings of EA not only as an antidote to EA's exaggerated claims but also as an example of how far wrong we can go even when we are trying very had to put the interests of other animals ahead of our own.

The Many Failings of EA

EA is incoherent. EA implicitly embraces care as a virtue by holding the reduction of suffering as a key value and by asserting that actual outcomes, rather than intentions or abstract principles, are what matter. On the other hand, EA encourages a kind of calculating dispassion that can lead to callousness. When EA adherents insist that the suffering of actual animals must be ignored in order to focus on reducing as much future suffering as possible, something has gone badly wrong with the reckoning.

EA encourages dishonesty. By setting themselves up as advisors to donors, acolytes of EA implicitly encourage activists to make out-sized claims. In the realm of animal advocacy, EA's insistence that promoting veganism is *the* most effective way to help animals has not only drawn donors away from literally life-saving projects but also encouraged those who do promote veganism to make false claims.

EA cannot be blamed for the bad habit of claiming that vegans "save" a certain number of animals per year—that predated the rise of EA within animal advocacy. But EA has taken that hyperbolic way of talking to new heights by giving favored interventions credit for vegan conversions and then multiplying those conversions by numbers of animals ostensibly saved in order to come up with a number of animals saved per dollars spent.

The primary problem here is that, except in the unlikely event that an intervention was the first and only time that the new vegan ever encountered the idea of not eating animals, the most anyone can claim is that their intervention was the tipping point. Unless the person never met a vegan or vegetarian, never heard a relative at Thanksgiving explain why she wasn't eating turkey, never saw an anti-meat billboard or read a newspaper article about some stunt pulled by PETA, never encountered even a single pro-vegan post on social media, the intervention didn't "make a vegan"—it simply closed the deal.

Even if an intervention had "made a vegan" all by itself, that doesn't necessarily mean that any animals were saved. As in the infamous case of "cheese-bombing" (wherein the dairy industry began loading more and more cheese into various pre-made products in order to make up for a decline in demand for liquid milk), animal-exploiting industries cleverly respond to any loss in their number of customers by inducing other customers to consume even more. And, of course, there is the matter of exports as well as the common practice of governmental purchases of surplus, which means that— uh oh!—both nebbishy leftists going to protests against the WTO and well-heeled lobbyists influencing the direction of trade and agriculture policies are also doing important work, even if they never directly promote veganism. Finally, even when we do succeed in reducing worldwide production of a particular animal product, we're not so much saving lives as we are preventing animals from being born into lives of captivity, suffering, and slaughter.

EA lacks rigor. Drawing inferences from data is a process of inductive reasoning that requires both honesty and rigor. Here are a few of the steps that EA usually skips:

1. Considering how the framing of the research question may limit what can be concluded from the findings;

2. Determining and disclosing the ways that the sample population may not be reflective of the population at large;

3. Reporting any possible ways that the study's methods might have skewed the results;

4. Imagining and fairly discussing alternative explanations for the find-

ings;

5. Putting the findings in the context of similar studies, especially those that have contradictory results;

6. Answering Roberta Flack's perennial question, "but compared to what?"

EA can't cope with complexity. The situations in which a single variable can be meaningfully affected by a simple intervention are vanishingly rare in the real world, which consists of nested and interlocking systems of physical and social relationships. EA makes no effort to utilize the advanced mathematics used for systems analysis, preferring instead to use the numerical results of simple calculations (e.g., dollars per vegan, number of animals saved per vegan, very basic statistical analysis of survey data, etc.) to signal that something scientific is happening. Real data scientists know it's not that simple.

EA can't cope with ambiguity. Every day at a sanctuary is a case study in decision-making under conditions of uncertainty. People like me thus must become adept at making decisions in situations that are both ethically and factually ambiguous. Often, these are literally life-or-death decisions. From this standpoint, I can report that the rudimentary mathematics of utilitarianism are not at all utile. Even in simple situations, any quest to decisively identify the greatest good for the greatest number often proves impossible.

EA harms worthwhile endeavors. In planning this essay, I found myself asking, "Is EA evil?" By evil, I meant both immoral and malevolent. You may protest: Whether or not we agree on what is or is not moral, surely effective altruists do not mean to cause harm and are therefore not malevolent actors. But is that true? First, doesn't EA itself insist that outcomes matter more than intentions? Secondly, has not EA set out deliberately to disadvantage some people who are trying to do good works? EA acolytes might argue that they seek only to advantage certain individuals and organizations by steering money and volunteers to them. But the very premise of the project rests on the fact that such resources are not infinite. More for those favored by EA equals less for everybody else. By seeking to advantage some charitable endeavors, EA seeks to disadvantage others. I can attest that EA has succeeded in that aim, causing both fiscal and emotional distress to activists engaged in truly useful work.

EA promotes callousness. It seems ludicrous that I should have to say this, but we will not awaken human hearts to animal suffering by becoming callous to that suffering ourselves. Yet EA insists that we harden our hearts to elephants in zoos... because there aren't that many of them. We must set aside any sympathy we may feel for ferrets or chimpanzees in order to focus our efforts on fishes and chickens. The loneliness, confusion, and terror felt by the last remaining members of an endangered species? Irrelevant! Unless saving that species will lead to lots of happiness for lots of other animals, we cannot waste our energy on them, and we must swallow our sorrow in order to be able to be as ruthlessly calculating as possible if we want to maximize our impact.

EA both enacts and encourages egotism. Everybody wants to do the most with what they have. But EA makes the self-centered wish to have an outsized impact the center of its project. Within animal advocacy, EA acolytes have done this by setting themselves up as the arbiters of the efficacy of the activism of others. Far from the muck and blood of animal rescue, they opine that such work is worthless while crediting themselves with saving thousands of lives. The hubris of this is so extreme that it seems I must be engaging in hyperbole myself by typing those words. But I have seen their websites with my own eyes and gaped at the numbers of animals some EA advocates have claimed to have saved—without ever once using their own muscles to actually save a single animal. Which brings us to classism and other forms of bias:

EA colludes with social injustice. Despite the fact that the majority of animal advocates, including the majority of organization founders, are women, the preponderance of organizations initially deemed highly effective by the self-appointed Animal Charity Evaluators were founded by men. Until quite recently, ACE failed to acknowledge good work by even a single organization led by people of color. Even as of this writing, one of the four "Top Charities" highlighted on the ACE website was founded by a known perpetrator of sexual assault and another was founded by a male friend of his who helped him evade consequences for many years. Coincidence? Maybe. A more likely explanation is that the sexism and racism are built into the evaluation criteria by favoring the kinds of simple and quantifiable single-issue tactics favored by white men and disadvantaging the kind of ecological, multi-issue, complex strategies favored by those who are committed to feminism and antiracism. Whatever the explanation, here is the fact: EA within animal advocacy has consistently steered funds toward organizations run by white men, thereby compounding the structural difficulties in raising funds faced by organizations run by people of color as well as by women-led organizations.

EA has vitiated the animal advocacy movement. In the process of further disadvantaging already disadvantaged activists, EA has discouraged all but the narrow sliver of potential tactics that it deems effective, thereby profoundly narrowing the strategic vitality of the movement. Long-term, multifaceted strategic plans often include actions that may not lead to any visible short-term gains. EA insists that such tactics not be funded, thereby forcing projects in need of funds to adopt a short-sighted approach focused only on near-term quantifiable results.

EA treats animals like objects. It is maybe not surprising that the overall effect of EA on animal advocacy has been to lessen overall efficacy, since EA does not and never has accorded due respect to animals, ironically treating them like numbers or tools in the same way that animal-exploiting industries do. Lately, some effective altruists have begun to concede that it might not be a complete waste of resources to care for animals at sanctuaries—but only if it can be proved that doing so promotes veganism. Within this is an implicit demand that sanctuary residents be put on display in some way that might motivate people to go vegan.

Queering EA

I have a confession to make: I sometimes give workshops on "Effective Activism," secretly hoping to divert interest in EA into more truthful and useful directions. In so doing, I bring my own queer history of tenant organizing, antiracist education, feminism, LGBTQ liberation, and animal rescue to students and grassroots activists struggling with the question that leads many to EA (and which began this essay): In a world of harm and hurt of so many kinds, how can I be most useful?

I don't often quote Mao, but when I do, it's "Let a hundred flowers bloom." What I believe, based on extensive study (and practice!) of activism, is that significant social change is most likely to occur when a variety of people approach the same problem from a variety of angles using a variety of tactics—ideally, although not necessarily, in cooperation with each other. That makes sense: Big problems tend to be complex situations in which social, cultural, economic, and material factors all play causal roles. It will rarely be the case that a single intervention can make a big difference. Even comparatively smaller problems, such as the need for a simple change at the local level, will be easier to solve if agitators are marching in the streets while insiders are simultaneously proposing practical solutions behind closed doors.

And so, I encourage workshop attendees to first inventory themselves—their skills, interests, standpoints, talents, and personality characteristics—and then look for existing projects that might need exactly those things. That's just one of many ways of doing the most: looking for the *best match* between what you have to give and the many different things that need to be done.

To go about that from another angle, I suggest choosing a problem and then listing all of the things that somebody should be doing about it right now. Which of those things aren't yet being done? Are you in a position to do one of them? Do that.

What is now VINE Sanctuary began when Miriam Jones and I found a chicken in a roadside ditch in the part of the USA where factory farming of chickens was invented and perfected. Right away, we saw that we were in a position, simply by converting a garage to a coop, to save lives. And so that's what we did. Twenty-plus years later, our multi-species community includes more than 700 nonhuman survivors of the war against animals, some of whom liberated themselves and others of whom were rescued by humans, often at significant risk to themselves. Along the way, we've seized every opportunity to do things we happened to be uniquely situated to do, from figuring out how to rehabilitate roosters used in cockfighting to helping LGBTQ people see the linkages between queer and animal liberation. We know we're not the only ones doing this work. We trust others to do the things they are better positioned to do.

Sometimes adherents of EA suppose that its opponents don't care about efficacy. For me, nothing could be further from the truth. It's just that my ideas about efficacy are more ecological, which is to say more queer. Animals are exploited (not to mention displaced and polluted) in a multiplicity of ways in a multiplicity of places, each of which is shaped by both material (physical) and social (economic and cultural) forces. That being the case, there's literally "something for everyone" in terms of things that need to be done.

We need people who are gifted with words or images to write and design leaflets, posters, websites, and other media. We need researchers with the patience to spend hours finding and compiling information. We need natural scientists to develop new and improved alternatives to vivisection, and we need computer scientists to implement those that involve computer modeling. We need botanists, economists, and agronomists to work out how to transition regions now dependent on animal agriculture to plant-based agricultural economies. We need lobbyists to convince state and federal government to quit subsidizing big "meat" and "dairy" and to pour that money into organic vegetable, fruit, nut, and grain cultivation instead. We need courageous people to engage in direct action of all kinds, whether it be undercover investigations or just walking in the woods with a booming radio during hunting season. And we always need artists and other creative thinkers to come up with new ways of awakening empathy, sparking imagination, and inspiring action.

Once, an artist-activist in another country told me that the multispecies community here at VINE Sanctuary exists in her mind as a source of inspiration, even though she's never visited. I want a way of thinking about efficacy that recognizes the value of that.

Four More Catastrophes Happened While I Edited This Essay

Seven to twelve additional calamities probably will have happened by the time you read these words. The world really is on fire. And here we are, together, unsure. Whatever we do or don't do will become part of the circumstances in which we and others exist. We must choose.

If you want to use utilitarianism to guide your own choices about what you will do to respond to the emergencies, that's fine by me. You do you. If tallying lives saved per unit of energy expended will motivate you to do your utmost, I will hand you a pad and pencil. All that I ask is that you refrain from deploying your own resources to try to stop others from doing good works.

If some people are doing something that seems less than maximally worthwhile to you, then... don't join them. Do something else. Wish them well, understanding that they might see or know things of which you are unaware. Hope that you're wrong and whatever they're doing will make a big difference. Especially now, when there is so much need and so little certainty, we all need to reject the injurious intolerance of Effective Altruism in favor of a more modest and generous mode of relating to the projects of others.

Remember the trees? Communicating with each other underground, exhaling the oxygen you need to breathe? They might have projects too. They need allies, not heroes, and so do the squirrels who (like us) depend on them for everything. If becoming more aware of the limits of human reason and more aware of perspectives other than your own leads you to become better able to perceive and work within the power of the larger-than-human world, then—by my reckoning—the time you spent reading this essay will have been effectively spent.

Works Cited

Gilligan, Carol. 1982. *In a Different Voice: Psychological Theory and Women's Development*. Cambridge, MA: Harvard University Press.

Kohlberg, Lawrence. 1964. "Development of Moral Character and Moral Ideology." In *Review of Child Development Research: Volume 1*, edited by Lois Wladis Hoffman and Martin L. Hoffman, 383–432. Thousand Oaks, CA: Russell Sage Foundation.

III. QUEERING ANIMAL LIBERATION

I quit eating meat as a teen in the mid-1970s, the same year that I attended my first gay rights rally, but I didn't understand how deeply those two choices were linked until decades later. In both cases, I now see, I seized my own heart's desire despite what the dominant culture told me I should want.

Shortly after we founded the sanctuary, Miriam and I scrambled to answer when invited to explain how we saw the intersections among queer and animal liberation. On the one hand, we could see so many conjunctions and sensed that there were many more we could not yet see. On the other hand, it was hard to express them pithily.

In the 20 years since, I've facilitated countless workshops and discussions in which activists came together to discover and discuss these linkages. I once challenged students in an LGBT studies course to explain how homophobia leads to global warming, and I've tried to explain that myself many times. The essays in this section represent but a subset of an ongoing process of inquiry into this topic, which will be the focus of both my next book *and* an edited collection of writing and art by others.

12

Conquistadors of the Senses

For a time, I regularly used holidays that I don't celebrate to write what I called "one day essays." This was written on Thanksgiving Day of 2006 and was published in the webzine *Freezerbox* and on various *IndyMedia* sites. I think it is the first time that I published something on the intertwined themes that run through this section: (1) linkages between harms done to animals and harms done to LGBTQ people; (2) the pivotal role of the conquest in bringing not only speciesism and homo/transphobia but also a host of other interrelated harms to the Americas; and (3) the likelihood that eros, in all its queerness, may be the only thing that can save us.

Conquistadors of the Senses

Throwing the homosexuals to the hounds sounds like a metaphor for the Republican Party's electoral strategy of recent years, but it actually happened back in 1513 in what is now Panama. Then, governor Vasco Nunez de Balboa condemned 50 homosexual Indians to be torn apart by dogs.

Seen by both Catholic Conquistadors and Protestant Pilgrims as a sign of godless animality, same-sex pleasure was ruthlessly suppressed throughout the process of the subjugation of the Americas. Today, the conquest of the senses continues, as billions of people and animals are forced to forgo all kinds of natural happiness so that a privileged few can enjoy the empty gluttony that has brought us to the brink of planetary catastrophe.

When Columbus blundered into the Caribbean, sexual freedom—including full acceptance of homosexuality—was the norm in the region. Did the invaders understand that such physical freedom would be a wellspring of resistance? Did they dimly suspect that people who don't need a reason to enjoy each other might be hard to control?

Whatever they knew, they threw themselves into the task of policing sexuality with a fervor that would satisfy any latter-day acolyte of Focus on the Family, mercilessly murdering those who transgressed the new world order of patriarchal heterosexuality. When the Tairona Indians on the Caribbean coast of what is now Colombia rebelled against the suppression of their sexual customs, which included divorce and homosexuality, the resulting repression nearly erased 80 communities. As Eduardo Galeano has remarked, it is one of the ironies of history that the Caribbean, where indigenous people physically fought for their right to same-sex pleasure, is now among the most homophobic regions of the world.

The Tairona were not alone. Same-sex coupling was recognized as natural by hundreds of indigenous South, Central, and North American peoples. In many cultures, homosexual men and women were not merely tolerated but fully integrated into the life of the people, often with designated routine or ritual roles that recognized their unique positions and perspectives.

Then came the Europeans with their guns and bibles. Disease, displacement, and missionaries dedicated to cultural genocide conspired to estrange many native peoples from their own traditions. New practices, such as Christianity and cattle ranching, became the new "traditions." These days, some gay and lesbian Native Americans who embrace the old ways are locked in struggles with conservative Christian elders over the same subject that brings Bush voters out in droves: gay marriage.

The glee with which our fellow Americans regularly run to the polls to deprive us of our civil rights is no surprise to LGBTQ people who know our own history. The Puritans whose survival is celebrated every Thanksgiving, like the Conquistadors of the Caribbean, often imposed the death penalty for homosexuality.

Anti-gay referenda are just one of many legacies of the European invaders. Historian Alfred Crosby has written that "one who watched the Caribbean islands from outer space during the years 1492 to 1550 or so might have surmised that the object of the game going on there was to replace the people with pigs, dogs, and cattle." Today, factory farms in which hundreds, thousands, tens of thousands, and even hundreds of thousands of animals are confined litter the landscapes of the Americas. Their effluents poison our water while the carbon dioxide and methane released by their operations are among the chief causes of climate change.

Some of the diseases that decimated indigenous people were deliberately introduced, as when Sir Jeffery Amherst distributed smallpox-infected blankets to Native Americans in 1763. Today, we live with the very real prospect of a pandemic of avian influenza that Dr. Michael Greger, in his new book Bird Flu, calls "a virus of our own hatching."

The conquest of the senses continues too. Gluttony of all kinds has replaced the natural pleasures that have been suppressed. Estranged from their own bodies, Americans have an

insatiable appetite for the bodies of others, conveniently converted into objects for consumption by butchery or pornography.

Homo Sapiens is just one of the hundreds of species of animals who enjoy homosexual activity either for transitory sensual pleasure or to form stable same-sex pair bonds. Nothing could be more natural. But, to the Europeans who invaded the Americas, our animal bodies were, like all of nature, profane objects to be exploited and controlled.

We've now reached the logical conclusion of behavior based in that mindset. At the brink of environmental catastrophe, we are profoundly disoriented animals living within a dangerously deranged biosphere. We are so out of touch with our senses and feelings that we cannot perceive the changing climate or feel the fear that motivates action in an emergency.

Among the Maya of Guatemala, the word for sex is "play." Play might seem beside the point in these dangerous days. But truly mutual animal happiness brings us into communion with each other and ourselves without hurting anybody else. Unlike the consumption of cancer-causing pork chops, paper sex objects, and plastic electronics, true play energizes people for the hard work ahead. So, if you're wondering what to do instead of shopping on Buy Nothing Day (or any other day), I invite you to come out and play.

13

Eros and Eco-Defense

This piece originally appeared in *Ecofeminism: Feminist Intersections with Other Animals and the Earth*, an essential collection edited by Carol Adams and Lori Gruen, which has recently been published in a second edition. Many thanks are due to Lori and Carol for kindly but firmly insisting that a sprawling draft three times the length of the finished essay be made more concise and coherent over the course of five iterations. Their patience and my persistence resulted, eventually, in a piece that I do think captures both the meaning and spirit of what I was trying to say.

Eros and the Mechanisms of Eco-Defense

Desire drives everything. Arising in our animal bodies, eros impels us to stretch and strive for what we want. What we want, most of all, is connection.

Rooted in patriarchal pastoralism, globalized via colonialism, serving the aims of capitalism, and furthered by slice-and-dice style science, the hegemonic economy of (re)production and consumption is the catastrophic antithesis of exuberant eros. It persists by damming and diverting eros along with rivers.

Sparked by rioting street queens and enacted in explicit solidarity with the Black, Chicano, Native American, and women's liberation movements of that era, the fabulous gay liberation movement of the 1970s has devolved into a fairly conservative movement that asks for only reactionary 'rights' like marriage and military service. We need a theory and praxis of animal liberation that resuscitates the queer spirit of rebellious and generous connectedness.

To be fully realized, the ecofeminist ethos of care[1] must be nourished and informed by eros. But "love don't come easy," as Diana Ross and the Supremes once sang. Eros can't be hurried, ordered around, or expected to march in anything like a straight line. To resuscitate eros, we must understand its queer ways.

Steps to an Ecology of Eros

"The diversity of modes of singing amongst birds is so great that it defies explanation"[2]

"We don't only sing, but we dance just as good as we want."[3]

---

1. Kheel, "From Heroic to Holistic Ethics: The Ecofeminist Challenge."

2. Catchpole and Slater, Bird Song, 234.

3. Archie Bell, introducing himself and the Drells on the 1968 recording of "Tighten Up"

The leaves of Bruce Bagemihl's 750-page encyclopedic account of animal homosexuality teem with "wuzzling" dolphins, "necking" giraffes, and "cavorting" manatees, not to mention "aquatic spiraling," "sonic foreplay," and a form of sexual stimulation known as the "genital buzz"—and all of that just in the few pages devoted to an overview of the "dizzying array" of ways that non-human animals court and show affection to one another.[4] In all, Bagemihl carefully reviews the documented accounts of same-sex courtship, affection, pair-bonding, parenting, *and sex*—did I mention "mounting, diddling, and bump-rumping"?—among the members of some 300 species of mammals and birds.

Zoo visits, televised nature programmes, and storybooks featuring stereotypically gendered characters teach us to think about other-than-human animals as relentlessly heterosexual despite "the much more prevalent sex diversity among living matter"[5] It's not just pop culture that gets it wrong. Bagemihl also documents the long, sorry history of scientific obliviousness, bewilderment, and heterosexist hubris in the face of same-sex sexuality among other-than-human animals. From the ethologist who decried the moral degeneracy of butterflies to the wildlife biologist who evicted a same-sex couple from the nest they had built together so that he could give it to a heterosexual pair, the litany of wrongs and wrong-headed writings is leavened only by the unintentional humor of the sometimes surreal extremes to which scientists have gone in order to avoid seeing (much less naming) the queer eros right in front of them.

Before we ascribe the bemusement of those scientists entirely to the mutually-reinforcing junction of ignorance and bigotry, consider this: The fungi known as *Schizophyllum Commune* swap genes by touching and have as many as 23,000 mating types (or, as we like to call them, sexes), thereby preventing "selfing" in a species in which any individual can both give and receive genetic material in order to produce progeny.[6] Confused? That's my point. Not only does non-reproductive sexuality flower in a variety of forms, but sexual reproduction itself occurs by means of a "remarkably diverse"[7] array of strategies. But—wait!—there's more: Not only some plants but also some

---

4. Bagemihl, Biological Exuberance: Animal Homosexuality and Natural Diversity, 13-18.

5. Hird, "Naturally Queer," 86.

6. Casselton, "Mate Recognition in Fungi."

7. Fraser and Heitman, "Evolution of Fungal Sex Chromosomes," 299.

animals reproduce by various asexual means, including parthenogenesis. As Catriolina Mortimer-Sandilands and Bruce Erickson note in the introduction to their important anthology, *Queer Ecologies*, this "diversity of asexual modes of reproduction as well as several multi-gendered ones... appear to defy dominant, dimorphic accounts of sexual reproduction altogether."[8]

Alaimo[9] and others have commented on the inadequacy of our conceptual categories in the face of all of this. As biologist J.B.S. Haldane famously opined, "the universe is not only queerer than we suppose, it is queerer than we *can* suppose." So it's not surprising that 18th, 19th, or even 20th century scientists unwittingly assimilated their observations of same-sex behavior into dualistic schemas they themselves couldn't see (because they seemed like reality).

Of course, just because mushrooms swap genes by brushing against each other is no reason to presume that we could or should do the same. Just because marsupials are also mammals does not—alas—mean that we can bound around with infants in our pouches. Nonetheless, this survey of the variety of (always embodied) animal eros offers us much more than an antidote to the still-too-common misconception that homosexuality is unnatural. First: Things we can't imagine right now might still be possible. And: We too may be queerer than we suppose.

People have courted, demonstrated affection, constructed households, and raised their children in a blooming profusion of different ways. And, while there's some doubt that we deserve the sobriquet of *sapiens*, there's no doubt at all about the *homo.* We not only sing to our same-sex sweethearts in almost as many languages and styles of music as there are varieties of birdsong, we also dance together in configurations that don't fit within the boy-girl two-step of the Western square dance—and not just in urban discos.

Since errors and erasures in this realm are almost as endemic as those concerning same-sex sexuality in non-human animals, a brief survey is in order. While gay or lesbian *identity* constructed in contradistinction to the relatively recently invented category of "heterosexual" is fairly new and geographically bounded,[10] same-sex erotic *behavior* has been "virtually universal in human

8. Mortimer-Sandilands and Erickson, "A Genealogy of Queer Ecologies," 12.

9. Alaimo, "Eluding Capture: The Science, Culture, and Pleasure of 'Queer' Animals."

10. Katz, The Invention of Heterosexuality.

societies,"[11] sometimes in defiance of cultural norms but often with cultural toleration or approval. From traditional marriages between African women[12] to casual sex "play" between Pakistani men[13]—neither considered particularly queer by the participants—expressions of same-sex desire continue to thrive even in regions where they are repressed or reputed not to exist.

None of this is news. Or, rather, none of this should be news, since the evidence—like that of animal homosexuality—has been hidden in plain view. For example, in Africa, where rock-solid scientific certainty of the absence of indigenous homosexuality delayed appropriate AIDS-prevention interventions for many years and where several states still justify anti-gay legislation with the idea that homosexuality is alien to the continent, indigenous same-sex sexuality "is substantially documented in scores of scholarly books, articles, and dissertations in a wide range of academic disciplines, in unpublished archival documents... in art, literature, and film and in oral history from all over the continent."[14]

In the Americas, culturally condoned expressions of same-sex sexuality were so common among indigenous peoples that this was frequently cited by invading Europeans as justification for cultural genocide.[15] In some North American native cultures, "two-spirit" people—those believed to have both male and female aspects due to their gender presentation and/or sexual orientation—were not only tolerated but esteemed.[16] Similarly, "there are striking examples of the recognition and acceptance of forms of same-sex desire in the history of important parts of Asia," including China, India, Japan, and Java.[17] Locals varieties of homoeroticism in Thailand and elsewhere in Asia-Pacific

---

11. Drucker, "'In the Tropics There Is No Sin': Sexuality and Gay–Lesbian Movements in the Third World," 75.

12. Morgan and Wierenga, Tommy Boys, Lesbian Men, and Ancestral Wives.

13. Khan, "Culture, Sexualities, and Identities."

14. Epprecht, Heterosexual Africa? : The History of an Idea from the Age of Exploration to the Age of AIDS, 7.

15. Galeano, We Say No; Katz, Gay American History; Smith, Conquest: Sexual Violence and American Indian Genocide.

16. Roscoe, Living the Spirit: A Gay American Indian Anthology.

17. Sanders, "Flying the Rainbow Flag in Asia"

were and remain truly diverse, confounding not only heteronormativity but also also easy explanations about what "homoeroticism" might mean.[18]

As Chou cautions about China, homosexualities of the past ought not be simplistically romanticized.[19] Some traditional patterns of same-sex sexual behavior, in that region and elsewhere, occurred within and were patterned by social inequalities that today we would condemn as unjust. Some historical reports of same-sex eroticism record its repression. Nevertheless, whether they have been esteemed, approved, tolerated, used, abused, or repressed—and however they have thought of or denoted themselves—people who sometimes or exclusively have sex with members of their own sex have existed in virtually every human population. We're just that kind of animal.

Many—perhaps most—of the people who have sex with partners of the same sex do not think of themselves as homosexual or even bisexual. At the same time, terms denoting homosexual identity (or something like it) abound. While the globalization of *gay pride* has led to the importation of the terms *gay* and *lesbian* and variants thereof into numerous languages, local terms both old and new express local ways of enacting and thinking about same-sex sexuality.[20] Again, it is necessary to resist idealization. While some contemporary same-sex practices challenge social inequalities or are integrated into egalitarian communities, others conform to—and perhaps reinforce—binary notions of gender and patriarchal conceptions of power.[21]

Nonetheless we can revel in the linguistic and conceptual creativity deployed in the service of same-sex sexuality. In China, some activists have repurposed the term *tongzhi*—a Chinese translation of a Soviet-era term for comrade, constructed from *tong* (same) and *zhi* (spirit, goal, or orientation)—as a way of denoting themselves in a manner congruent with cultural values.[22] In Uganda, the previously derisive term *kuchu* is now claimed with pride.[23] In the United States, many Native Americans have embraced the term *two-spirit* as "an ex-

---

18. Jackson, "Pre-Gay, Post-Queer;" Wieringa, Blackwood, and Bhaiya, Women's Sexualities and Masculinities in a Globalizing Asia.

19. Chou, "Homosexuality and the Cultural Politics of Tongzhi in Chinese Societies."

20. Katyal, "Exporting Identity."

21. Blackwood and Wieringa, "Globalization, Sexuality, and Silences: Women's Sexualities and Masculinities in an Asian Context."

22. Chou, "Homosexuality and the Cultural Politics of Tongzhi in Chinese Societies."

23. Tamale, "Out of the Closet: Unveiling Sexuality Discourses in Uganda."

pression of our sexual and gender identities as sovereign from those of white GLBT movements."[24]

Diversity in self-identification also flowers within populations. Thailand's national lesbian organization uses the term *ying-rak-ying* (women who love women) to describe its constituency; at the same time, many Thai women who do love women reject that term in favor of *tom* (short for tomboy) or *dee* (short for lady), because these better express their sense of themselves within the rigid gender system in which their sexualities operate.[25]

Which brings us to gender. Recently, Czech archaeologists unearthed neolithic skeletal remains of a biological male who had been buried—4,500 to 5,000 years ago—in the manner in which females of that time and place usually were interred.[26] Considerable diversity in ideas about gender has been documented in the human cultures that have arisen in different times and places since then, both in terms of whether gender is mutable[27] and how many genders there might be.[28] Communities also have varied in the ways that they have coped with or explained persons who don't quite fit into any of the categories created by their culture's gender system.[29]

The multiplicity of sexualities and exuberant diversity of gender expression among *Homo sapiens* suggests that some measure of flexibility—or, at least, a capacity for and tendency toward variability—is intrinsic to our species. The rigid enforcement of a two-gender system that goes hand in hand with rigid insistence on relentless heterosexuality is an artifact of a particular set of circumstances, seeming natural only because of its tendency to reproduce itself.

Televised nature programs tend to portray evolution as an urgent quest in which every animal attempts to spawn as many offspring as possible. Some scientists, too, have implicitly defined evolutionary success as reproduction of the individual rather than the survival of the family, population, or species. Some 'evolutionary psychologists' attribute virtually every characteristic and

---

24. Driskill, "Stolen From Our Bodies."

25. Blackwood and Wieringa, "Globalization, Sexuality, and Silences: Women's Sexualities and Masculinities in an Asian Context."

26. Karpova, "Third Sex Prehistoric Skeleton Found."

27. Nanda, Gender Diversity; Ramet, Gender Reversals and Gender Cultures.

28. Davies, Challenging Gender Norms: Five Genders Among Bugis in Indonesia; Roscoe, Changing Ones: Third and Fourth Genders in Native North America.

29. Epprecht, Heterosexual Africa?"

behavior to the reproductive imperative implicit in this presumed law of nature.

But, if incessant reproduction is the law, we've got an awful lot of animal scofflaws. In some species, only a few individuals even attempt to reproduce. In many species, females—for whom reproduction is often a physically perilous affair—actively avoid pregnancy by means of a variety of strategies.[30]

Natural selection in the sense of helpful genetic mutations passed along to offspring who then disproportionately survive to reproduce certainly does occur and certainly does explain many evolutionary changes. But exclusive focus on the reproductive success of individuals ignores the interlocking material and social circumstances that also evolve. It's not *quite* right to say that organisms adapt to their environments, since organisms are *part of* their ecosystems, which themselves constantly change as their participants evolve.[31] Furthermore, natural selection acts upon not only physical traits but also behaviors, many of which are transmitted by social learning.[32] Moreover, cultural and physical traits often co-evolve.

Natural selection acts upon groups as well as individuals. The overall fitness (or lack thereof) of the social group—family, flock, tribe, or troop—significantly influences likelihood of individual survival. Some circumstances—such as high rates of predation—do mandate that everyone at least attempt to reproduce for the population to survive, but in most instances the problem faced by populations is the opposite. The long-term survival of any group requires that its population be calibrated to the availability of resources. Same-sex sexual activities (and non-reproductive heterosexual erotic activities) allow for pleasure, bonding, and other benefits without risk of reproduction. Hence, queer eros enhances group fitness.

Adults who don't reproduce help groups in other ways. Homosexual pairs adopt orphaned offspring in many species. Adult animals who do not reproduce—including but not limited to exclusively homosexual animals—tend to contribute more to their social group than they take out. In all social circumstances where adults cooperate to provide protection and resources to juveniles, those who do not reproduce contribute without withdrawing. Those adults

30. Bagemihl, Biological Exuberance.

31. Oyama, The Ontogeny of Information.

32. Avital and Jablonka, Animal Traditions : Behavioural Inheritance in Evoloution.

also have more energy to devote to activities that benefit the group, whether these be writing operas or looking out for predators.

The simplistic view of natural selection and the European mindset in which it emerged both presume a struggle for scarce resources as the precondition of life. This way of thinking about the world makes sense in its own ecological context. Even after the decimation of the plagues and purges of the centuries just past—the traumatic impact of which must still have been reverberating in European psyches—the population of Europe remained too high to be satisfactorily supported by its deforested and depleted ecosystems. Within such simultaneously barren and crowded surrounds, the Hobbesian view of each against all must have seemed self-evidently true.

But, in fact, plenitude rather than scarcity is the norm in nature. Most animals—like most people, prior to the successive waves of conquest and consequent population explosion that have globalized the environmental crises from which they arose—spend comparatively little time securing food and shelter, with plenty of time left to play. Virtually every human culture has produced music, visual art, and sport of some sort. All of these—along with non-reproductive sexuality—can be seen as exuberant uses of the abundant energy that shines down from the sun every day.[33]

Bagemihl contrasts his theory of biological exuberance with the notion that homosexuality serves as a natural check on population, but I see those ideas as complementary and mutually reinforcing. The exuberant upsurge of queer eros keeps populations in check, thereby setting the stage for even more exuberance. Suppression of queer eros thus injures populations, and their enveloping ecosystems, as well as individuals.

Reproduction and its Discontents

In zoos and vivisection labs, animals are assorted into boy-girl pairs and forced to mate if they do not do so willingly. Often, this involves breaking up same-sex pair bonds or preventing females from fleeing unwanted penetration. Likewise, in animal agriculture—whether on factory farms or family farms—everything depends on reproduction. From the electro-ejaculation of bulls to the confinement of fragile "broiler breeder" hens with heavyweight roosters made sex-mad by starvation, numerous cruel and unusual strategies ensure that no farmed animal opts out of compulsory heterosexuality.

33. Bagemihl, Biological Exuberance.

Even animal lovers join in the superintendency of animal sexuality. Dog lovers who decry puppy mills still feel free to decide whether, when, and with whom the canines under their control will partner. Animal advocates pursue the laudable goal of reducing animal homelessness and execution by demanding that all companion animals be deprived of reproductive freedom rather than by abolishing the for-profit traffic in dogs and cats. Animal sanctuaries, with similarly pragmatic rationales, routinely prevent their residents from choosing to reproduce.

Meanwhile, homosexual or transgender behavior or identity remains a risky endeavor for people in many places. In some 35 countries, homosexual behavior remains a crime punishable by imprisonment. In South Africa—the first country in the world to enshrine non-discrimination on the basis of sexual orientation in its national constitution—lesbians still confront an everyday threat of "corrective rape." Here in the United States, a gay male cofounder of Mercy for Animals was gay-bashed nearly to death only a few years ago.

The structural function of homophobia is the maintenance of the man-on-top binary gender system.[34] That system dates back to the days when both daughters and dairy cows were the property of males who presumed the right to force females—whether they be called wives, slaves, or livestock—to bear more or different offspring than they would otherwise choose. Patriarchy and pastoralism both require fairly relentless preoccupation with and control of reproduction (and, hence, sexuality). The traditional pastoralism from which today's factory farms evolved *necessarily* involved hands-on control of the reproduction of captive animals.[35] Tools and tactics first used to gain and maintain total control over nonhuman animals were adapted for use with enslaved humans.[36] The process of conquest by which men who viewed women, land, animals, and people of other races as property created a globalized economy also carried homophobia around the world.

In today's topsy-turvy world in which Uganda's Christian president condemns homosexuality as a foreign import despite the fact that Christianity comes from elsewhere while the indigenous Langi people allowed marriage between men and biologically male *mudoko dako* people,[37] it may be important

34. Pharr, Homophobia: A Weapon of Sexism.

35. Patterson, Eternal Treblinka.

36. Spiegel, The Dreaded Comparison.

37. Tamale, "Out of the Closet: Unveiling Sexuality Discourses in Uganda."

to repeat that queer eros flowered in a variety of flavors prior to the era of European colonialism and imperialism. While cultures varied in their attitudes towards homosexual behavior, toleration appears to have been the norm,[38] including in places where homophobia is now most marked.

What happened? First, European Christians brought their atypical antipathy to homosexual behavior with them when they invaded the Americas, in some instances using native sex and gender norms as excuses for cultural genocide.[39] Obversely, Europeans were vested in the notion that Africans were like animals—and, hence, relentlessly heterosexual. "The prevailing prejudice was that Africans were uncivilized and close to n ature.... The emerging consensus on homosexuality thus required that Africans conform to the expectation of a supposedly natural heterosexu ality."[40] The mechanisms by which African sexual diversity was denied or suppressed eerily echo those by which homosexuality among non-human animals was elided from the record for so long. Anthropologists failed to see, refused to record, hesitated to publish, or explained away instances of same-sex sexuality of which they were aware.

These colonial cover-ups were in many instances compounded by post-colonial leaders eager to avoid any suggestion of the luridly 'exotic' spectacles of African sexuality promulgated by National Geographic and the like.[41] Many of these leaders were men eager to enjoy the subordination of women facilitated by homophobia.[42] Meanwhile, the post-colonial wave of trade globalization brought commodified conceptions of "gay," "lesbian," and "transgendered" identity to regions where indigenous cultures had other ways of conceptualizing same-sex activity.[43] Rooted as they are in European ways of thinking about identity, these may or may not prove to be useful to queer people elsewhere—or to our shared struggle to bring ourselves into balance with the biosphere—but

38. Epprecht, Heterosexual Africa?"

39. Galeano, We Say No; Smith, Conquest: Sexual Violence and American Indian Genocide.

41. Epprecht, Heterosexual Africa?"

42. Tamale, "Out of the Closet: Unveiling Sexuality Discourses in Uganda."

43. Katyal, "Exporting Identity."

they certainly have provoked a fresh wave of homophobia-fueled violence in many places.[44]

How did "gay" or "lesbian" get to be nouns instead of adjectives (or, even better, verbs) anyway? In short, the same Enlightenment ideas that brought us scientific racism engendered a way of thinking that led eventually to the categorization of people on the basis of what we now call sexual orientation. "The rise of evolutionary thought in Charles Darwin's wake generally coincided with the rise of sexological thought in Richard von Krafft-Ebing's"[45] As we've seen, sexual selection is but one aspect of natural selection. Yet, perhaps because of the preoccupation with reproduction implicit in patriarchy/pastoralism, that element of evolution became the center of evolutionary theory. In consequence, "sex became a matter of fitness, and individual attributes could now be evaluated based on their apparent adaptiveness to an organism's reproductive capacity."[46]

That was bad news for eros. The medicalization of homosexuality arose at the same time, and from the same train of thought, as eugenics and scientific racism. Many of the medical assaults on people who were (or were perceived to be) either homosexual or non-gender-normative "occurred in the context of Race Hygiene and Race Betterment movements"; not only queers but also deaf, disabled, or dark-skinned people were considered "literally, biological enemies of the human species."[47] All of these efforts to improve the species presumed and sought to preserve the position of *Homo sapiens* at the top of an imagined hierarchy, the scientific rationalization of which continues to make speciesism feel logical even to those who now know that evolution is not an upwards affair.

Along with delusions of grandeur and a perverse preoccupation with reproduction, the process of conquest that has led us to the present juncture exported an ethic of exploitation and a fantasy of infinity. That ethic, and the fantasy that enables it, have since been codified into the economic rules by which European powers still force the rest of the world to play.

Capitalism demands and indeed requires incessant growth—new markets for new goods, which must come from somewhere—in order not to collapse. Unlike economies in which participants cooperate to trade fairly, capitalism is

44. Blackwood and Wieringa, "Globalization, Sexuality, and Silences: Women's Sexualities and Masculinities in an Asian Context."

45. Mortimer-Sandilands and Erickson, "A Genealogy of Queer Ecologies," 7.

47. McWhorter, "Enemy of the Species," 76.

mathematically unbalanced by the removal of profits into private pockets and thus requires constant infusions of fresh resources. Thus, it requires not only incessant reproduction—whether of factory farmed chickens, assembly line automobiles, or worker-consumers to build those cars and eat those birds—but also the diversion of desire. Every natural impulse, whether for self-expression or social contact or—yes—sex, must be detoured toward the purchase of some product (for which, of course, one must earn the money to buy). And so now queer eros, where it is not still actively suppressed, faces the same dispiriting fate as heterosexual romance—the destination wedding!

Having integrated virtually every place on earth into its economy of empty rapacity, late consumer capitalism has run out of places to go for fresh supplies of worker-consumers. Everything now depends on getting everybody to buy *more*—which is of course the opposite of what everything actually depends on.

Seven billion people now stand on an overheated planet. "Humans have already changed the biosphere substantially, so much so that some argue for recognizing the time in which we live as a new geologic epoch, the Anthropocene."[48] Climate change comes down to "patterns of human behavior, particularly over-population and over-consumption,"[49] both of which follow directly from the suppression and diversion of eros in all of its exuberant diversity.

Preoccupation with reproduction characterizes most present-day human cultures. Reproduction remains an obligatory duty to family and community even as we confront the catastrophic environmental effects of overpopulation. Parenthood remains conflated with adulthood in many minds. This "repro-centric"[50] logic is both cause and consequence of suppression of queer eros. If reproduction is the paramount goal, then non-reproductive eros must be suppressed; if non-reproductive eros is suppressed, eros will seek satisfaction in socially sanctioned reproduction and consumption.

Unless...

Consciousness of Lost Limbs

48. Barnosky et al., "Approaching a State Shift in Earth's Biosphere," 57.

49. Oskamp, "A Sustainable Future for Humanity?" 496.

50. Mortimer-Sandilands and Erickson, "A Genealogy of Queer Ecologies," 11.

In 2001, the mass trial of 52 Egyptian men arrested for dancing together at a floating nightclub rightly drew international attention to the ongoing persecution of homosexuals in that country.[51] But let's notice something else: These were men who *knew* they faced prosecution for homosexual activity. And they were *dancing*. To *disco*. On a *boat*.

From "Fiddler on the Roof" to "Mississippi Masala" (not to mention "Romeo and Juliet" and all of its remixes), pop culture thrums with tales of young lovers defying parental prohibitions to follow their hearts. In the real world, eros often leads lovers of all ages to disobey even more powerful authorities. Here in the United States, in South Africa, and elsewhere, laws prohibiting miscegenation aimed to maintain oppressive racist regimes, but men and women of different races persisted in partnering, the threat of jail notwithstanding. All around the world to this day, same-sex couples come together despite real and menacing threats ranging from social ostracism to the death penalty.

"Beneath the paving stones—the beach!" Like half-forgotten dreams, anarchist slogans like that Situationist gem from the 1968 student rebellion in Paris pop up on walls and burst from the mouths of black-clad teenagers smashing shop windows with baseball bats. Tattooed survivors of childhood sexual abuse tuck battered copies of the CrimethInc Ex-Workers Collective Manual *Days of War, Nights of Love* into backpacks, to read while sitting in endangered trees. Vegan punks bake cupcakes for each other, just to bring some sweetness to their struggles.

Eros is right there—ready—to show us where we need to go and give us the energy to get there. Yet eros is also so easily deadened or misdirected. Eros can help us save ourselves and each other, and quit wrecking the planet along the way, but to do so it must be deliberately cultivated.

It might seem counterintuitive to pursue the aim of checking human hubris by cultivating human eros. But true eros, unlike plastic pleasures purchased from profiteers, is both enlivening and relational. Eros is exuberant, sometimes jumping up when and where you least expect it. Eros begins in the body but always reaches outward, seeking connection.

By "eros" I mean not only physical love and sexual desire but also what Black lesbian feminist poet and activist Audre Lorde called the "sharing of joy, whether physical, emotional, psychic, or intellectual, [that] forms a bridge

51. Hawley, "Anger over Egypt Gay Trial."

between the sharers."[52] Eduardo Galeano reports that among the Maya of Colombia, the ancestors of whom rose up against the sexual constraints imposed by the Conquistadors, the word for sex is "play." Eros *is* playful. Queer eros is both cause and consequence of a happy state of affairs in which life is *not* a grim struggle to reproduce in the face of scarcity but, rather, joyous usage of the surplus energy that shines down from the sun every day.

Because eros is inherently surplus and always oriented outward, genuine eros is always generous. We share smiles with sweethearts and give gifts and kisses to beloved others. It *feels good* to do this. Eros awakens feelings of all kinds—including the ones that ought to be telling us this is an emergency and giving us the energy to do something about it. As Lorde wrote in her classic essay on the uses of the erotic, "as we begin to recognize our deepest feelings, we begin to give up, of necessity, being satisfied with suffering and self-negation, and with the numbness which so often seems like their only alternative in our society."[53] Our feelings are fuel, and the good news is that they are renewable sources of energy.

Eros arouses not only desire but also curiosity, creativity, and courage. It has abidingly proven to be more powerful than guns or governments in motivating human behavior. Inherently ecological, because it begins in our animal bodies, eros undammed and undiverted will flow in the direction of biospheric balance.

Greta Gaard points out that "dominant Western culture's devaluation of the erotic parallels its devaluations of women and of nature" and that "these devaluations are mutually reinforcing."[54] As with all of the intersections of oppression, the upside of seeing the junction is recognizing opportunities for intervention. And so, when we nurture wombats, women, or weeds genuinely and with generosity, we also are cultivating eros. But, if we hope to use eros to reanimate ourselves while animating our environmental efforts, we will have to come to better terms with our own animality.

The Animal Problem

The Eurocentric logic of mind-over-matter tells us that we should transcend our animal bodies by means of our very fine minds. That's the same log-

52. Lorde, Sister Outsider, 56.

53. Ibid., 58.

54. Gaard, "Toward a Queer Ecofeminism," 115.

ic, however, that divides and conquers the world into male-over-female, white-over-black, and straight-over-gay. My favorite flavor of ecofeminist theory extends the feminist understanding of intersectionality to include earth and animals, deepening our analysis of race, gender, and other social constructs along the way.

Neither homophobia nor speciesism (nor any other ism) is a disembodied idea. They are *practices* (and accompanying rationalizations) that arose at particular times and places for particular purposes. Perhaps the most important purpose, for both of those and for sexism and racism too, is control of reproduction. Thinking about that intersection forces us to face not only our own animality but also our complicity in the ongoing subordination of other species by our own. That raises the question of how to go about animal liberation.

Neither we nor the other animals we propose to liberate are abstract entities. Actual animal liberation is all about bodies—theirs *and* ours—and is therefore all about eros.

Without eros, ethos risks slippage into the realm of disembodied abstraction. Suppression of eros is suppression of our animal selves and is thus antithetical to the project of animal liberation. Suppression of eros severs us not only from our desires but also from others, deadening our feelings and relationships in the process. It's difficult to imagine how a liberatory ethos of care could be adequately enacted by beings who are cut off from themselves and others.

What would an *erotic* ethos of care bring to the project of animal liberation? First, eros is always embodied and therefore always actual. Animals don't care about our pretty ideas or pure intentions—what matters is what actually happens. An ethos of care rooted in eros would therefore mandate that care be actually enacted, that our ideas interact with that practice, and that both theory and praxis be constantly adjusted in response to what actually happens.

Next, eros is all about desire. Different animals want different things. Salmon want streams that haven't been dammed or diverted. Frogs want unpolluted ponds. Chickens want *out* of those battery cages. Dogs want other dogs. All of these desires are located in bodies. Their frustration is felt physically. So, again, this brings us back to the actual. But also, the animal rights movement as it is currently constituted does not, in my view, make an adequate effort to wrestle with that diversity of desires, preferring to focus on rights that are most important to animals like us (e.g., legal liberty). An ethos of care rooted in eros would mandate a much more thorough reckoning of animal desires and a consequent (and continuing) adjustment of aims and tactics.

Third, eros is all about relationships. An ethos of care rooted in eros would therefore mandate that such deliberations flow from, insofar as possible, real relationships with the animals in question.

Which brings me to my expanded conception of the organic intellectual—let's call it my theory of the veganic intellectual. As conceptualized by Gramsci, the organic intellectual—a person who conceptualizes and articulates the ideas of a class of people in which zhe is enmeshed—is essentially a function of the social group, both growing out of and acting upon the group.[55] Whether or not they have formal education, organic intellectuals both learn and teach in the context of active engagement with the struggles of their group, whether that group be an economic class or some other aggregation.

Roosters have helped me not only to think through several important subjects but also to apply the resulting ideas in ways that help other roosters. When the first avian resident of what would become VINE Sanctuary turned out to be a rooster rather than a hen, he refused to allow my stereotyped ideas about roosters define him or our relationship. This forced me to think deeply about where I got those ideas, which in turn led me to investigate the role of animals—real and imagined—in the social construction of gender. Similarly, a bonded pair of male foie gras factory refugees provoked me to commence a series of workshops at which participants considered the intersections between queer and animal liberation.

Then, in flew a group of two dozen roosters who had been living together for years. They schooled both me and the young orphans from factory farms in the methods and morals of flock life. Their habit of sleeping in the trees rather than in buildings eventually led our sanctuary to be the first in which chickens rewilded themselves. That wouldn't have happened if we hadn't decided to listen to the roosters themselves—who expressed themselves very clearly using their voices and bodies—on the question of how to balance freedom against safety from predation.

Our sanctuary was the first to figure out how to rehabilitate former fighting cocks. I say "our sanctuary" deliberately because this was a collective effort. The process involves not only soothing but also socializing these abused birds. I certainly could not have conceptualized that process without having first been taught about roosters by roosters, and the process cannot be implemented unless there are roosters willing and able to model the social behaviors that former fighters must learn in order to resolve conflicts without injury.

55. Gramsci, Selections from the Prison Notebooks.

The veganic intellectual, then, plays the same role as the organic intellectual, but for a group that includes nonhuman animals. The veganic intellectual does not claim to be "the voice of the voiceless," but rather recognizes and listens to animal voices. The veganic intellectual—I think of Karen Davis[56] with chickens and Lori Gruen[57] with chimps—thinks in conjunction with nonhuman animals, exercising both empathy and careful observation, and then shares any arising ideas with people who don't have the same opportunities for communion.

The Return of the Repressed

Desire drives everything. It's easy to maintain patriarchy once you've tricked little girls into dreaming of their wedding days, and it's not so hard to control the working class if a preponderance of grown men are addicted to pornography and flat-screen TVs. Conversely, it can be difficult to engender progressive change while wild eros is dead-ended into such socially constructed cravings.

According to a warning recently published in *Nature* by more than 20 researchers in biology and allied fields, we seem to be "approaching a state shift in Earth's biosphere."[58] wherein "the biological resources we take for granted at present may be subject to rapid and unpredictable transformations."[59] Reductions in *both* "world population growth and per-capita resource use"[60] will be necessary if we hope to avoid or even mitigate the coming cataclysmic changes.

Scientists haven't had much luck in using rational argumentation to persuade people to change our patterns of resource consumption (much less our mania for reproduction). Maybe we'll get lucky (in both senses of that phase) if we focus on feeling instead, cultivating queer eros in all of its manifestations, including not only love among animals but also topophilia and biophilia. That project will depend on our ability to put people in touch with their most heartfelt desires (which won't tend to be wedding dresses or artisanal cheese),

---

56. Davis, "Thinking Like a Chicken: Farm Animals and the Feminine Connection."

57. Gruen, "Attending to Nature."

58. Barnosky et al., "Approaching a State Shift in Earth's Biosphere," 52.

59. Ibid., 57.

60. Ibid.

and that in turn will require us to embrace our own animality, including its queer eros.

Works Cited

Alaimo, Stacy. 2010. "Eluding Capture: The Science, Culture, and Pleasure of 'Queer' Animals." In *Queer Ecologies: Sex, Nature, Politics, Desire*, edited by Catriona Mortimer-Sandilands and Bruce Erickson, 51–72. Bloomington, IN, USA: Indiana University Press.

Avital, Eytan, and Eva Jablonka. 2000. *Animal Traditions : Behavioural Inheritance in Evoloution*. Port Chester, NY, USA: Cambridge University Press.

Bagemihl, Bruce. 1999. *Biological Exuberance: Animal Homosexuality and Natural Diversity*. New York: St. Martin's Press.

Barnosky, Anthony D., Elizabeth A. Hadly, Jordi Bascompte, Eric L. Berlow, James H. Brown, Mikael Fortelius, Wayne M. Getz, et al. 2012. "Approaching a State Shift in Earth's Biosphere." *Nature* 486 (7401) (June 7): 52–58.

Blackwood, Evelyn, and Saskia E. Wieringa. 2007. "Globalization, Sexuality, and Silences: Women's Sexualities and Masculinities in an Asian Context." In *Women's Sexualities and Masculinities in a Globalizing Asia*, edited by Saskia E. Wieringa, Evelyn Blackwood, and Abha Bhaiya, 1–21. New York: Palgrave MacMillan.

Browne, Kathe, Jason Lim, and Gavin Brown, ed. 2007. *Geographies of Sexualities : Theory Practices and Politics*. Brookfield, VT, USA: Ashgate Publishing Group.

Casselton, Lorna A. 2002. "Mate Recognition in Fungi." *Heredity* 88 (2) (February): 142–147.

Catchpole, C. K., and P. J. B. Slater. *Bird Song: Biological Themes and Variations*. 2nd ed. Cambridge University Press, 2008.

Chou, Wah-Shan. 2001. "Homosexuality and the Cultural Politics of Tongzhi in Chinese Societies." *Journal of Homosexuality* 40 (3-4): 27–46.

Crimethinc Workers Collective. *Days of War, Nights of Love: Crimethink For Beginners*. Crimethinc, 2001.

Davies, Sharyn Graham. 2006. *Challenging Gender Norms: Five Genders Among Bugis in Indonesia*. Independence, KY, USA: Wadsworth Publishing.

Davis, Karen. 1995. "Thinking Like a Chicken: Farm Animals and the Feminine Connection." In *Animals and Women: Feminist Theoretical Explorations*, edited by Carol J. Adams and Josephine Donovan, 192–212. Duke University Press.

Driskill, Qwo-Li. 2004. "Stolen From Our Bodies: First Nations Two-Spirits/Queers and the Journey to a Sovereign Erotic." *Studies in American Indian Literatures* 16 (2): 50–64.

Drucker, Peter. 1996. "'In the Tropics There Is No Sin': Sexuality and Gay–Lesbian Movements in the Third World." *New Left Review* 1 (218): 75–101.

Epprecht, Marc. 2008. *Heterosexual Africa?: The History of an Idea from the Age of Exploration to the Age of AIDS*. Athens, OH, USA: Ohio University Press.

Fraser, James A., and Joseph Heitman. 2004. "Evolution of Fungal Sex Chromosomes." *Molecular Microbiology* 51 (2): 299–306.

Gaard, Greta. 1997. "Toward a Queer Ecofeminism." *Hypatia* 12 (1): 114–137.

Galeano, Eduardo. 1992. *We Say No*. New York: W.W. Norton & Company.

Gramsci, Antonio. 1971. *Selections from the Prison Notebooks*. Edited by Quintin Hoare and Geoffrey Nowell Smith. New York: International Publishers Co.

Gruen, Lori. 2009. "Attending to Nature: Empathetic Engagement with the More Than Human World." *Ethics & the Environment* 14 (2): 23–38.

Hawley, Caroline. "Anger over Egypt Gay Trial." *BBC*, August 15, 2001, sec. Middle East.

Hird, Myra J. 2004. "Naturally Queer." *Feminist Theory* 5: 85–89.

Jackson, Peter A. "Pre-Gay, Post-Queer: Thai Perspectives on Proliferating Gender/Sex Diversity in Asia." *Journal of Homosexuality* 40, no. 3/4 (2001): 1–25.

Karpova, Lisa, trans. 2011. "Third Sex Prehistoric Skeleton Found." *Pravda*, July 4.

Katyal, Sonia. 2002. "Exporting Identity." *Yale Journal of Law and Feminism* 14 (1).

Katz, Jonathan. 1976. *Gay American History*. New York: Avon.

Katz, Jonathan Ned. 2007. *The Invention of Heterosexuality*. University of Chicago Press.

Khan, S. 2001. "Culture, Sexualities, and Identities: Men Who Have Sex with Men in India." *Journal of Homosexuality* 40 (3-4): 99–115. doi:10.1300/J082v40n03_06.

Kheel, Marti. 1993. "From Heroic to Holistic Ethics: The Ecofeminist Challenge." In *Ecofeminism: Women, Animals, Nature*, edited by Greta Gaard, 243–271. Philadelphia, PA: Temple University Press.

Lorde, Audre. 2012. *Sister Outsider: Essays and Speeches.* New York: Random House.

McWhorter, Ladelle. 2010. "Enemy of the Species." In *Queer Ecologies: Sex, Nature, Politics, Desire*, edited by Catriona Mortimer-Sandilands and Bruce Erickson, 73–101. Bloomington, IN, USA: Indiana University Press.

Morgan, Ruth, and Saskia Wierenga. 2006. *Tommy Boys, Lesbian Men, and Ancestral Wives: Female Same-Sex Practices in Africa*. Jacana Media.

Mortimer-Sandilands, Catriona, and Bruce Erickson. 2010. "A Genealogy of Queer Ecologies." In *Queer Ecologies: Sex, Nature, Politics, Desire*, edited by Catriona Mortimer-Sandilands and Bruce Erickson, 1–47. Bloomington, IN, USA: Indiana University Press.

Nanda, Serena. 2000. *Gender Diversity: Crosscultural Variations.* Long Grove, Il, USA: Waveland Press.

Oskamp, Stuart. "A Sustainable Future for Humanity? How Can Psychology Help?" *American Psychologist* 55, no. 5 (2000): 496–508.

Oyama, Susan. 2000. *The Ontogeny of Information: Developmental Systems and Evolution*. Duke University Press.

Patterson, Charles. 2002. *Eternal Treblinka: Our Treatment of Animals and the Holocaust.* New York: Lantern Books.

Pharr, Suzanne. 1997. *Homophobia: A Weapon of Sexism*. Inverness, CA: Chardon Press.

Ramet, Sabrina Petra, ed. 1996. *Gender Reversals and Gender Cultures: Anthropologial and Historical Perspectives.* London: Routledge.

Roscoe, Will, ed. 1988. *Living the Spirit: A Gay American Indian Anthology*. New York: St. Martin's Press.

———. 2000. *Changing Ones: Third and Fourth Genders in Native North America*. New York: Palgrave Macmillan.

Sanders, Douglas. 2005. "Flying the Rainbow Flag in Asia:" Conference paper. https://digitalcollections.anu.edu.au/handle/1885/8691.

Sandilands, Catriona. 1994. "Lavender's Green? Some Thoughts on Queer(y)ing Environmental Politics." *Undercurrents: Critical Environmental Studies* (May): 20–24.

Smith, Andrea. 2005. *Conquest: Sexual Violence and American Indian Genocide*. Cambridge, MA, USA: South End Press.

Spiegel, Marjorie. 1996. *The Dreaded Comparison: Human and Animal Slavery*. Mirror Books.

Tamale, Sylvia. 2007. "Out of the Closet: Unveiling Sexuality Discourses in Uganda." In *Africa after Gender?*, edited by Catherine M. Cole, Takyiwaa

Manuh, and Stephan F. Miescher, 17–29. Bloomington, IN, USA: Indiana University Press.

Wieringa, Saskia E., Evelyn Blackwood, and Abha Bhaiya, ed. 2007. *Women's Sexualities and Masculinities in a Globalizing Asia*. New York: Palgrave MacMillan.

Wu, Peichen. 2007. "Performing Gender Along the Lesbian Continuum: The Politics of Sexual Identity in the Seitô Society." In *Women's Sexualities and Masculinities in a Globalizing Asia*, edited by Saskia E. Wieringa, Evelyn Blackwood, and Abha Bhaiya, 77–100. New York: Palgrave MacMillan.

14

Queer Eros in the Enchanted Forest

This essay, my sentimental favorite, appeared in a special 2019 issue of *QED: A Journal in GLBTQ Worldmaking* commemorating the 50th anniversary of the Stonewall rebellion. I love this piece because it comes closest to conveying the experience of VINE Sanctuary, which *Zoopolis* co-author Sue Donaldson has called "an unparalleled place for thinking anew about ideas of individual flourishing in community, and respectful inter-community relations." Special shout-out to Fiona Probyn-Rapsey of the University of Wollongong for setting up the ecofeminist writing retreat at which I wrote part of this piece and to the wombats and kangaroos at the site of that retreat, the Bundanon Land Trust.

Queer Eros in the Enchanted Forest

The Spirit of Stonewall as Sustainable Energy

I live in an enchanted forest. In the hundred-acre wood occupied by the denizens of VINE Sanctuary, an animal refuge established by LGBTQ people, beech trees synchronize their photosyntheses so that all may share the sugar. Flying squirrels nest with birds in the cavities of hollow trees and might stick their heads out to see who's there if you come knocking at dusk. Wild turkey hens collaboratively raise their young, sometimes taking them on walks to visit Pete and Repeat, two captive-born toms who share a coop with chickens rescued from egg factories.

In the wooded back pastures, a cow who rescued herself and her calf from a beef farm mingles with dozens of similarly self-possessed bovines. If you hike up to visit, their pheasant friend—who rewilded himself after being hatched to be hunted—might fly alongside you for a moment before returning to his own projects. Down at the duck pond, feral descendants of birds purchased at pet stores socialize with wild waterfowl. Back at the barn, sheep give rides to survivors of egg factories, and a group of peace-keeping geese help with the project of rehabilitating roosters formerly used in cockfighting.

One of those roosters—Sharkey—once teamed up with a Muscovy duck called Ready to co-parent a duckling who had been cast out by her own mother. Along with their friend Rocky the peacock (who had a crush on Sharkey), they co-created a vibrant community of care without regard for what people think about who should love who. In so doing, they transgressed manmade categories, stereotypes, and boundaries, motivated by the joy of mutual affection rather than the demands of procreative productivity. That's the spirit of Stonewall, and it may our only hope to avert climatic catastrophe.

As ecofeminist Val Plumwood has said, "our relationships with nature are currently failing."[1] Repairing those relationships will require us to surrender

1. Plumwood, "Decolonizing Relationships with Nature," 52.

the prideful idea that humans are separate from and superior to everybody else on the planet, but—as anybody who has ever fallen in love knows—decentering yourself can feel delicious and prompt creative activity. Since animals have been knocking down fences and other artificial barriers built by people for millennia, we might be able to learn something about resistance too. So let's make friends with queer ducks and other transgressors of Eurocentric conceptions of sexuality and identity.

Queer Ducks

The first time I saw Jean-Paul and Jean-Claude having sex, I thought they were fighting and promptly separated them. Three times, I broke up what seemed to be a vicious attack, removing the victim to another part of the sanctuary, only to later discover that he had climbed a fence, walked thought the woods, walked down a road and up a driveway and then climbed one more fence to reunite himself with his... *boyfriend*? Yes, even though I knew that ducks are among the hundreds of nonhuman animals for whom same-sex relationships are common,[2] some combination of speciesism and internalized homophobia had led me to separate a bonded pair who remained together (albeit not monogamously) until the end of their lives.

Jean-Paul and Jean-Claude were survivors of a foie gras factory where they had been confined in the dark without adequate access to water and force-fed massive quantities of grain in order to induce the fatty liver disease that defines that cruel delicacy. Let us pause for a moment to reflect upon the courage and tenacity Jean-Claude displayed in finding his way back to Jean-Paul again and again despite their forcible separation by a mystifying mammal. We know how it feels, don't we, to want to be with somebody—whether lover, comrade, friend, or family—that much?

Let's call that heartfelt drive for relationship *eros* and join Audre Lorde in recognizing the erotic as our most sustainable source of power. *Eros* is the Greek word for love in all of its manifestations, including but not limited to the sexual. In her germinal essay "The Uses of the Erotic," Lorde calls upon us to seize "the power which comes from sharing deeply any pursuit with another person,"[3] noting that "recognizing the power of the erotic within our lives can give us the

---

2. Bagemihl, Biological Exuberance: Animal Homosexuality and Natural Diversity.

3. Lorde, Sister Outsider, 56.

energy to pursue genuine change within our world."[4] Along with other forms of renewable energy, eros may be the key to averting planetary catastrophe engendered by human folly.

Queer Planet

Biologist J.B.S. Haldane famously suggested that "the Universe is not only queerer than we suppose, but queerer than we *can* suppose."[5] Two-spirit Native American poet and scholar Qwo-Li Driskill, who also recognizes Lorde's conception of eros as essential, reminds us of the "complex realities of gender and sexuality that are ever-present in both the human and more-than-human world, but erased and hidden by colonial cultures."[6] Those colonial cultures include present-day USA, where queer eros continues to encounter stone walls built by the "rationalist dualisms that oppose reason to nature, mind to body, emotional female to rational male, human to animal, and so on."[7]

Those binaries abide in our own minds, making it difficult to perceive our own diversity and complicating any quest to liberate ourselves or others. Even concepts and terms that feel and are freeing in some ways to some people in some places at some times may be hurtful in others, because they inadvertently include and cannot help but replicate antiquated European ideas about sexuality, family, and selfhood. We keep adding letters and asterisks to our acronyms because the idea of sexual-orientation-as-identity and conceptions of trans-ness rooted in (or in opposition to) the European-style gender binary cannot adequately cope with the actual diversity of human sexuality and gender expression. Exported around the world for the fine purpose of fostering LGBTQ rights, our neocolonial notions may inhibit rather than facilitate the liberation of eros.

Worse, the consolidation of erstwhile 'queer' people into normalcy within the reprocentric culture that has brought us to the brink of climatic catastrophe, while perhaps soothing to those who crave the comforts of conformity, only adds to the emergency. While late consumer capitalism requires more and more people buying more and more things and is therefore thrilled to

---

4. Ibid., 59.

5. Haldane, Possible Worlds and other Essays, 286.

6. Driskill, "Stolen From Our Bodies," 56-57.

7. Plumwood, "Decolonizing Relationships with Nature," 52.

sell destination weddings to same-sex couples while promoting the patriarchal notion that parents are paragons of productive adulthood, the others who share our increasingly stressed habitat probably would prefer that we remain queer. As we celebrate the 50th anniversary of Stonewall, let's remember that many of the bar-going stone-throwers that night were people who transgressed not only the norms of straight society but also the strictures of a nascent gay/lesbian rights movement that was busy telling straights "we're just like you" and hoping to one day be blessed by the state.

Stonewall Was a Riot

Eros upsurged despite and in direct contradiction to the state at the Stonewall Inn one night in 1969. Drag queens and other subversives literally turned the tables on the cops, barricading them into the bar they had come to raid. Fifty years on, Stonewall is a national monument authorized and delimited by the state. Could it be that the state celebrates its loss in that skirmish in its years-long war against queer eros? Or does the monument, like most war memorials, reflect a victory for the state?

I can't say that I don't feel any subversive glee at the idea of park rangers, who are a kind of police, protecting the memory of a night that queer folk fought back against cops, even as I feel queasy about the embrace of the armed state implicit in every smiling selfie taken in front of the plaque commemorating the site. All of our emotions are queer in the sense of refusing to march in the straight lines demanded by logical consistency.

I feel admixed myself here. I came out as a teen in 1976, the same year I quit eating meat. Both choices were the result of eros resisting diversion by the dominant culture. Whatever society said I should want, I did not, in fact, want a boyfriend. Nor did I wish to kill a cow. I wanted romantic relations with women, and I wanted harmonious with my nonhuman kin. By 17, I was the "co-coordinator" of the first college gay liberation organization in my state, where the newness of our endeavor allowed us to take a playful approach to creating change. In some ways, the question we wrestled with—how to be joyously queer (we were ahead of our time in reclaiming that word) without scaring the straights into attacking us even more—has been my abiding preoccupation ever since: How can we unsettle people enough to provoke them to reach for their most heartfelt desires but not so much that they retreat into the perceived safety of stasis? How can we infuse our most pragmatic strategies with erotic energy, always remembering the end goal of liberation even as we pursue dismal necessities like "rights" within the inherently violent existing legal system?

I love rainbows and everything they represent about our blurry multihued existence and the promise of sunshine after a storm. But I began to feel queasy, working at a lesbian bookstore in the 90s, when the rainbow decals, badges, jewelry, t-shirts, trinkets, and flags began to outnumber the books. And then the Pride flags flew at the 1993 March on Washington, where many participants pleaded for the right to get married and carry guns for the government, and my concern shifted from the commodification of queer identity to the attenuation of queerness itself by means of the very 'pride' that was supposed to liberate us.

The Pride flag is a *flag*. First used on battlefields and then to denote militarized nation-states, flags continue to signify combative identity. As ethno-nationalisms around the world upsurge, we cannot pretend that pride in identity isn't inherently hazardous. Yes, of course, persecuted people often find both communal solace and a center around which to organize resistance by embracing a subordinated or despised identity. At the same time, perpetrators of the worst atrocities tend to be inspired by identity. Again and again, people have fled persecution only to persecute others. Again and again, people with genuine grievances have been tricked by malicious leaders into perpetrating genocide. This is something that people do, often enough that we ought to be wary whenever we feel both prideful and aggrieved, even when both of those feelings are justified. I also worry that all forms of prideful identity carry within them the injurious imaginary border between people and nature.

Because the elevation of humanity above all others also entails a separation of humans from all others, we find it difficult to perceive, much less be mindful of, the multiplicity of ecological, material, and social systems in which we participate. Sure of our superiority, we literally cannot imagine what we might learn if we stepped down off our self-constructed pedestals and looked around.

Speciesism confuses us not only about other animals but also about ourselves. The Aristotelean notion of 'man' as a uniquely 'rational animal' leads us not only to discount the cognitive capacities of other animals but also to overstate the role of reason in our own lives. In truth, we are social animals who are all-too-easily swayed by advertising, propaganda, and peer pressure. Most of our cognition occurs outside of conscious awareness. We are motivated more by desire than by reason.

That's not necessarily bad news. Noticing how people actually act, as opposed to how members of the imaginary superior species act, can lead us to discover strategies more likely to bring about the more equitable, peaceful, and sustainable communities we all want. As I have argued elsewhere, "Eros begins in the body but always reaches outward, seeking connection."[8] If we can tap into that wellspring of wishing for true communion, it will help us see what we need to do *and* give us the energy to do it. We can forge bonds not only with other oppressed people but also with other entities who have been disgraced and displaced by the dominant culture, and these can be based on felt solidarity rather than identity.

If we're going to feel pride, let's be proud of what we *do* rather than what we *are*. And if we must fly a multi-hued banner, let it stand for variety, including not only the blooming profusion of ways that people desire each other and express themselves but also biodiversity.

As the World Turns

Somewhere near you stands a tree. That tree communicates with insects and with other trees by means that may seem quite queer to you, using fungi as telephone lines or sending off messages encoded in scents. You send and receive scent messages too, although you may not be aware of this. More importantly, you are among the animals dependent on that tree. Do you breathe? Thank photosynthesis, which has been there for you, day in and day out, since the day you were born.

How much longer can you count on trees? The droughts, floods, and wildfires of recent years are but the tip of the melting iceberg that has already begun to submerge the lands on which we stand under rising tides for which our own reprocentric rapacity is to blame. In order to ensure the things we need — fresh water to drink, clean air to breathe, enough food for everybody to eat — then we will need to set aside socially constructed cravings in favor of our most heartfelt desires.

As social animals, we want relationships more than anything. The same drive for queer communion that propelled the Stonewall Rebellion can power a quest for other kinds of connectedness, bringing us back into vibrant relationship with the talking trees, polyamorous ducks, and other queer beings who share this queer planet with us. In turn, those improved relations can animate our struggles for social justice, increasing our ability to think imaginatively and act creatively within systems that confound the constraints imposed by Eurocentric logic.

8. jones, "Eros and the Mechanisms of Eco-Defense," 101.

I live in an enchanted forest. So do you. The forest is on fire. Eros can save us, but only if we are willing to forswear pride in order to rejoin the joyful worldwide resistance against humdrum human hegemony.

Works Cited

Bagemihl, Bruce. *Biological Exuberance: Animal Homosexuality and Natural Diversity*. New York: St. Martin's Press, 1999.

Driskill, Qwo-Li. "Stolen From Our Bodies: First Nations Two-Spirits/Queers and the Journey to a Sovereign Erotic." *Studies in American Indian Literatures* 16, no. 2 (2004): 50–64. https://doi.org/10.1353/ail.2004.0020.

Haldane, J.B.S. *Possible Worlds and other Essays.* London: Chatto and Windus, 1927.

jones, pattrice. "Eros and the Mechanisms of Eco-Defense." In *Ecofeminism: Feminist Intersections with Other Animals and the Earth*, edited by Carol J. Adams and Lori Gruen. New York: Bloomsbury Academic, 2014.

Lorde, Audre. *Sister Outsider: Essays and Speeches.* New York: Random House, 2012.

Plumwood, Val. "Decolonizing Relationships with Nature." In *Decolonizing Nature : Strategies for Conservation in a Postcolonial Era*, edited by W. M. Adams and Martin Mulligan, 51–78. London, GBR: Earthscan, 2003.

15

Becoming More Queer

This brief piece was published in 2020 in a special tenth anniversary edition of the Spanish magazine *Parole de Queer*. I wrote with LGBTQ+ people who might not yet be in solidarity with animals or the larger-than-human world in mind. I do truly believe that such solidarity can make us both less alone and more queer. This piece was published in Spanish, so this is the first time it appears in English. I include it here because it so concisely encapsulates many of the messages I feel to be most urgent at this moment of worldwide emergency.

Becoming More Queer

Right now, as you read, trees are talking to each other via telephone lines made of fungi. Insects send and receive invisible scent messages carried by breezes. Small woodland mammals listen to songbirds, whose alarm cries warn of danger and whose cheerful chirps signal safety.

Pause for a moment to imagine this.

Now imagine that the forest is on fire—because it is.

As we celebrate *Parole de Queer*'s tenth anniversary, we must simultaneously realize that ten more years have gone by during which we have *not* done what we need to do to about human-engendered climate change. Wildfires rage as islands disappear, all because of a 500+ years-long war against the queer that began when Europeans set out to colonize the planet, carrying dangerous ideologies along with their weapons.

By "queer," I mean much more than LGBTQ+. I mean every body, whether human or otherwise, who has been deemed inferior because of difference from the presumed norm of the able-bodied European heterosexual masculine male human. It's important to understand how the different aspects of this Eurocentric, androcentric, and anthropocentric point of view fit together.

For nearly 20 years, VINE Sanctuary has organized "Queering Animal Liberation" workshops at which participants collectively try to answer questions such as:

Where do speciesism and homophobia/transphobia overlap? What are their shared features? What are their common roots? Does one support, compound, or amplify the other in any way?

How are animals used to make homosexuality seem unnatural? How are LGBTQ+ people hurt by this? How are animals themselves hurt by this?

How are animals used in the social construction of gender stereotypes? How are LGBTQ+ people hurt by those stereotypes? How are animals hurt by those stereotypes? By their use as avatars of femininity or masculinity?

You may find it useful to work through such questions yourself or in conversation with comrades. Let me focus on just two factors that have emerged from our conversations, which work together to create climate crisis: reprocentrism and toxic masculinity.

"Toxic" masculinity, which hurts everybody, defines manhood as the power to control others without showing weakness. This way of thinking categorizes certain human characteristics and occupations, such as emotions or care-taking, as feminine and therefore inferior. Within this gender regime, boys and men strive to be seen as masculine. Abuses of animals such as hunting, cockfighting or bull fighting may be used to demonstrate masculinity. This way of being masculine also leads directly to violence against women as well as to homophobic and transphobic behavior.

"Reprocentrism" measures the worth of every person by their ability to produce children and/or profits. Both humans and animals are subjected to involuntary reproduction. For animals, this is a matter of forced reproduction at farms, zoos, labs, and other sites of exploitation. For humans, forcible reproduction sometimes happens, especially during wartime, but the most common methods of compelling reproduction are social norms, including compulsory heterosexuality.

How do these work together to create climate change? Late consumer capitalism, which requires more and more people buying more and more things, has brought patriarchal reprocentrism into a new millennium. Meanwhile, research shows that men who embrace toxic notions of masculinity are less likely to engage in "green" behavior such as going vegan or carrying reusable shopping bags.

To respond to this, I believe that we need to become more queer, not only resisting the norms of reprocentrism and toxic masculinity but also by finding new ways to feel and express solidarity with those whose brains, bodies, and ways of communicating are different than our own. Yes, nonhuman animals think and communicate and form families and communities differently than we do. Let's stop seeing such differences as markers of inferiority and instead embrace the biodiversity that literally makes life possible. Let's recognize that animals might be able to teach us things that we desperately need to learn.

VINE runs a humane education program in which children consider serious questions while in the midst of our multi-species community, where LGBTQ+ people care for more than 600 nonhuman animals. Here, children see that an alpaca can be friends with a pig, and they learn that it is both possible and pleasurable to extend respect and care across differences. They see roosters rescued from cockfighting getting along with each other, and they learn that is it possible to be more peaceful than you were raised to be. They see a giant ox taking care not to step on a tiny bird as they feast together on donated vegetables, and they learn that true strength includes generosity and restraint.

I remind you: As you read this, fungi and trees cooperate to make it possible for you to breathe. Birds and bees pollinate the plants upon which all life depends. If you can bring yourself into better relationship with them, you will be less alone as well as more queer.

IV. DIRECT ACTION GETS SATISFACTION

"We're here, we're queer, we're not going shopping!"

In the 1990s, flamboyantly outfitted LGBTQ+ people affiliated with ACT UP or Queer Nation sometimes took over malls and shopping centers chanting that refrain, interrupting the everyday machinations of capitalism to draw attention to the lethality of homophobia. The disruption itself was the point. While I now retroactively wish we had been more explicit in elaborating some of the linkages discussed in the previous section, I still see value in simply stopping people from shopping, if only for a fleeting moment in which it might be possible to imagine a world in which the Mall of America—which features an underground aquarium where sea turtles, sharks, stingrays, and jellyfish swirl helplessly beneath the feet of midwestern spendthrifts—no longer exists.

In my decades of activism before co-founding VINE Sanctuary, direct action was, along with the formation of unlikely coalitions, a persistent theme. I organized rent strikes and kiss-ins. As a member of ACT UP/Ann Arbor, I brought bleach and clean needles to a protest encampment of unhoused people, several of whom showed up in court to cheer me on when I went on trial for handing out condoms and AIDS information in front of a high school. I also questioned tactics commonly mistaken for direct action, such as splashy protest marches that don't interrupt anything at all. So, of course, after Miriam Jones and I had set up a refuge for chickens literally surrounded by factory farms, I began to think about direct action in the struggle for animal liberation.

The essays in this section all delve into direct action as an activist tactic: What it is, how it works, and how it can fit into the diversity of activities that can add up to successful social change strategies.

16

ALL-CITY RENT STRIKE

Originally published in February of 1999 in Ann Arbor's independent newspaper, The Agenda, this is more of a feature article than an essay but I have included it here because the whole story illustrates how direct action can be used, alongside other tactics, to bring about substantial and long-lasting change. As the coordinator of the Ann Arbor Tenants Union for four years in the early 1990s, I saw first-hand how the practical tactics of community organizing can simultaneously solve problems in the here-and-now while educating and empowering people to reshape their communities into the future. I have edited the article down by removing some details of strictly local interest.

Tenants Strike Back

The All-City Rent Strike of 1969-71

"Landlords have money and power... tenants have each other."

With those words, a group of University of Michigan students launched an event that reverberates to this day. The Ann Arbor Tenants Union's "all-city rent strike" of 1969-71 began 30 years ago this month and may be said to have never ended. The story is instructive as well as dramatic.

Once upon a time, rental housing conditions in Ann Arbor were among the worst in the nation. Students fought with one another for the chance to crowd into over-priced, dilapidated apartment houses near campus. Low-income renters faced similar conditions on the outskirts of town.

This was in the late 1960's, a time of great national and local upheaval. Frightened by the rising tide of urban uprisings, lawmakers across the nation turned to studies and commission reports, most of which listed housing problems and powerlessness as sources of potentially violent discontent. In Lansing, lawmakers responded with the Warranty of Habitability (MCLA 554.139), which requires all elements of a rental unit to be fit for the use intended and compels landlords to abide by applicable city and state housing codes.

Meanwhile, in Ann Arbor, the University of Michigan campus had become a hotbed of student activism. Frustrated by their own housing problems and angered by the conditions faced by tenants living in poverty, a group of graduate students decided to test the new law. Since the Warranty of Habitability appeared to imply that tenants had a contractual right to withhold rent when landlords did not fulfill their responsibilities, a rent strike seemed to be the most promising tactic.

The young organizers of Ann Arbor's tenants union knew that tenants living in poverty had organized successful rent strikes elsewhere — most notably in Harlem in 1963-64 — but they also knew that Michigan's law was yet untested and that low-income renters would be most vulnerable were they to strike and fail. In contrast, students could fall back upon parents or dorm housing. A student rent strike could win benefits for all tenants without exposing the most vulnerable tenants to the threat of eviction.

The organizers targeted ten local landlords believed to be among the worst offenders. They publicized the impending strike and collected signatures of students who pledged to strike. Along the way, they obtained the endorsement of a number of diverse campus groups, including the Engineering Council, the Black Law Student Association, and the student government.

The proposed strike was big news in Ann Arbor through the fall of 1968 and into the winter of 1969. The Ann Arbor News and the Michigan Daily were filled with articles, editorials, and letters about tenant rights, landlord abuses, housing prices and conditions, and other related issues. While the newspapers may not have intended to do so, they furthered the cause of the strike by helping to spread the word and by teaching renters about their rights. Thus the new tenants union won its first victory before the first dollar of rent was withheld.

On the evening of February 13, 1969 the tenants union announced that the goal of 2,000 signatures had been reached. The strike began the next day and lasted into 1971. Along the way, what had been a local controversy turned into a spectacle closely attended by the national media.

While educating tenants, coordinating the strike, and helping to strikers to defend themselves in court, the tenants union scrambled to defend itself and striking students from other forms of landlord retaliation. Some landlords locked-out striking tenants, throwing their belongings on the street. Others achieved the same end by cutting off utilities. A few landlords threatened and physically intimidated striking tenants, leading to the creation of a tenants union 24-hour mobile defense team.

Local attorney Jonathan Rose, who joined the tenants union in 1969 and served as its attorney in 1970, recalls the exciting tenor of the times. "The tenants union was a high energy, optimistic undertaking. The tenants union shared the lobby of the Student Activities building with the student government. The Black Action Movement (BAM) was organizing outside the window while the tenants union was working inside.... There was a high spirit of grassroots organizing." When the BAM strike against the University began, the tenants union organizers encouraged rent strikers to participate in the BAM-led general strike. An AATU flyer printed at the time noted that the high cost of housing in Ann Arbor contributed to low Black enrollment and concluded that "the general strike [is] the only tactic left to force the University to grant the BAM demands."

The student organizers of the tenants union also had to grapple with the University. Then, as now, the university played a significant role in the city's housing woes. Then, as now, the University provided a captive market of unsophisticated consumers for landlords, was slow to respond to student demands for additional on-campus housing, and drove up property tax rates by removing land from the city tax rolls. But, rather than supporting its students' attempts to obtain more habitable housing, the University chose to respond to the rent strike by threatening striking students with academic sanctions.

While the University never followed through on its threat to sanction striking students, its preparations to do so set the stage for one of the most dramatic incidents of the strike. A local bank agreed to provide the University with the names of students who were holding rent in escrow. In response, the tenants union called for all students to withdraw all of their funds from that bank on a single day. The students responded, withdrawing more than $100,000 and closing 400 accounts. Students stood on the street corner burning their bank books. The bank closed early that day, and went out of business soon thereafter.

Other local tenants were encouraged by the success of the student rent strike. Public housing tenants launched a 1971 rent strike complaining, among other problems, of ankle-deep mud in ground-floor apartments.

Positive outcomes of the rent strike of 1969-1971 were not limited to court victories and local tenant empowerment. Because of the national attention directed at the strike, which included articles in such venues as *Business Week* and the *New York Times*, student tenant associations modeled on the Ann Arbor Tenants Union sprang up across the country. Some, like the AATU, have survived and thrived into the present. Ann Arbor's successful rent strike also helped to spark the national consumer rights movement, which would become so important later in the 1970s.

While AATU has turned out to be one of the most stable local entities of the late 1960s, its organizers had not intended to found a permanent organization. Their original goal was simply to organize an effective strike, bringing the tactics of democratic unionism to landlord-tenant relations. However, as the strike progressed, tenants' desires for a permanent and more extensive tenant association prevailed. The new AATU opened itself to non-striking tenants and began to take action on a number of issues.

One of the most pressing concerns of local renters was the University's failure to adequately house its students. In a precursor to the tactic used by homelessness activists in the 1990s, the AATU constructed a 'tent city' on the U-M campus in the fall of 1970. For three weeks, student protesters lived in tents in order to protest dorm over-crowding and publicize the University's role in the local housing crisis. That protest ended only when a hepatitis scare caused health officials to order the tent city destroyed.

Another dramatic series of early AATU actions involved State Crime Commissioner Louis Rome. The AATU staged a number of demonstrations intended to show that while Rome was enforcing the law in Lansing, he was breaking the law as a landlord in Ann Arbor. A 1970 demonstration in Lansing paved the way for Rome's resignation as State Crime Commissioner — which he tendered only hours before pleading guilty to criminal charges stemming from excessive Ann Arbor Housing Code violations in his buildings.

Following the close of the all-city rent strike, the AATU found itself with little money and a lot of responsibilities. While financial support for the strike itself had come from a number of sources, including a large donation from the UAW and a benefit concert by Joan Baez, the AATU had a harder time finding support for more mundane tasks like following up on court cases in the appeals phase, providing day-to-day tenant counseling services, and working to expand the rights of renters in Michigan. Tenants who could not afford to pay AATU dues wanted and needed AATU services, but the costs of providing those services had to be covered somehow.

The AATU sought and gained funding from the U-M student government and agreed in exchange to provide the benefits of AATU membership to all students without charge. That agreement has persisted, in various permutations, to this day. Then, as now, services to low-income non-student renters were funded by donations and grants while non-student renters who could afford to do so were asked to pay AATU dues in exchange for AATU services.

In addition to providing educational services to individual tenants and helping groups of tenants to organize rent strikes, the AATU in the 1970s worked to enhance the rights of all Michigan tenants. In Lansing, the AATU helped to pass the 'lock-out law' (which prohibits landlords from using extra-legal tactics like changing locks or shutting off utilities to evict tenants), a law that prohibits retaliatory eviction, the Truth in Renting Act, and the Security Deposit Act. Each of these laws is strongly pro-tenant, and every Michigan renter now enjoys their protection. The AATU also worked in coalition with other organizations to support passage of the state's consumer protection and anti-discrimination laws.

This list of legislative victories might seem to suggest that the AATU had become a tamer and less controversial organization. Nothing could be further from the truth. During this period, the AATU continued to organize hotly contested rent strikes and to use the tactics of dramatic demonstration in order to publicize pressing problems. Such efforts concerning the plight of low-income mobile home residents led to the extension of tenants rights to those who rent space in mobile home parks.

AATU actions of the 1970s were not always so successful at achieving wider ends. While most strikes concerning poor conditions or landlord abuses continued to result in court victories or out-of-court settlements favoring tenants, strikes for lower housing prices or collective bargaining agreements were less effective. One exception to that general rule was the Trony strike of 1976, which resulted in a unique collective bargaining agreement between the landlord and the AATU.

As always, AATU rent strikes were emotional affairs. Recalling her participation in the 1976 strike against Edith Epstein's Reliable Realty, bookstore owner Lynden Kelly says that she and other tenants felt "very scared... but also empowered." In lawsuits arising from that strike, tenants represented themselves with the assistance of the AATU and won significant victories. Kelly reports that the process was "easy, once you got over your nervousness" and that negotiating "as a bloc" rather than as individuals was a useful strategy.

In the 1980s, the AATU turned its attention to local housing legislation, helping to revise the Ann Arbor Housing Code and working with environmentalists to pass the Weatherization as Responsible Management (WARM) ordinance. As the 80s progressed, the AATU, like other housing organizations across the country, focused increasing attention on the critical lack of affordable housing.

Since the chief complaint of Ann Arbor renters has always been high prices, the AATU had always worked for fair rents. As homelessness increased, the problem became more urgent. Local efforts to institute rent control had been repeatedly thwarted and were now moot due to a provision in state law forbidding localities from imposing rent control. This left local housing activists with only a few options for dealing with the problem. AATU efforts to encourage public funding of new affordable housing, preserve the existing stock of low-income housing by forcing landlords to make necessary repairs, and pressure the University to build more student housing have played an important role in the ongoing local struggle against homelessness. Since eviction is the most common immediate cause of homelessness, AATU anti-eviction efforts on behalf of low-income tenants prevent homelessness on a case-by-case basis.

The AATU's emphasis on service to individual tenants combined with activism on behalf of all tenants has continued into the 1990s. In this decade, the AATU has worked in coalition with a diverse set of organizations in order to achieve common goals. For example, the AATU worked with feminist organizations to pass a privacy ordinance, with gay and lesbian organizations to open University housing to same-sex couples, with disability rights organizations to enforce fair housing laws, and with anti-racist organizations to contest police harassment at public housing sites. This coalition work has proceeded on top of the day-to-day work of the AATU despite a significant backlash against tenant rights.

The effects of that backlash cannot be overstated. During the years that I coordinated the AATU, we spent a lot of our time simply blocking landlord efforts to overturn or dilute existing tenants rights. Every year, the state House of Representatives considered outlawing — yes, outlawing — the mandatory housing inspections required many Michigan localities. The integrity of our local Housing Code is constantly threatened by landlord demands for exceptions and revisions.

Perhaps the most serious local threat to tenant rights in this decade was posed by the Ann Arbor 'Y' which claimed — with the strong support of the Mayor and several City Council members — that its tenants were not entitled to the rights provided by state and federal law. The 'Y' case provided me with one of the most chilling moments in my association with the AATU. I cannot describe how it felt to hear the attorney for the 'Y' assert — in open court — that people with psychiatric disabilities did not deserve the same due process rights in evictions as other tenants.

Another highly-publicized AATU action of the 1990s, the Baker Commons rent strike of 1994-95, inspired all of the AATU staff and associates who worked on it. Baker Commons is a public housing site serving seniors and people with disabilities. Responding to requests from tenants, the AATU organized a rent strike to compel the Housing Commission to make urgently needed repairs. While about a third of the building's tenants began the strike, threats and misleading information from the Housing Commission soon reduced the number of strikers to a handful. The Housing Commission then sued to evict the remaining strikers but dropped the suit as soon as they realized that the tenants had a lawyer — the same Jonathan Rose who had represented the AATU back in 1970.

Negotiations dragged on and then failed. The tenants sued the Housing Commission, asking the judge to order the repairs made. In the strike's 16th month, the case was settled out of court since most of the repairs had been made or were in progress. The settlement allowed the tenants to permanently retain almost all of the rent that they had withheld.

Speaking at an AATU educational seminar in 1993, founding member Steve Burkhart said that the students who organized the rent strike of 1969 succeeded in part because they wholeheartedly believed that they could. The same could be said of the Baker Commons tenants. Commenting on the staying power of the AATU, Burkhart stressed the importance of relationships in community organizing.

In a sense, unionism is nothing other than the creation and maintenance of relationships. The AATU has survived against the odds precisely because of the relationships — both among people and between people and the organization — that it has engendered. Unlike many other organizations, the AATU has never chosen between service and activism. In the absence of activism, social services provide short-term solutions for long-term problems. On the other hand, activism aimed at long-term solutions often leaves people without solutions for the problems they face right now. While it has often taken heat from every direction for doing so, the AATU has steadfastly insisted on providing immediate assistance while working for structural change.

The AATU's preference for the tactics of direct action is another reason for its continued existence. I define 'direct action' as any tactic that actually does something about the problem it seeks to address. Demonstrations just... demonstrate. While the common tactics of marches and rallies do have expressive value and do provide some education to the public, they no longer have the power to bring about change by themselves. New activists fed on a diet of only demonstrations and marches soon become depleted and demoralized. In contrast, direct action offers something to do with all of the energy stirred up by demonstrations and provides visible results at every turn.

Rent strikes are direct action: the target (the landlord) is actually affected by the action from the moment that it commences. Other forms of direct action used by various movements include needle exchange programs, reclamation of abandoned buildings, and physically blocking the destruction of environmental resources. Each of these examples of non-violent direct action actually does something about the problem while at the same time, through media coverage, educating the public about the problem and its potential solutions. By consistently including non-violent direct action in its spectrum of activities, the AATU has ensured that the struggle will continue until everybody has access to safe and affordable housing.

17

MOTHERS WITH MONKEYWRENCHES

The late Karen Davis of United Poultry Concerns was responsible for the existence of this essay. Having written her own chapter for *Terrorists or Freedom Fighters? Reflections on the Liberation of Animals*, she noticed that the volume contained too few contributions by women and none from a feminist perspective. Although the manuscript was otherwise ready for the publisher, she insisted that the editors invite me to write a chapter, pausing the publication schedule long enough for me to do so. To their credit, they did. Although written in haste quite early in the evolution of my thinking about the conjunctions in question, this chapter helped me to begin to find my way toward a methodology of animal advocacy that simultaneously centers animals themselves and attends adequately to the nexus of social circumstances that both engender their oppression and inhibit their liberation. Thanks to Karen for the boost and to Miriam Jones and the late Marti Kheel for useful comments on the first draft.

Mothers with Monkeywrenches

Feminist Imperatives and the ALF

"Its necessity is its excuse for existence." Elizabeth Gurley Flynn, *Sabotage*, 1916[1]

I

The black cat arches her spine, glancing back before springing ahead. It was she who inspired the Yellow Turban Rebellion and the Boston Tea Party. She gives breath to the Shakers and Quakers and Sufis who even now weave their bodies in dances of defiance. She sat down with Rosa Parks and stood shoulder to shoulder with Wobblies on wildcat strikes. The tunnels of the Underground Railroad still echo her name. Call her Krazy, but she knows that direct action brings satisfaction. Call her Mehitabel because she is always hopeful, *toujours gai*, despite the horrors she confronts every day. Call her Felix because she's never without her bag of tricks.[2]

---

1. Elizabeth Gurley Flynn (1890-1961) was an organizer for the Industrial Workers of the World (IWW) and a founding member of the American Civil Liberties Union.

2. The Yellow Turban Uprising of c.e. 184 was a peasant uprising staged by Taoists. The Boston Tea Party was a night of property destruction staged by American colonists protesting British rule. Shakers, Quakers, and Sufis all have been condemned as heretics and all use motion in pursuit of spiritual goals. Contrary to popular belief, Rosa Parks sat down in the white section of a segregated bus as part of a deliberate strategy for change, rather than just because her feet hurt. IWW members are called Wobblies. Wildcat strikes are staged by workers without the sanction of a union recognized by the employer. Harriet Tubman and others used the Underground Railroad as an avenue of freedom for enslaved people of African descent. Krazy Kat was the black cat of indeterminate sex who appeared in the George Herriman comic strip of the same name. Poet e.e. cummings wrote that Krazy's "ambiguous gender doesn't disguise the good news that here comes our heroine." Mehitabel appears in archy and mehitabel by Don Marquis, which is a novel in verse about a roach and a black cat. Mehitabel the cat has an "extensive past," proclaims herself to be "toujours gai" [always happy] in the face of deprivation, and says that "the things that i had not ought to/ i do because i ve gotto." Felix the cat is a more modern cartoon prankster known for his bag of tricks.

Today the black cat rides on the backs of the women and men who sabotage animal research labs, delivering very real kittens from death. She graces the shoulders of tree huggers, road blockers, and the black-clad "night gardeners" who uproot test plots of genetically modified monstrosities.[3]

Along with the sabot and the monkeywrench, the black cat has long been a symbol of direct action. Direct action is often misused as a synonym for civil disobedience or flamboyant protest. But, in fact, mass arrests and dramatic street theatre may or may not add up to direct action, depending on the context. Direct action includes only activist tactics that, like boycotts and sabotage, are intended to have an immediate impact on a problem or its causes. In contrast, indirect action aims for future change through more circuitous routes, such as education, legislation, and symbolic demonstrations of opinion. Actions may include both direct and indirect elements. Ideally, direct action will illustrate or illuminate the problem at the same time as it interferes with its causes or effects. The very best direct action contributes to a long-term strategy for future change even as it offers tangible results in the here and now.

Direct action is best understood by example. People who have integrated segregated lunch counters, put their bodies in the paths of troop transport trains, distributed illegal clean needles or birth control devices, boycotted chocolate or Coca-Cola, staged rent strikes, or built very visible "tent cities" for the homeless have all taken direct action against one or another form of oppression. Direct action for animals is similarly diverse. People who interfere with hunts, deface fur coats or egg cartons, stage open or covert rescues, provide sanctuary to escaped and rescued animals, block the entrances of slaughterhouses, destroy the laboratory equipment of vivisectors, or simply stop buying animal products all immediately impact the lives of actual animals.

Specific Examples may help to clarify the distinction between direct and indirect action. When the Berrigan brothers destroyed draft records during the Vietnam war, that was direct action, because the destruction of the records actually impeded the conduct of the draft. More recently, when massive crowds have protested the attacks on Afghanistan and Iraq by marching through the

---

3. For many years, women in the Chipko Andolan (the hugging movement) in India have blocked bulldozers by wrapping their bodies around trees. [See Ynestra King. "Healing the Wounds: Feminism, Ecology, and the Nature/Culture Dualism." In Irene Diamond & Gloria Feman Orenstein (Eds) Reweaving the World: The Emergence of Ecofeminism, Sierra Club Books, 1990.] Many of the activists who block environmentally destructive road development in Britain are "eco-pagans" who blend an appreciation of fairy mythology with the hardcore realities of direct action. [See Andy Letcher, "The Scouring of the Shire: Trolls and Pixies in Eco-Protest Culture," Folklore, October 2001.] Night gardeners uproot and otherwise interfere with plantings of genetically modified plants.

empty streets of the District of Columbia, that was indirect action aimed at changing the hearts and minds of citizens in the hopes that they would, in turn, influence or replace their elected officials.[4]

Symbolic demonstrations can be designed to be direct action as well. When the Field of Dreams Hunting Club went out in a huge yellow rubber ducky, shooting into the air in order to scare the birds away from the real hunters, that was both direct and symbolic action because it saved bird lives while mocking hunters. In contrast, trying to pass legislation to ban certain types of hunting is indirect action, since there are very many steps between the activists who may or may not succeed in convincing enough legislators and the wildlife officials who may or may not effectively enforce any new regulations.

Direct action for animals may be legal or illegal, overt or covert, sardonic or strictly sober. The one thing all forms of direct action have in common is that they without doubt relieve the suffering of animals or obstruct the activities that cause that suffering. This is in contrast to the more speculative nature of indirect action, wherein success depends on both an accurate theory of social change and an effective implementation of that theory. Harriet Tubman may well have had a theory of social change concerning how her actions might lead to abolition but did not need such a theory to know that leading specific slaves to freedom would result in liberation for them. In contrast, when Sojourner Truth made abolitionist speeches, she was working according to the theory that rhetoric can change people's minds and that changing people's minds will lead them to change their behavior. Tubman's actions were certain to bring the desired results as long as she didn't get caught. In contrast, success for Truth depended upon both the accuracy of her theories about relationship between beliefs and behavior and the effective enactment of her theories about rhetoric.

In direct action, one often risks physical injury or loss of freedom; in indirect action, one wagers time and energy on strategies that may or may not bear fruit. Thus, direct action tends to require more courage while indirect action tends to require more faith. Both require skill and dedication. Neither is entirely effective without the other. Analysis of other social movements in history suggests that our best bet will be a strategy that includes a diversity of direct action tactics in coordination with a diversity of other types of tactics.

The black cat of direct action is usually presumed to be female, perhaps because of the association with witchcraft and the left-handed, or feminine,

4. For more on the distance between purely symbolic demonstrations and effective direct action, see my "Marching in Circles: The Tactics of Dizziness and Despair."

nature of transgressive activity. The black cat usually symbolizes the most secret and subversive forms of direct action, such as those utilized by the ALF. The kitten in the laboratory is the captured kin of the black cat. It is her ongoing and inescapable pain that makes direct action against vivisection necessary. We must remember that kitten, and the cow crying for her calf, and the hen driven mad by the battery cage whenever we assess the allegedly extreme tactics used by the ALF to free animals and interfere with the industries that abuse them.

II

Like the black cat, feminism doesn't ask whether ALF actions adhere to the law or conform to abstract philosophical principles. Like the black cat, feminism asks: Do ALF actions cause, create, or contribute to the effective expression of care for animals?

Why should we care what feminism asks of the ALF? Because animal liberation is a feminist project. Speciesism and sexism are so closely related that one might go so far as to say that they are the same thing under different guises. Women and animals, along with land and children, have historically been seen as the property of male heads of households. Patriarchy (male control of political and family life) and pastoralism (animal herding as a way of life) appeared on the historical stage together and cannot be separated, because they are justified and perpetuated by the same ideologies and practices.[5]

Both women and animals are seen as less rational and more constrained by biology than men. Both suffer by being reduced to their bodies or, worse, their body parts. As Simone deBeauvior wrote in *The Second Sex*: "Woman? Very simple, say the fanciers of simple formulations: she is a womb, an ovary; she is a female — this word is sufficient to define her. In the mouth of the man the epithet *female* has the sound of an insult."[6]

---

5. For recent scientific evidence concerning the link between pastoralism and patriarchy, see "Cattle Ownership Makes it a Man's World" in the 01 October 2003 issue of New Scientist magazine, which summarizes Holden and Mace (2003), "Spread of Cattle Led to the Loss of Matrilineal Descent in Africa: A Coevolutionary Analysis" in Proceedings of the Royal Society: Biological Sciences, DOI 10.1098/rspb.2003.2535

6. Simone deBeauvior's 1952 The Second Sex helped to launch the modern feminist movement. Her 1948 Ethics of Ambiguity provides an easy to understand explanation of the ethical implications of the existential principle that existence precedes essence. I would argue that this principle means, for example, that one becomes an environmentalist by making environmentally sustainable choices and that one cannot be an environmentalist if one's choices run counter to the best interests of the ecosystem.

The word *animal* also has the sound of an insult. Women are derided as 'fat cows' and condemned for 'cattiness.' Meanwhile, as Karen Davis has pointed out, even people who claim to venerate 'wild and free' animals display only contempt for the farmed animals "whose lives appear too slavishly, too boringly, too stupidly female."[7] Tactics such as objectification, ridicule, and control of reproduction have been and continue to be used to oppress and exploit both women and animals.

This can be seen more easily by looking at specific issues generally assumed to be within the sphere of either feminism or animal liberation...

Milk is a feminist issue. Milk may be defined as the exploitation of the reproductive capacities of the cow in order to produce profits for the dairy industry. Cows are forcibly and repeatedly impregnated so that their bodies will produce the milk intended to sustain their calves. People then steal both the milk and the calves. The cows suffer painful physical ailments, such as mastitis, as well as the emotional distress of having their children and their own freedom torn away from them. Meanwhile, milk products are responsible for an unhealthy acceleration in the onset of menses in girls and are also correlated with breast cancer in women. Thus the mammary glands of cows are exploited in order to produce a product that harms the mammary glands of women.

Rape is an animal issue. One out of every three women is sexually assaulted in her lifetime — one in four before the age of 18. Experts agree that rape is about power, not sex. Rape puts into action the idea that women and children are objects that can be used for pleasure without regard for their own wishes or subjective experiences. The same attitude underlies a host of abusive practices toward animals, ranging from circuses to factory farming. Animals are raped too, sometimes for the pleasure of the male human rapist (as in so-called "bestiality") but more often to control their reproduction so that corporations can have the pleasure of profits (as when bulls are electro-ejactulated and cows forcibly impregnated on what dairy farmers sometimes call "rape racks.")

Cockfighting is a feminist issue. Sex role stereotypes hurt both human and non-human animals. In cockfighting, the natural behavior of roosters is perverted in order to force them to act out human ideas about masculinity. The birds are traumatized and then deliberately placed in harm's way so that their handlers can feel like big men.

---

7. "Thinking Like a Chicken: Farm Animals and the Feminine Connection" by Karen Davis is one of several important essays in Carol J. Adams and Josephine Donovan (Eds.), Animals and Women: Feminist Theoretical Explorations, Duke University Press, 1995. This essay is also online at the United Poultry Concerns website.

They die in stylized spectacles of masculinity that have nothing to do with natural bird behavior and everything to do with human ideas about gender. Meanwhile, human boys are also traumatized in order to make them conform to cultural ideas of masculinity. Those who do not may find themselves "gay bashed" to death.

Domestic violence is an animal issue. Domestic violence is one way that men maintain control of the women, children, and animals in their households. The World Health Organization has identified domestic violence against women as a global public health emergency of the highest order. Here in the United States, partner violence is the number one reason women visit the emergency room and at least two out of every ten pregnant women are beaten by their male partners. Very often, domestic violence includes abuse of companion animals as a way to frighten, traumatize, or control women. Many women remain in dangerous households because battered women's shelters do not accept animals and they are afraid of what will happen to their animal companions if they leave them alone with the abuser. No one knows how many companion animals have been killed by domestic abusers or how many women are dead because they stayed to protect a companion animal.

...and the list goes on and on.[8] Eggs, sex tourism, Premarin,[9] lack of the legal rights enjoyed by adult males — all of these and other problems have both sexist and speciesist components. This is why so many of us insist that neither women nor animals can truly be free until both speciesism and sexism are abolished.

The ALF seeks the abolition of animal enslavement and exploitation. Hence it is legitimate to ask whether it is consistent with feminist theory and practice. That's not so easy to do because there are so many varieties of feminism, each of which is a matter of ongoing debate. Below, I examine the ALF from the perspectives of ecofeminism, anarcha~feminism, radical feminism, and feminist ethics *as I understand them.* Some may disagree with my demarcations or descriptions of these feminisms but I trust that no one will fail to agree that all of the ideas and principles I discuss fall somewhere within feminism.

---

8. For more examples of links between sexism and speciesism see Carol Adams' The Sexual Politics of Meat and The Pornography of Meat.

9. Premarin is a hormone replacement medication made from the urine of cruelly confined pregnant horses and given to women who have been led to believe that the natural life cycle of menopause should be treated like a disease. The Women's Health and Ethics Coalition at is an innovative international alliance of feminists and animal advocates using a multifaceted strategy against Premarin and its derivatives.

ALF & Ecofeminism

The world is round. Everything that happens on it, happens in it. Mystics have intuited it and scientists have proved it: everything is connected to everything else. That means that the old anarchist slogan — "no one is free while others are oppressed" — is literally true.

Ecofeminism understands that exploitation of ecosystems, animals, and women are interconnected and that the solution to these problems resides in the resituation of people within, rather than outside or above, the web of life. From tree huggers in India to tree sitters in the USA, from oil refinery occupiers in Nigeria to road blockers in the UK, ecofeminists express their kinship with people, plants, and animals by using their own bodies to block the bulldozers and chainsaws coming to kill their relatives.[10]

Abstraction is the antithesis of ecofeminism, which is all about embeddedness, embodiment, and embrace. "Theoretical ecofeminism" is a contradiction in terms. This does not mean that theory is useless, only that it is impossible to be an ecofeminist only in theory — one can only *be* an ecofeminist in practice. The best ecofeminist theory arises from and interacts with practical experience.[11]

Ecofeminist principles must be *lived* to be meaningful. Thus, just as the Declaration of Independence asserts the right *and the duty* to rebel against illegitimate authority, the credo of ecofeminism might be said to mandate sabotage and other forms of direct action.

The ALF is also all about action. Anyone who liberates animals and/or interferes with animal abusers in accordance with the ALF principle of non-violence can consider herself a member. Absent such action, one cannot claim membership in the ALF, no matter how pretty one's political opinions or earnest one's intentions.

---

10. Tree sitters such as Julia Butterfly Hill live in the branches of trees that have been marked for felling, protecting the trees with their bodies. In Nigeria, women have challenged the environmental and economic practices of Chevron-Texaco by occupying a major facility and stopping production.

11. We all think about and come up with theories to make sense of our lives and the world. In his Prison Notebooks (International Publishers, 1971), Antonio Gramsci identified the "organic intellectual"as someone who conceives and articulates ideas that are rooted in experience rather than education. Organic intellectuals exists in all classes and can play key roles in liberation struggles. The slaughterhouse worker who perceives and articulates a connection between her company's inhumane treatment of animals and its disregard for the safety of workers is fulfilling the function of an organic intellectual. Her observations will be more accurate and persuasive than the speculations of a theorist who has never seen the blood of butchered animals mingling with the blood of injured workers on the floor.

Thus, the ALF is the antithesis of an abstraction. It coincides precisely with a group of people engaged in the difficult and dangerous work of actually liberating animals. In this existentialism, the ALF is entirely consistent with ecofeminism.

Being based in an awareness of the intrinsic and practical value of biodiversity, ecofeminists understand that both beauty and survival require a balance of diverse elements. Scattered everywhere like seeds, each flowering freely within the context of set parameters, ALF "cells" are diverse in comparison with each other while also offering a necessary balance to the more conservative aims and tactics of other animal activists.

Deeply rooted in natural reality, as well as analysis and spirituality, ecofeminism agrees with abolitionist and suffragist Frederick Douglas that it's not possible to have "rain without thunder" or "the ocean without the awful roar of its many waters." ALFers are always ready to 'bring the thunder,' consequently facing not only the risk of arrest but also the hostility of allies who do not understand the role of the ALF in the natural order of the animal liberation movement. Ecofeminists do, or at least ought to, recognize the ALF as an agent of change that may, in retrospect, prove to have been as vital as carbon dioxide to photosynthesis.

ALF & Anarcha~Feminism

Just as the ALF is often viewed with annoyance by both mainstream animal advocates and the left, anarcha~feminism has been angering male anarchists and mainstream feminists since the early 1970s. Anarcha~feminists insist on actually putting into practice the principles that spring from feminist and anarchist analyses of the dynamics of oppression. Thus, anarcha~feminists believe that liberation movements and organizations must be non-hierarchical and unselfish in order to overturn an oppressive social order that is based on private property and an algebra of hierarchical dualisms (e.g., men over women, people over animals, culture over nature, etc.).

The ALF is non-hierarchical and unselfish. No one runs the ALF and no one who is truly ALF tries to take credit for it. Unselfish action intended to undermine the people over animals paradigm is its reason for existence.

Most anarcha~feminists do their work in other movements and few bother to explicitly identify themselves as such. Nonetheless, anarcha~feminist principles have been elaborated by women working within anarcha~feminist collectives. Peggy Kornegger notes that anarcha~feminists work to dissolve power rather than to seize it, value both collectivity and individuality, and favor both spontaneous and organized action.[12]

Anarcha~feminists believe, as one manifesto put it, that "the world obviously cannot survive many more decades of rule by gangs of armed males calling themselves governments." Thus, anarcha~feminists seek to destabilize and replace, rather than join and reform, governments. The ALF is anarchistic in both aims and means. The goal is abolition of illegitimate authority. Actions are aimed at undoing, rather than revising, power over animals. ALF activists takes matters into their own hands, rather than waiting for governments to get around to liberating the animals.

Anarcha~feminists believe in individuality within collectivity, valuing both the creativity of the individual and the power of the group. Similarly, anarcha~feminists value spontaneity within the context of a set strategy. In its cell structure, the ALF embodies the principle of individuality within collectivity. Individual cells are free to be as creative as they please within the guidelines of the limits set by the minimal ALF principles.

Thus, the ALF appears to be consistent with both ecofeminism and anarcha~feminism. That is not surprising, since it also turns out to be consistent with radical feminism in general.

ALF & Radical Feminism

Radical feminists and radical lesbian feminists of the 1960s and 1970s took direct and often flamboyant action concerning many of the problems that have since been addressed more moderately by mainstream feminists. It was radical feminists who first established safe houses for battered women and brought previously unspeakable topics like rape and child sexual abuse into the public discourse. Radical feminist activism persists to this day but the dominant tone of the feminist movement is now determined by quieter and less troublesome women.

Radical feminism aims to find and undermine the very roots of sexism, understanding that the original subjugation of women under patriarchy has served as the template for all subsequent intra-species oppression. Thus, radical feminists also do the intellectual, cultural, and educational work of undoing the often unconscious categorical thoughts that pattern our perceptions about sex and gender.

---

12. For more on anarcha~feminism, see Quiet Rumours: An Anarcha~Feminist Anthology.

Any investigation into the roots of sexism has to go back to the origins of patriarchy, which turn out to be entirely entangled with the origins of pastoralism. Again and again, enslavement and exploitation of women and animals appear together in the historical record and it is impossible to say whether one preceded the other or they arose contemporaneously.[13] Thus, the radical feminist project of exposing and uprooting the sources of sexism will necessarily require uncovering and dislocating the roots of speciesism.

The distinction between radical and mainstream feminists is not unlike that of animal liberationists and animal welfarists and may best be understood by example. Radical feminists talk about women's liberation rather than women's rights. Seeing the police as the muscular arm of the patriarchal state, the radical feminist works to directly protect and empower girls and women rather than asking for more police protection against rape and domestic violence. Radical feminists write the names of date-rapists on bathroom walls and subvert the billboards of companies that exploit women's bodies for profit. They shout and stomp and don't think its a crime to feel and express anger. They do not implore or compromise. You probably want a mainstream feminist to argue for you in court or congress, but you hope that a radical feminist will be around when the fundamentalists are menacing your picket line or the cops are banging on your head.

Who do you hope will be around if you are ever confined in a cage or about to be forcibly impregnated?

Both animal liberationists and radical feminists take what are seen as extreme positions on fundamental questions and are often willing to use what are seen as extreme means to achieve their aims. Quiet as it's kept, many of the so-called suffragettes were radical rock throwers and fire starters who ended up in prison — where they more often than not asked for vegetarian meals. Like many radical lesbian feminists of the 1970s, many of the most radical women's advocates in Edwardian England found that their feminism led them naturally to vegetarianism.[14]

---

13. Although deeply flawed by its reliance on Reichian assumptions, DeMeo's "The origins and diffusion of patrism in Saharasia c. 4000 BCE: Evidence for a worldwide, climate-linked geographical pattern in human behavior" (World Futures, 30, 247-271) gives an accurate presentation and thought-provoking analysis of key facts concerning the origins of patriarchal societies in various regions. While he does not stress this fact, all of the original patriarchal cultures he discusses were also pastoral (animal herding) cultures.

14. For more on radical vegetarian women in Edwardian England, see Leah Leneman, "The Awakened Instinct: Vegetarianism and the Women's Suffrage Movement in Britain," Women's History Review, Vol. 6, No. 2, 1997.

Radical feminists of more modern times coined the phrase, "the personal is the political." The implications are often uncomfortable and go well beyond the prescription of veganism for those who believe that animals are not property. Every time you walk past a dog on a chain, the radical feminist or ALF activist might remind you, you are making the political choice to allow that animal to spend his or her days in lonely anguish. These kinds of difficult political choices face us every day, making us all complicit to some degree in the ongoing abuse of animals. Radical feminists demand that we learn to live with the feelings that awareness of such realities brings. Only in so doing can we make our ethical choices with necessary modesty, honesty and empathy.

ALF & Feminist Ethics

The ALF is the metaphorical mother of all animal activism. Like a mother, the ALF rushes to the rescue of endangered youngsters. Like a mother, the ALF labors behind the scenes, rarely getting credit for the results of its productivity. Like a mother, the ALF says "eat your vegetables" and "just because everybody does it doesn't mean it's right."

It's not an accident that women were the actual mothers of the early antivivisection and animal welfare movements or that women continue to far outnumber men in virtually all animal advocacy and liberation organizations including, so far as we know, the ALF. Carol Gilligan's groundbreaking research demonstrated that, for a complex constellation of reasons, women tend to make their ethical decisions on different bases than men. While there are always individual departures from the norm, boys and men tend to make their decisions on the basis of laws or abstract principles while girls and women tend to make their decisions on what is best characterized as an *ethos of care.*[15]

When asked if it is justifiable to steal medicine to save the life of someone who cannot afford to purchase it, boys and men will tend to talk about the illegality of stealing versus the principle that life must be valued above all else. In contrast, girls and women will tend to talk about who gets hurt and who needs care. They may reach the same conclusion by different routes, a boy concluding that the value of life trumps the value of private property while a girl concludes that the harm suffered by the shopkeeper if the medicine is stolen is less than the harm suffered by the sick person if it is not. Feminist ethics assert that this ethos as care is at least as valid a method of moral reasoning as the rule-based method preferred by men.

The ethos of care is pragmatic rather than theoretical, and particular rather than abstract. The ethos of care infuses the activities of ALF activists, who exercise actual care for actual animals who would otherwise suffer almost unimaginable harm.

"But," one might ask, "what if ALF activities slow down or hinder efforts to improve the conditions for animals in general? Wouldn't that contradict the ethos of care?" That seems a reasonable objection until one realizes that there is no evidence whatsoever that ALF activities on behalf of specific animals will in any way inhibit the efforts of other activists to free or improve the welfare of animals in general.

"But," the argument often goes, "they make us look bad and that makes us less effective." Another common argument is that ALF activities make our opponents angry and thus unwilling to compromise with us. These are understandable but baseless concerns. As other liberation movements have learned through hard experience, it doesn't matter how 'good' you are — they will always find someone to mock or condemn in an effort to discredit your movement. It's no good telling gay boys to stop swinging their hips or women to stop showing their emotions; those who benefit from the oppression are always going to find some person or organization to point to with derision or censure.

People enjoy their privileges and don't give them up without a struggle. It's trying to take away their privileges that makes them mad, by whatever manner or means you try to do it. People enjoy the material and emotional benefits of owning and feeling superior to animals; corporations enjoy the profits they obtain through animal exploitation. That means that ALF efforts on behalf of specific animals, by interfering with the process of extracting profits from animals, may make the ultimate liberation of all animals more rather than less likely. Just as the pig farmer may switch to organic vegetables if the costs of complying with new environmental regulations make pork less profitable, so corporations have scaled back animal exploitative operations due to real or imagined ALF-related costs. In this way, the ethos of care for particular animals furthers the cause of caring for animals in general.

III

If ALF principles and practices are consistent with ecofeminism, anarcha~feminism, radical feminism, and feminist ethics, are there any critiques or challenges feminism might offer the ALF? Since feminism never lets anybody get away without some sort of challenge, they answer to that is, of course, yes.

Like speciesism, sexism is inherently violent, requiring constant force (or threat of force) to maintain itself. While men like Mohandas Gandhi and Martin Luther King, Jr. have tended to get the credit for the theory of nonviolent social change, it has been women who have most consistently deployed nonviolent tactics against violence throughout recorded history. From the Sumerian priestess who wrote the first war protest poem circa 2300 b.c.e. to the women who set up the Greenham Common peace encampment in opposition to nuclear weapons in the 1980s, women have used creative and nonviolent means to contest violence against themselves and others.[16]

Hence, the primary feminist challenge to the ALF is to find ways to ensure that individuals and cells considering themselves ALF do, indeed, act in accordance with the ALF principle of non-violence. It's not good enough to simply disclaim any actions that are violent by using the circular reasoning that "the ALF is non-violent, hence any violent actions are not ALF." If, indeed, violent actions are taken by persons inspired by or believing themselves to be ALF, then the ALF bears some responsibility.

Maintaining disciplined adherence to principles across widely distributed secret cells is difficult but not impossible. One must learn, as feminists have done concerning issues like domestic violence, to be able to quite firmly say, "that's not okay," and be willing to back up that assessment with action.

This means that it will be necessary for ALF cells to immediately disclaim any alleged spokesperson who implicitly threatens or condones violence, as one self-proclaimed ALF spokesman recently has done when answering media inquiries about a non-ALF action. Spokesmen who cannot be trusted to voice the collective position of the ALF without straying into the realm of personal opinion must be jettisoned in favor of spokespeople with the discipline and reserve required to place the needs of the group above their own wish to give voice to heroic fantasies of violent resistance.

This might more easily be done by setting aside the practice of the single, stable spokesperson altogether. Allowing a single person to call himself the

---

16. For further information on women and nonviolent social change, see Pam McAllister (Ed.) , Reweaving the Web of Life: Feminism and Nonviolence, New Society Publishers, 1982. For further information on past and present women's activism against war, see Daniela Gioseffi, Women on War, The Feminist Press, 2003.

spokesman for the ALF gives that person more power than anyone should have in a non-hierarchical organization. Furthermore, there's simply no way to ensure that this person does, in fact, speak for all of the widely distributed and secret cells of the ALF. Better for individual cells or sets of cells to call upon a rotating set of spokespeople who can be trusted to say only what they have been given explicit permission to say and to make clear that they are speaking for only a small subset of the ALF. This would bring the ALF's method of communication with the outside world into better agreement with both ALF and anarcha~feminist principles concerning distribution of power and individuality within collectivity.

The ethos of care requires one to actively prevent foreseeable harm. This raises the question of arson as a means of property destruction. I would argue that fire always involves an inherent risk of harm to firefighters and ecosystems and thus is not consistent with either ALF principles or the ethos of care. More creative effort must be expended to discover alternative methods by which to interfere with or raise the costs of exploitative operations. Remembering the proverbial monkeywrench in the machine, it may be possible to identify the point in a complex system where a simple intervention can have a profoundly destabilizing effect.

Just as people may disagree when interpreting abstract rules, differences may arise when invoking the ethos of care. For example, some feminists have argued that the tactic of picketing the houses of vivisectors should not be permitted when there are children in the home, because the children might be frightened or traumatized by the idea that their parents are not able to make home a safe place. Others argue that it does children no favor to collude with the deceptions of violent parents and that therefore, so long as the picket lines are peaceful and no invective is hurled at the children, such demonstrations are not only permissible as direct action against vivisection but also may have

the side benefit of encouraging the children of animal abusers to look outside of their families for role models.

It takes discipline and self-restraint to maintain the proper attitude during actions in which care must be taken to avoid harming people or other animals. An uncomfortable issue that cannot be avoided is the potential for disaffected and potentially violent young men to use the ALF as an excuse to vent their anger in inappropriate ways. Studies of the violent racist right have established that, prior to recruitment, the young men involved could have gone either way — right or left. Filled with pain and rage and desperate for a feeling of belonging, these young men are drawn to any extreme movement that will help them feel less powerless and alone.[17] It stands to reason that the ALF, which offers the opportunity to defend the powerless in a powerful manner, would be attractive to young men fitting this profile. The animal liberation movement can offer such young men the opportunity to develop the discipline and maturity needed to channel their emotional energy into productive activism. But the combination of macho posturing by ALF spokesmen, the unstructured nature of the ALF cell system, and the essential lawlessness of the ALF itself makes it equally if not more likely that such young men will use the ALF as an excuse for destructive behavior.

One way to mitigate this potentially very serious problem would be to put a feminine face on the ALF. What mental image comes to mind in response to the phrase "Animal Liberation Front?" Probably a black-clad young man. What happens when you change that mental image to a young woman or a grey-haired grandmother? One thing that happens is that the ALF suddenly becomes much less attractive to young men motivated more by macho ego than by compassion. Such a paradigm shift easily could be accomplished by deliberately choosing female spokespersons and using images of women on t-shirts and other promotional materials.

Putting a feminine face on the ALF would be accurate, since the US ALF was founded by a woman and we have no reason to believe that the gender balance of the ALF is any different than the rest of the animal liberation movement. Such a shift might help the ALF to accomplish the other feminist challenge facing it, which is to ensure that the ALF does not in any way hamper total animal liberation by contributing to the oppression of human animals.

Obviously, since people are animals, total animal liberation will not have been achieved until both human and non- human animals are free. That explains why all animal liberationists must, at minimum, avoid contributing to the ongoing oppression and exploitation of women and other persecuted groups. At best, animal liberation activists will forge alliances with social justice activists and sometimes structure their actions so as to illustrate one of the many connections between speciesism and sexism, racism, militarism and economic exploitation.

For the ALF, this means that, in the selection of targets and tactics, care must be taken to ensure that ALF actions are never used as an excuse to express sexist or racist aggression. In addition, ALF cells must consciously attend to gender

17. For an insightful analysis of violent young men drawn to extreme organizations, see Rafe Ezekiel's The Racist Mind: Portraits of Neo-Nazis and Klansmen.

dynamics so that common problems do not occur. Thanks to sex role socialization in childhood, it's very easy for women and men to slip into unequal relationships without realizing that they have done so. In group discussions men may interrupt and dominate while women wait politely before giving up and giving in. This can lead to an illusion of consensus. In allegedly non-hierarchical groups, an unofficial leader often arises and often just happens to be the most masculine person in the group. Sexual harassment or sexual assault may be perpetrated by one member on another. Partner violence might be an issue when two group members are dating. Such problems are always difficult for groups to process and even more difficult when the group is underground and group members may feel that it would be disloyal to confront the rapist or batterer.

In confronting these often unconscious dynamics, it's important to remember that, just as we were all taught to think about animals in certain ways, we were all taught to think about men and women in certain ways. It takes just as much conscious work to undo sexist socialization as it does to undo speciesist socialization. In both instances, the job is never entirely done. Ongoing unlearning and relearning is necessary.

Thinking through such issues might aid ALF activists in framing actions and communiques that illuminate the connections between exploitation of animals and exploitation of women. In this way, and by helping cells to become more equitable and effective, confrontation of sexism can increase the ALF's contribution toward total animal liberation. For example, ALF cells might elect to challenge sexism by questioning what Marti Kheel has called an "heroic ethic" in which nature and non-human animals are reduced to "damsels in distress" awaiting rescue by the muscular hero.[18] Of course, many captive animals are, indeed, powerless to effect their own escape and thus in need of rescue. Our cultural conditioning makes it very easy for us to slide from that fact into the fantasy of the helpless feminine victim who is entirely dependent on the powerful masculine hero. This, in turn, can lead us to fail to take the animals' own agency and opinions into account when planning our actions on their behalf. Seeing ourselves as their voice, we can forget to listen to them.

Thus, the feminist challenge to the heroic ethic leads us to a renewed appreciation of the animals' participation in their own liberation. How this might be put into action will vary according to circumstance. For example, ALF

---

18. Marti Kheel's "From Heroic to Holistic Ethics: The Ecofeminist Challenge" is but one of many illuminating essays in Ecofeminism: Women, Animals, Nature edited by Greta Gaard. This essay is also available online.

cells in relevant regions might seek to understand the patterns of and put themselves into alliance with the recent upsurge in elephant escapes and attacks on property. In the United States, sanctuaries and those who staff them offer opportunities to get to know individual animals, so that plans can be grounded in their hopes and experiences rather than our fantasies and theories. This, of course, is a prescription that applies to all animal advocates, not just those associated with ALF.

IV

Feminism also offers challenges to all animal activists — ALF and non-ALF alike — concerning cooperation, coordination, coalition, and communication. Because social change struggles have always been most effective when a diversity of tactics have been deployed within the context of a coordinated strategy, these principles of feminist practice can help us to build a more effective animal liberation movement.

Cooperation means, at minimum, not impeding the actions of one's allies and, at best, facilitating their work. The rest of the animal liberation movement must recognize ALF activists as allies and vice versa. Mainstream animal advocates need not jump to distance themselves from the ALF and certainly should not find reasons to criticize the ALF in public. Similarly, ALF activists ought not harshly condemn liberationists who include within their work efforts to improve the lives of animals until such time as freedom is achieved. There's simply no evidence to support the idea that either ALF actions or welfare reforms in any way inhibit the long term struggle for animal liberation. Both ALF actions and welfare reforms seek to improve the lives of actual animals right now and the animals have not given us any indication that they believe we should cease such efforts on their behalf.

Cooperation beyond mutual respect extends to coordination of efforts. Coordination need not involve discussions across the above-ground/underground divide. For example, if news of an ALF raid on an egg factory appears in the media, above-ground groups might strike while the iron is hot by immediately staging events, lobbying lawmakers, or publishing educational material or letters to editors about battery cages. From the flip side, if an ALF cell were to notice that an above-ground organization in its region was mounting a campaign about eggs, that might be the time to gather and release some footage revealing what goes on behind closed doors at the local egg factory.

Coalition goes a step beyond coordination and does require some communication, if only through a trusted third party. The potential benefits are worth the effort. If, for example, a diverse array of organizations were to agree to focus for a set period of time on milk — with each tackling the topic from its own perspective and with its own favored tactics — then the public and the government would encounter different aspects of the problem at every turn, as they did when both the Black Panthers and the Southern Christian Leadership Convention were among the diverse groups fighting segregation.

Honest and responsible communication is another important principle of feminist practice. This could go a long way toward bridging the divide between the ALF and mainstream animal advocates. In the context of communication, responsibility and honesty mean owning one's feelings, being willing to back up opinions with fact, and ruthlessly examining one's own assumptions. Thus, in debate with an ally, one doesn't say "you're making it hard for the rest of us" or "you don't really believe in liberation" but rather "I believe your tactics are counterproductive because..." or "I feel uncomfortable with your approach because..," offering evidence to support any assertions of fact. You can even say, "it's not okay with me that you... because... " as long as you stick to talking about behavior and refrain from making assumptions about the feelings or motivations of others. Feminist practice requires assuming that the other person (or group) is acting in good faith unless you have solid evidence to the contrary. That means refraining from calling ALF activists "reckless" or "destructive," as if they were not actuating a legitimate, if debatable, strategy for social change. That also means taking people at their word when they say that they believe working for welfare reforms can eventually lead to liberation. Open debate is great as long as we all admit that there's no way to say for sure what will work to achieve total animal liberation until we have done so. But the confrontation of thesis with antithesis will never lead to synthesis in an atmosphere of name-calling and character assassination.

It bears repeating that one's circle of communication ought not be confined to human animals. Debates about animal liberation tactics quickly become sterile in the absence of the viewpoints of actual animals. The challenge to all of us is to improve our ability to listen to the animals for whom we purport to speak and act.[19] Only then can we trust ourselves to be the allies they so desperately need.

V

The need for animal liberation remains as urgent as ever. Despite arguments and pleas for vegetarianism dating back to antiquity, *per capita* meat production and consumption is at an all-time high in the USA and around the world.[20] Meanwhile, genetic engineers are designing ever more perverse methods of vivisection and exploitation. While significant gains have been made against a few specific forms of animal exploitation, such as veal and fur, we must admit that our efforts on behalf of animals cannot yet be described as successful.

More of the same is not enough. All of us — ALF and non-ALF alike — must be more creative and cooperative. Feminist analyses and practices can help to guide us. The ALF is implicitly feminist but often not explicitly so. While the ALF must remain underground, its inherent feminism need not stay under cover. More conscious use of the principles of ecofeminism, anarcha~feminism, radical feminism, and feminist ethics will make the ALF an even more effective component in the multi-faceted struggle for total animal liberation.

The black cat stalks the slaughterhouses and haunts the dreams of vivisectors. Strong and stealthy, fierce and fearless, she taunts and tricks the rapists and the child abusers too. Sometimes, in quiet moments, you can feel her watching you. The ALF should follow her, because she knows what to do.

---

19. If you have no idea how you might go about taking the opinions of animals into account, that's a sign that you have not paid enough attention to the problem of how to listen to the animals before attempting to be their voice. Given the limitations of cross-species communication, one must take particular care to learn whatever it is possible to learn about the hopes and fears of the non-human animals one hopes to help. There are two intersecting avenues of approach: empathy and observation. Getting to know animals — either by spending time with them or by learning from trustworthy people who have spent time with them — allows one to use empathy accurately. That means asking not "what would I want if I were in a battery cage?" but "what would I want if I were a chicken in a battery cage?" Careful observation — either directly or via the factual reports of trustworthy people — allows one to make inferences about animal preferences based on the actions they have taken on their own behalf. That means asking not "what do the experts believe that these animals want?" but "what do the actions of these animals tell anybody willing to listen about what they want?"

20. Up to date statistics concerning US and worldwide per capita meat production and consumption may be retrieved from the US Department of Agriculture and the UN Food and Agriculture Organization.

18

Stomping with Elephants

In many ways, this essay, originally published in 2006 in the AK Press collection entitled *Igniting a Revolution: Voices in Defense of Mother Earth*, represents a continuation and elaboration of the prior chapter. Here, the themes of animal agency and feminist direct action recur, this time within an analysis of human hubris and cluelessness in the context of an escalating climate emergency. Rereading it now, I am struck by how many years have gone by during which the gap between the urgency of that crisis and the fecklessness of our collective response has gaped ever wider. Thus it seems even more important to me to come to understand the roots of human error and the means by which we might bring ourselves into better relationship with the larger-than-human world, both of which have been foci of my subsequent writing.

STOMPING WITH THE ELEPHANTS

FEMINIST PRINCIPLES FOR RADICAL SOLIDARITY

"Pull or stab or cut or burn,

She will ever yet return."

— Robert Graves, Marigolds

1. Evening

It's nighttime in Zululand and the men who have been working in the Thula Thula Exclusive Private Game Reserve are ready to retire, having captured and corralled several antelopes for a breeding program. The frantic antelopes mill about restlessly, not knowing what to do. Out of the twilight comes a herd of elephants. They encircle the enclosure, inspecting the situation. The people keep their distance, apprehensive of the elephants. The matriarch of the herd steps forward and uses her trunk to unlatch the bolts and open the gate. The antelopes escape into the enveloping darkness. The elephants disappear back into the night.

Witnesses use the word "rescue" to describe what they saw that night.[1] Whatever their previous beliefs about animals, they could not help but recognize the deliberate and purposeful nature of the actions of the elephant called "Nana" by local conservationists. Trusting their own eyes, they learned something that most people — including most animal and environmental activists — fail to appreciate: people aren't the only ones acting to undo the damage that people have done.

Putting ourselves in the place of the antelopes that night, we can learn something too: the outlook is very scary but help is at hand.

---

1. "Elephant unlatches gate to save South African antelopes," AFP (8 April 2003); "Elephants on a rescue mission," South African Press Association (9 April 2003)

2. Emergency

I live at a sanctuary for chickens. The roosters are very loud. All day long, they check in with each other by crowing, which evolved as a way to maintain contact in the dense Asian forests where the wild jungle fowl still thrive.

Roosters raise a ruckus whenever they spot a predator or other threat to the flock. All the chickens within earshot respond immediately, taking cover until the the danger has passed. In the event of a continuing hazard, the hens and other roosters add their voices to those of the roosters who raised the original alarm. The meaning of the ensuing cacophony is clear to anyone with ears to hear: This is an emergency.

If only human beings were so sensible! Every day, including today, we go about consuming and spending as if we had no knowledge of impending ecological disaster. Some people lash out at the "roosters" who issue warnings about global warming and other emergent crises. Most people ignore them. Even those who do heed the warnings do so without a sense of urgency proportionate to the dangers that face us. There's a breach between what we think and what we feel, a gap between what we know to be true and what we actually do.

As any earthquake survivor can tell you, disjunctions can be hazardous to your health. And, indeed, every day brings more evidence of the dangers of disconnection. In the wake of the Tsunami of 2004, Sri Lankan wildlife officials were stunned to discover that all of of the animals at the Yala National Park had survived. Park workers and tourists perished as floodwaters surged through the refuge but the animals evidently sensed the danger in advance and retreated in time.[2] Accustomed to scanning the newspaper or the television rather than the skies, modern men and women do need a weatherman to know which way the wind blows. Like the park rangers of Sri Lanka, even people who are relatively more attuned to the natural world have lost their animal ability to sense and respond appropriately to impending natural disasters.

How else to explain our dumb numbness in the face of the facts? Nine of the ten hottest years on record have occurred since 1990. Thirteen percent of the planet's plant species are in danger of extinction.[3] One out of every ten bird species are likely to be extinct within the century.[4] Our own lives are in peril too. The World Resources Institute predicts that at least 3.5 billion people —

---

3. *Threatened Plants of the World* by UNEP World Conservation Monitoring Centre (2001)

4. "Researchers Predict Massive Avian Decline" by Roddy Scheer, *E Magazine* (22 December 2004)

that's more than half of us — will experience water shortages by 2025. And, of course, we all are vulnerable to the escalating effects of climate change. For all species, the primary cause of extinction is habitat destruction. In these days of disappearing islands and catastrophic cataclysms, can there be any doubt that we have endangered ourselves?

Much of the damage cannot be undone. In the mountains of Mexico, the wild grasses that are the living ancestors of all maize have been forever polluted by genes from genetically engineered corn. The individual frogs and fish born with missing limbs or extra sex organs will never be the animals they would have been if their mothers had swum in water untainted by antibiotics and pesticides.[5] Shattered rocks and punctured atmospheres cannot be put together again.

How long will it be until we do whatever *can* be done to stop the violence and repair the damage? To what contortions of body and behavior will the progeny of today's sex-crossed fish and five-legged frogs descend in the interim? How does it feel to fly home after a season at the winter place to find that all of the food and housing has been chopped down or washed away? What, exactly, is a bird or a butterfly to do when she finds herself famished and homeless after a long migration? When will well-fed people, safe in *their* houses, *feel* the wing-flapping, heart-pounding, fur-raising sensation that says: "This is an emergency"?

Emergencies mandate immediate and effective direct action.[6] Both critics and proponents of radical environmental activism ought to ponder the implications of that obligation. Those who would condemn radical direct action on behalf of earth and animals might first consider the fine line between complicity and underactivity. If they want their work to be fruitful, those who purport to be radical environmental activists must think carefully about efficacy in

---

5. For examples of the latest traumas endured by animals due to human impact on their habitats, see "Pollution triggers bizarre behavior in animals" by Andy Coghlan in *New Scientist* (01 September 2004).

6. Only tactics that have an immediate impact on some element of the target problem qualify as direct action. Indirect action seeks change via more circuitous routes, such as seeking to change citizens' minds in the hope that they will, in turn, change their voting behavior and that this will, in turn, lead to changed government policies. Rent strikes, boycotts, blockades, and demonstrations that substantially interfere with business as usual are direct action. Petition drives, letters to editors, community education, and demonstrations that are limited to symbolic expressions of opinion are indirect action.

order to avoid wasting scarce resources on symbolic activities that might be emotionally satisfying but hardly meet the criteria for direct action.[7]

Particular care must be taken when contemplating actions that may lead to incarceration. Since we are in a state of emergency, we cannot afford to pay the price of years of relative inactivity for the dubious benefits of symbolic acts. All of which is to say that we must think strategically. In order to do so accurately, we must understand not only our own limitations but also the root causes of the problems we hope to solve.

3. Faultlines

How do you break a wild animal? The key can be found in the word itself: You sever connections.

To break, or domesticate, an animal you must first physically isolate the individual from the natural world. Then, you must cut all natural bonds to other animals by controlling sexual relations, interrupting the relationship between mother and child, and rupturing the structure of the extended family. You must alienate the animal from herself, so that she no longer expects her own will to control her own body. Finally, you must break the spirit, by humiliating and violating the animal in every possible way, including physical and sexual assault.

It's no accident that these are the same tactics used by abusive husbands to control their wives or that analogous methods are used to bring wild plants under "cultivation." After all, "husbandry" refers to the breeding of plants and "livestock" while "grooms" are both breakers of horses and takers of brides.

We tend to think about sexism, speciesism, and environmental exploitation as separate, if sometimes intersecting or interlocking, problems. In truth, they are just different symptoms of the same injury.

While we don't have a word for this violation, we know it when we see it. It's the fault line running underneath all of the social and environmental disruptions that plague us and the planet. You can read all about it in Genesis or the platform of the Republican Party: Men have the right and the duty

---

7. Flamboyant transgressions may be civil disobedience without being direct action. Similarly, sabotage that substantially interferes with ecologically destructive activities is direct action while sabotage that expresses the emotions of the activist but does not significantly prevent, hinder, mitigate, stop, or heal the effects of harmful activities must be considered indirect action. Whether such acts of sabotage are *successful* indirect action depends upon whether they really do have the intended impact (such as changing people's minds or inspiring them to change their behaviors). Successful social change strategies generally require a coordinated combination of direct and indirect action tactics.

to subdue the earth, the animals, their own families, and the men of other faiths. You can see this ethos in action everywhere from the detention camps at Guantanamo Bay to the dead zone in the Chesapeake Bay.

At the heart of the problem is alienation, separation, dissociation. To imagine that you "own" a piece of land, you must first alienate yourself from it, psychologically tearing yourself out of the seamless fabric of your ecosystem in order to lay claim to part of it. In order to demarcate "your" land, you must create artificial boundaries, perhaps even erecting physical fences to separate it from the rest of the world. In creating and enforcing those borders you will probably hurt or scare animals and other people. To do so, you must dissociate yourself from your natural empathy for fellow beings.

To feel comfortable breaking the body or mind of another human or non-human animal, you must first wrench yourself out of the web of relationships that define ecosystems. Doing so necessarily culminates in disruptions to those systems.

To fail to perceive the detrimental ecological impact of your actions, particularly when you own health or life is threatened by the pollution or disruption you have created, you must divorce yourself from the evidence of your senses. Healthy animals notice dirty water or smoky air. Only a profoundly disoriented animal fails to respond to a perceptible change in climate.

Estrangement is both cause and consequence of the problem. We are cut off from the earth, other animals, each other, and ourselves. Those disconnections in turn allow us to do terrible things to the earth, other animals, each other, and ourselves. These actions increase the estrangement, and the cycle of violation and separation continues.

What started the cycle? Did it begin with the first "wife" or the first "livestock"? Was terror or hubris the motivation for that first enslavement? Did the story of "God the father" — alone in the sky, sacred and separate from his profane creations — predate and motivate the original denigration of the earth or did men make up the story after the fact to rationalize what they had done?[8]

We may never be able to answer those questions about the origins of our disconnection but we can and must recognize and repair the ruptures that we

8. The foundational texts of all of the patriarchal "faiths" — which many ecofeminists, like me, believe to be misogynist and speciesist political propaganda dressed up as spirituality — explicitly mandate the exploitation of women, earth, and animals. Like the violence that they promote, these ideologies are part of the problem and thus cannot be part of the solution. That is the reason why so many radical feminists, eco-activists, and animal liberationists embrace either atheism or earth-based spirituality.

have created within ourselves and in the world. We must learn to see, and act within our awareness of, the similar ways that women, plants, animals, and the planet are exploited and abused. We must recognize and cultivate our relationships with each other, with other animals, and with the ecosystems in which we are enmeshed. And we must make sure that our own hearts, minds, and hands are always connected. We must work to ensure our own basic integrity, so that what we think and feel and do are always consistent.

If breakage is the problem, then integrity is the answer. That means that we must embrace integrity as both end and means. That may mean using force to stop the violence.

4. Violence

Did the elephants who freed the antelopes commit violence? Some critics of radical environmental activism would say yes, since they tampered with locks and probably caused some property damage. But the very word "property" ought to give you a clue as to why such actions, whether undertaken by elephants or adolescents, ought not be considered violent under any definition of the term.

Those who decry or defend "violence" in defense of the earth and animals often fail to first answer the question: What is violence? To adequately answer that question, one must attend to both concepts and context.

What is "violence"? Words tend to reflect what most people mean when they say something. When most people say "violence," they are talking about some sort of *violation* by means of actual or threatened physical *force.* Both aspects—force and violation—must be present for an act to be considered violent. Passing a basketball involves physical force but is not violence. Forging a signature may cause emotional or economic injury but is not violence. Thus, in law as well as in popular imagination, there is a distinction between violence and justifiable use of force as well as a distinction between violent and non-violent crime.

Most people consider intention when thinking about violence. Physical injuries caused accidentally are generally not considered the result of violence, unless the person who caused them could or should have known that they might occur. Similarly, acts that would be considered violently aggressive in some circumstances are considered to be justifiable use of force when undertaken in self-defense, unless the force used was excessive in relation to the threat.

The exceptions to the commonsense definition of violence, and the qualifications of those exceptions, highlight the importance of context, which is another factor that knee-jerk opponents and proponents of "violence" tend to neglect. Here, feminist ethics offer an avenue through what might seem like a jungle of ambiguity.

Like most women, many feminist ethicists tend to suspect invariable moral rules that leave no room for considerations of context. Thus, feminist viewpoints on nonviolence tend to be more nuanced and practical than abstract condemnations or defenses of "violence."

If we understand *violence* to be *injurious and unjustified use of force,* then we can never discern whether or not an act is violent apart from its context. We don't have to waste time arguing about abstractions because, as a matter of practical fact, violence always occurs within a material context. Furthermore, we can stop arguing about whether violence is ever okay. Justifiable use of force isn't violence. Instead of trying to justify "violence," we can turn attention instead to the rather more pressing problem of figuring out how much force is justified in defense of earth, plants, animals, and ourselves.

Where is the line between force and violence? We must attend carefully to that question. Violence is at the heart of the problems we seek to solve. Using violence to address those problems is like using genetic engineering of plants to solve the problem of pesticides. Adding fuel to the fire is not likely to put out the flames. At the same time, physical force often is required to defend ancient redwoods and baby seals from the chainsaws and clubs that menace them. In the long run, physical force may become more and more necessary to counteract the very great power of those who profit from the continued exploitation of people, plants, animals and the earth herself.

In the context of the escalating environmental emergency, force may be necessary but violence is never okay. Force is necessary when material problems require a physical solution that will not otherwise be forthcoming. Violence, as I have defined it, is intrinsically wrong and is particularly wrong-headed as a solution to problems that are founded in violence.

Where is the line between force and violence? That question can only be answered with reference to the details of the context in which it arises. An act that would be violent in one setting may be a justifiable use of force in another setting. Pushing a child so hard that she flies several feet in the air before hitting the ground is a justifiable, and perhaps even heroic, use of force when a little girl is standing in the path of an onrushing truck but would be severe child abuse if done by an angry parent at the head of a flight of stairs.

In contemplating use of force in any given situation, we must ask, first, whether the action contemplated really is likely to result in a defined desired outcome. Next, we must ask whether the same outcome might be achieved as quickly and certainly (or, perhaps, even more quickly or certainly) by some other means. We also must ask whether the force contemplated is proportionate to the harm we are seeking to correct or prevent. Most people think that it would be okay to bash a man over the head, using potentially deadly force, if he were in the act of raping a child but not if he were in the act of cheating a senior citizen out of $20.

Returning to the question that opened this section, is property damage violence? The question can only be answered by asking other questions. We must ask: What objects will be damaged? For what purpose? Using what kind of force? Will any living being be injured in any way? If the only potential "injury" is to "property rights," then I would argue that the act is not violent. Property rights are suspect within the worldview that holds that neither land nor animals are objects to be owned. In many instances, property rights are themselves violence or, at minimum, the result of past violence. The creation of "property" generally involves a process wherein land or animals are forcibly enclosed or wherein people or animals are alienated from the products of their labor. These are inherently violent processes, since they involve actual or threatened use of force to and do cause injury. Moreover, continuing violence is often needed to maintain property. From electrified fences around lakes to armed guards at grocery stores, the violence implicit in property is hidden in plain view every day.

Because violation of life is perhaps the most important cause of the problems that plague our planet, environmental activists and their apologists must take particular care to avoid a rhetoric of violence. Instead of reveling in militaristic terms that implicitly glorify violence, we must distinguish between legitimate use of force and violence, which is always illegitimate. We can and should valorize those who dare to use justifiable force, putting their own bodies on the line in the process. We must not glorify those who use the plight of mother earth as an excuse for reckless aggression or selfish violence. By building strong relationships with each other and with others who are working for earth and animal liberation, we will more easily see the difference between force and violence and better able to have the courage to use force when necessary and the forbearance to always avoid violence.

5. Flower Power

All life depends on photosynthesis. People and all other animals depend on the bodies of plants for food, fuel, and shelter. People and all other animals also require the oxygen that is a by-product of the almost magical process by which plants convert light into food. Without plants, we could not live.

Without photosynthesis and its complement, photorespiration, plants could not live.

Photosynthesis requires light, water, and carbon dioxide in proper proportions.[9] Plants can die or are damaged by too much or too little light, water, or carbon dioxide. Despite the fact that our lives depend on it, humans have tampered with each of these essential elements of photosynthesis. Around the world, people have distorted and destroyed plant habitats by pumping, flooding, depleting, and tainting water; by cutting, burning, uprooting, and transplanting shade trees; and by poisoning the air that the plants need to breathe. At the same time, our collective folly has interfered with the global atmosphere. We have torn the protective mantle of the ozone layer, exposing the plants that sustain us to increased levels of the kind of ultraviolet light that can interfere with photosynthesis.

Meanwhile, human activities such as burning fossil fuel have radically increased the amount of carbon dioxide in the atmosphere. The resulting climate changes will surely alter growing conditions such as temperature as well as availability of water. We don't know what impact the ever-increasing amount of carbon dioxide in the air that we share will have on plant photosynthesis and photorespiration or, in turn, what impact that will have on the availability of oxygen for the animals of the world.[10]

Like the spark of life itself, the energic exchange at the heart of photosynthesis cannot be faked or even fully explained. Scientists know, or believe that they know, quite a bit about *what* happens, but much remains unknown in the realms of *why* and *how*. Common sense dictates that life-or-death mysteries be approached with hesitation and respect but some scientists are confronting the carbon dioxide conundrum not with more caution but with ever greater

---

9. Different plants have evolved to grow under a broad range of circumstances, including extremes ranging from deserts to rainforests. However, each plant requires a certain balance of water and light in order to thrive. Desert plants can drown if given too much water while shade-loving plants can die from too much direct sunlight. Similarly, plants vary in their reactions to levels of carbon dioxide.

10. See the International Council for Local Environmental Initiatives briefing on climate change at for more information on the impact of increased levels of carbon dioxide in the atmosphere. See the chapter on photosynthesis in *Plants* by Irene Ridge (Oxford University Press, 2002) for a detailed discussion of the interaction of photosynthesis, photorespiration, and atmospheric carbon dioxide.

recklessness. Even though we don't really know how or why plants balance photosynthesis (in which they consume carbon dioxide and release oxygen) and photorespiration (in which they consume oxygen and release carbon dioxide), some scientists intend to tamper with plants' genes to reduce photorespiration.

Thanks to the promiscuity of pollen, both food crops and wild plants already have been contaminated by the genes of plants engineered to resist pesticides and it's possible that the genes of plants engineered to produce pharmaceutical or industrial chemicals also have gone astray.[11] Imagine what could happen if genes engineered to interfere with the mechanics of photosynthesis were to cross into wild plant populations.

The idea of using genetic engineering to tamper with the process upon which virtually all plant and animal life depends is an extreme case of the everyday hubris that leads humans to assume that they know best. Given the length of the list of things that seemed like a good idea at the time but turned out to be disastrous, this is a remarkably foolish assumption.

Since human animals are responsible for the ecological emergency in which we find ourselves, we do have an especial obligation to stop the violence, undo whatever damage can be undone, and ease the suffering of those who have been harmed. However, we must do so humbly, remembering that other species have a vested interest in our efforts and rejecting the preposterous idea that we alone know what needs to be done.

So much destruction has devolved from our failure to attend to and act in concert with other species. We neither look nor listen carefully enough to perceive the patterns and rhythms of the actions of other species as they maintain balances with each other and their environments.

Our so-called "scientific" method requires us to deliberately narrow our range of perception, accepting as valid information only decontextualized "data" falling within the preset parameters circumscribed by our own experimental methodology. Most often, this means that we simply do not perceive anything that we did not previously conceive. Any stray sensations or ideas that penetrate this powerful perceptual filter are laughed off as illusory, brushed off as irrelevant, or (if all else fails) warped into a form that fits our fixed ideas. The

11. "Crops 'widely contaminated' by genetically modified DNA" by Fred Pearce, *New Scientist* (23 February, 2004)

extent to which ostensibly objective scientists have twisted their perceptions to fit their preconceptions would be comical if it weren't so tragic.[12]

Our ideas about plants are rigid and dismissive. We demonstrate contempt by both belittling plants and tinkering with their genetic integrity, as if they were our playthings rather than the source of all that we need to survive.[13] Such an attitude is only possible in the context of radical dissociation. We are so estranged from the rest of the world that we don't recognize our place in it. We think of ourselves as the owners and bosses of those without whom we could not survive. Anyone less alienated from the natural world might be mystified by our unjustified ideas about human singularity.

Plants and other animals appear better able than we to perceive and respond to each other's needs in a mutually gratifying manner. Countless animal pollinators and seed distributors help to propagate the plants that feed them without, apparently, feeling the need to claim credit for the process or to assert ownership of the resulting seedlings. For their part, plants have managed to feed themselves and the rest of us despite all manner of impediments imposed by people.

Plants are not passive, however inert they may seem to the human eye. Probing, probing, probing into the ground, roots seek out resources, break through barriers, and share information with other plants. Reaching, reaching, reaching toward the light, limbs and vines position leaves so that they can do what we all need them to do: transubstantiate light into food. While we do not now and may never know anything about plant intentionality, we do know that plants are, indeed, actively responding to pesticides, genetic modification, and other assaults on their bodies.

---

12. One thinks, for example, of *Drapetomia,* which was the term coined in 1851 by Dr. Samuel Cartwright for the "disease" that led slaves to run away. See *An Early History: African American Mental Health* by Vernellia R. Randall for more examples of tragically inane "scientific" ideas about race.

13. Male attitudes toward women are remarkably similar to human attitudes toward plants. In both instances, the denigrated being has life-giving capabilities not possessed by the allegedly superior being, who depends upon the subordinated being for the continuation of life. In both instances, invasive scientific tinkering with the bodies of the denigrated beings stands in the stead of healthy respect for their reproductive capabilities. While feminist scholars and activists have focused increasing attention on the linkages between exploitation of women and exploitation of animals, we've not yet broken ground for the digging that needs to be done to get to the root of the earth-plant-animal-women conjunction.

What do plants know? What do they feel? Do they have projects? Are their efforts to counteract the harms done by humans intentional? Does it matter? What can we learn from them either way?

Some fundamentalist Christians laughingly dismiss the idea that people make choices or in any way control their own fates. To them, it seems self-evident that God — and only God — makes choices. Whatever they might *seem* to be doing, everyone else is just dumbly acting out God's will.

Most people take a similar view concerning the self-determination of plants and non-human animals. To them it seems self-evident that people — and only people — make choices. Whatever else they might *seem* to be doing, everyone else is just dumbly acting out laws of nature.

Our constructions of such concepts as consciousness and purpose have a built-in bias favoring animals in general and human animals in particular. We have a hard time even imagining how awareness or intention might be realized in beings very different from ourselves. That's okay. We don't need to know or even be able to imagine everything. As long as we recognize that there are limits to our knowledge and imagination and that things may be true even though we cannot perceive or prove them, then we can avoid the folly of unfounded assumptions loosely rooted in ignorance.

Are plants that participate in happy mutualisms with insects, fungi, or other plants *cooperating* with other beings? Are the "super weeds" that have evolved in response to pesticides trying to tell us something? In the end, what we think we know about such questions is irrelevant. We can and should learn from what plants are *doing*, taking guidance from the measures they have taken to preserve themselves and their ecosystems. Even if we don't know what the trees are "thinking," we can still follow their lead.

6. Terrorists

When US Secretary of Defense Donald Rumsfeld tried to hold a press conference in New Delhi in 2003, the press corps were greeted by scores of jeering Macaques monkeys, who shouted at them from the window ledges of surrounding buildings, literally making a mockery of the event.[14] In New Delhi, monkeys regularly break into the offices of the Defense Ministry, rifling through file cabinets and otherwise interfering with business as usual.

---

14. "Monkeys terrorize India workers, tourists " by Andrew Wang, AP (2 November 2003)

As with the witnesses to the antelope rescue, witnesses to these events know what they are seeing. "Monkeys are very furious," said Ujagar Singh, spokesman for the Patiala district in India, where pink-faced Rhesus monkeys have uprooted lawns and trashed houses.[15]

If the frequency of news reports are any guide, direct action by animals is on the rise. Elephants, apes, and monkeys in various regions of Africa and Asia are refusing to cede to the ideas that people have about who belongs where and who owns what. From baboons in South Africa, who break into houses not only to take food but also to pull clothes out of closets and urinate on them, to elephants in Indonesia, who have returned again and again to destroy the cash crops on a particular plantation, non-human animals in many places are actively contesting the privileges claimed by human beings.[16] Meanwhile, attacks by sharks, leopards, and even elephants are on the rise worldwide.[17]

Wildlife officials and other experts in the affected regions are unanimous in their assessment of the cause of the apparent increase in human-animal conflicts: habitat loss due to pollution or other human intrusions. Reading reports of animal responses to human activities, it seems to me that they can be divided into three categories: (1) incursions and attacks for the purpose of obtaining food or other necessities; (2) destruction, defacement and/or occupation of structures and locations claimed by people; and (3) expressions of discontent. The first category is relatively self-evident and includes some, but not all, of the attacks on the bodies of people. The third category includes acts against people or property that appear to have no material purpose other than the expression of anger or frustration. While we must be careful in relegating acts to this category, since there may be material ends that we are not able to discern, we must also remember that people are not the only animals who have feelings. Monkeys who engage in seemingly senseless acts of property destruction may well, like some human eco-activists, have mixed motives that include both emotional and rational aims.

Acts falling into the second category of animal reactions to human activities often are equivalent to the work undertaken by radical environmental activists.

---

15. "Pesky, protected monkeys doing hard time in jail" by Kim Barker, Chicago Tribune (16 September 2004)

16. See, e.g., "Baboons on rampage in South African town," AFP (16 June 2004) and "Indonesian worker escapes rampaging elephants," New Straits Times (26 December, 2001).

17. See, e.g., "Dead zone may boost shark attacks," BBC (4 August 2004); "Wild leopards on human killing spree in Bombay" by Jayashree Lengrade, Reuters (5 June 2004); and "Sierra Leone Villagers flee deadly elephants, " Reuters (29 July 2004).

Indian elephants who repeatedly demolish cash crop plantations remind me of Indian farmers who demolish fields of genetically modified crops. Both are using the most direct method to remove noxious human introductions from the environment.

Animals have taken even more assertive measures to protect their habitats from human exploitation. I think, for example, of a region in Sierra Leone, which had been controlled by animals during a recent war but into which people now wish to relocate; the elephants have fought back, chasing people away and killing those who do not flee. Similarly, elephants killed 130 people in two years in the Indian state of Assam.

When animals use deadly force to protect their homes, ought they be considered "violent?" Recalling the number of extinctions due to habitat loss, not to mention the number of individual animals who have starved or otherwise perished when their homes have been invaded or polluted by people, the concept of justifiable force in self defense comes to mind. Many animals also confront hunters who deliberately seek to kill them, sometimes for food but sometimes for fur or trinkets. Hunters have found ever more insidious and violent ways to kill elephants, including jackfruit bombs, poisoned salt licks and water holes, electrified foot paths, and nets made out of nails.[18] Should we really be surprised when some elephants elect to fight back?

People almost always kill animals by some means when they fence off, cultivate, or build on land. When the new construction or cultivation is not, strictly speaking, necessary, ought not those killings be considered aggressive violence?

When, as is so often the case, poverty forces people into places formerly controlled by animals, then tragedy is sure to follow. One way or another, somebody who doesn't deserve to die is going to end up dead. People in the aggregate already have more than we need but because resources are not shared equitably, starving people often end up competing with starving animals on the outskirts of so-called civilization. This is why the struggle for earth and animals will never be won in the absence of social justice and *vice versa*.

When animals resist human expansionism, they often face reprisals. In India and elsewhere, villagers have poisoned and speared elephants in retaliation for crop raids.[19] Despite government protections, baboons have been shot in South Africa and monkeys have been killed *en masse* and dumped in sacks in

18. "Hunters find ingenious ways to kill elephants" by Shali Ittaman, Hindustan Times (1 May 2003)

19. See, e.g, "Angry villages in India's northeast kill five elephants for raiding crops" by Wasbir Hussain, AP (11 October 2002).

India. Because killing monkeys is illegal in India, the Punjab state has instituted a monkey jail. As of 2004, more than a dozen monkeys were imprisoned for life in a 15 by 15 cell, some for "crimes" no more serious than destruction of property.

Like human rebels, animals who refuse to respect property rights or other ideas made up by people are increasingly called "terrorists" or accused of creating "terror" whether or not they have engaged in acts that might be considered violent. In the Punjabi struggle between the people and the monkeys, one local newspaper referred to a captured animal as a "terrorist monkey." Similarly, local news media report that elephants in the states of Assam and Tripura invade human settlements not only to find food but also "to create terror."

When people rise up against their oppressors, solidarity movements spring up around the world. When people are imprisoned for acts of resistance, whether these be in defense of earth, animal, or human rights, like-minded activists extend comfort and support to them. In India, Maneka Gandhi has stood up for the imprisoned monkeys but, otherwise, overt extensions of solidarity to animal rebels have not been forthcoming from animal advocates or other environmental activists.

Dare we step forward to say that rebel elephants are as deserving of solidarity as Zapatistas or Irish Catholics? Dare we assert that monkeys locked up by people are political prisoners and that their indefinite detention is just as unjustified as the permanent imprisonment of suspected "terrorists" now contemplated by the US government? Shouldn't we support all defenders of the earth, regardless of their species?

Officials have implored citizens not to feed the monkeys who occupy government buildings in New Delhi but people come weekly, bearing bananas, anyway. Such common-sense expressions of material and moral support are heartening and ought be emulated wherever animals are under fire for transgressing human rules.

One need not need live near elephants or monkeys to find opportunities to express solidarity. In the US state of Virginia, for example, turkey vultures — who serve a vital ecological function in addition to being intrinsically valuable as individuals — have been literally under fire for their failure to respect suburban notions of cleanliness. With the aid of the federal government, local officials have shot these allegedly protected birds and hung them by their feet from the trees (purportedly to scare off others of their species) solely in order to spare humans the trouble of washing bird dropping from their cars and barbecue equipment.[20] In the state of Louisiana, bees bit back when children threw rocks at their hive. 40,000 bees — who also serve a vital ecological function in addition to being intrinsically valuable as individuals — were killed and another 80,000 captured in retaliation for the stings suffered by the aggressive children.[21]

We can and should support non-human rebels, whether they are fighting for their own lives or for the ecosystems that they share with other beings. As with the plants, we must also seek to learn what we can from the patterns of their actions. Escalation of attacks, property destruction, or other rebellious acts in a particular region may signal that the animals in the area, like those who sense the onrush of the Tsunami, may be more aware than we of impending ecological disaster. They also may know better than we what needs to be done to arrest or mitigate the detrimental effects of ongoing human activities.

7. Morning

"In the course of history, there comes a time when humanity is called to shift to a new level of consciousness... That time is now."

-- Wangari Maathai[22]

None of us evolved in isolation, whether as individuals or species. Evolution always occurs in context and in relationship with others. For example, humans and dogs co-evolved. Like plants and pollinators or ants and aphids, the progenitors of dogs and humans got together for mutual benefit. For all we know, our species might not have survived were it not for the extra reproductive success we gained through the association of proto-humans and proto-dogs. At night they helped to keep us safe and warm. But then, in what must be among

---

20. "Virginia City Trying to Scare Away Vultures," Associated Press (03 December 2001)

21. "Kids plus rocks equals 120,000 angry bees," Reuters (16 August 2004)

22. Wangari Maathai recently won the Nobel Peace Prize for planting trees. She is the first African woman and the first environmentalist to win the prize and she did it by founding and maintaining, despite vehement and at time violent opposition, an uncompromising program of direct action. For detailed information about Wangari Maathai's work, see her book, *The Green Belt Movement*, published by Lantern Books. Two wide-ranging and very interesting interviews with Maathai may be accessed online courtesy of *Satya* and *Mother Jones* magazines.

the most brazen betrayals in natural history, humans turned around and made slaves out of their trusted friends.[23]

The good news is that evolution is ongoing. We can choose another path. We can recognize our kinship with other beings. We can recognize without being terrified by our dependence on them and act accordingly.

If we really want to wage a war on "terror," then we need to learn to be less afraid. We don't need to enclose or control those upon whom our lives depend.

If we can recover our kinship with our non-human relatives, then we won't have to hide behind barricades because we won't be alone anymore.

Can we do it? Yes. Will we do it? I don't know. I do know that we are not alone in the struggle to save the earth. The sooner we see that and act accordingly, the sooner we can begin to end our own awful estrangement and help to heal those we have hurt.

The current situation is more dangerous and perverse than any nightmare. Yet most people, including many who consider themselves to be environmentalists, slumber fitfully within the uneasy dream of human singularity. For the sake of the rhinos and the redwoods, and the canaries and the cornflowers too, I hope we wake up soon.

---

23. As Raul Valadez Azúa recently wrote in the official publication of the *Asociación Mexicana de Médicos Veterinarios Especialistas en Pequeñas Especies*, "an important process of familiarity and posterior coevolution between Canis lupus and Homo erectus" lasted for about 40,000 years until Homo sapiens came along and "took advantage of familiarity" to capture puppies and begin the process we euphemistically call 'domestication.'

19

I Know Why the Caged Birds Scream

The legendary Patty Mark and her comrade Debra Tranter kindly consented to be interviewed for this piece, which appeared in the February 2006 issue of *Satya* magazine. Patty Mark invented one of the most effective methods of direct action: Open Rescue. Ducks Jean-Paul and Jean-Claude, who feature so prominently in VINE Sanctuary history and in my thinking about queering animal liberation, were liberated from a foie gras factory in the course of an open rescue operation. This is an example of how direct action can carry the struggle into the future even as it saves lives right now.

I Know Why the Caged Birds Scream (SPLIT)

Three women walked past the electrified fence and onto the Happy Hens Egg World compound, which confines 220,000 hens in rusty cages 60 miles west of Melbourne, Australia. As the women began documenting the deplorable conditions in the sheds, videotaping the sights and sounds of crowded birds in constant misery, they were set upon by seven male employees of the egg factory, demanding they leave. The women agreed to leave voluntarily but the men attacked them anyway, pushing and shoving them through the dim and dusty shed.

Hearing her comrade cry out in distress, one of the activists grabbed the wall of the shed and said that she would not leave without her friend. The youngest worker grabbed both her breasts and squeezed them hard, putting his mouth next to her ear and snarling, "that made you move, didn't it?" She screamed and fell on the floor. The men grabbed her by the ankles and dragged her body along the length of the grimy walkway.

"During moments like this funny thoughts pop into your head," she said later. "Every time I enter a battery hen shed, the noise of hens screaming is almost deafening. I silently stare into their cages documenting via video their suffering. As I was being dragged along the floor by my feet, I remember looking up at five tiers of cages and all the hens were completely silent, their necks were stretching out of their cages and their eyes were looking down on me. I was the one screaming and they were witnessing my suffering."

By the end of the ordeal, animal rescue team member Debra Tranter was covered in filth and bruises. Pictures of her and Animal Liberation Victoria (ALV) founder Patty Mark leaving the scene show strong women shaken by a traumatic experience. Nonetheless, their first press statement after the incident stressed their ongoing determination to protect and rescue hens. Some days later, they went back to the same shed and did so, dodging guard dogs and barbed wire, to rescue as many hens as they could carry away into the night.

Unhappy Hens

Most of the eggs eaten by people come from hens caged in egg factories, who spend their days standing on sloped mesh in cages so small that the birds crowded into them cannot open their wings or even lie down comfortably. They are fed just enough to keep them laying eggs and not one iota more. Dim lighting and the constant cries of birds in distress create a sense of chaos. Ammonia from the manure pits below the tiers of cages hangs heavily in the air.

Animals deprived of everything that is natural to them behave unnaturally. Deprived of freedom, normal social relations, and cognitive stimulation, birds may vent their frustrations on themselves or each other. To prevent economic losses from this, the people who run egg factories burn off the tips of the birds' beaks in a painful and disfiguring operation known as "debeaking."

In the U.S. right now, 270 million birds are caged in egg factories—sprawling complexes in which as many as 250,000 birds may be confined in each building, and a total of more than a million birds at the mercy of men like those who assaulted Patty Mark and Debra Tranter.

Numbers can be numbing. 270 million is too many to contemplate. Imagine a single hen crowded with seven others in the middle of a battery of cages containing thousands of others. Imagine you are that hen.

Have you ever been bored? Frustrated? Uncomfortable? Cranky? Imagine yourself crowded into a cage, often thirsty and always a little hungry, with nothing to do other than jostle your cage-mates. They're not your friends—they're your competitors. There's never enough space and never enough food for everybody to feel satisfied. You can't ever get comfortable. There's no place to go to get away from each other. And there's never anything to do!

One of your cage-mates keeps screaming. She won't shut up! Another is slumped in a stupor. She won't move out of the way! Somebody else is dying. No—she's dead. Your eyes burn. Your feet throb. Your wings ache to open. You can't turn around or lie down. You wait.

Ten minutes. Five hours. Three weeks. Eight months. Two years. Two years you may wait for relief from the tedium and pain. Then the cage opens but you are not released. Instead you are trucked to a painful and terrifying death at a slaughter factory or, if no buyer has been found for your bedraggled body, simply buried alive in a landfill.

Animal Liberators to the Rescue

The July 2005 ALV raid on Happy Hens Egg World was what's known as an "open rescue." Open rescue teams do not mask themselves or their intentions. They record every phase of the process of saving animals who are in dire need of food, water, or veterinary care. They replace any locks that they break and sometimes call to ask the police for help in taking abused animals to safety. If they end up in court, they use the "necessity defense," arguing that any crime they committed (such as trespass) was justified by the need to prevent a greater crime and using the trial as an opportunity to get evidence of extreme yet routine cruelty to animals into the public record.

First used by an ALV team in Australia in 1992, the tactic of open rescue has since spread to several European countries and U.S. states. The German organization Befreite Tiere (Liberated Animals) has undertaken 36 open rescues in the past two years, rescuing 1,031 hens, ducks, geese and pigs along the way. In Sweden, a group calling itself Raddningstjansten (The Liberation Service) has coordinated a series of raids on egg factories. In one, four activists calling themselves "Action Group Pippi" (after the character Pippi Longstocking) took 60 hens from cages, leaving behind a letter for the farmer. In the U.S., local organizations such as Mercy for Animals of Ohio and the Animal Protection and Rescue League of California have used the open rescue method to document abuses at egg factories.

Still photos and video footage gathered during open rescues alert activists and the public to the atrocities that go on behind closed doors in factory farms, puppy mills and vivisection labs. The brave animal advocates who break into these houses of horror risk their own safety and sanity, confronting unthinkable cruelty and unspeakable suffering, to bring abused animals and their stories into the sunshine.

On the night of the incidents at Happy Hens Egg World, Patty Mark was still awake and shaky at two a.m. In the weeks following her assault, Debra Tranter wrestled with depression and struggled with questions about the futility of her activism. Both say that the expressions of empathy and solidarity that poured in from animal advocates around the world kept them afloat during the difficult days following their misadventure.

Solidarity Against Sexual Abuse

Debra Tranter was not the first woman sexually assaulted at an egg factory (nor the first woman sexually assaulted while trying to protect or rescue animals). In 2002, the Equal Employment Opportunity Commission determined that supervisors employed by DeCoster Farms, which had egg factories in Iowa and Maine, sexually assaulted several female employees. Because the women were undocumented workers, their supervisors were able to use threats to keep them silent and compliant in the face of sexual exploitation.

That kind of behavior should come as no surprise. Debra Tranter is perhaps in the best position to explain why. In the moment of the sexual assault, she says, "as well as feeling shocked and violated I also felt in complete solidarity with the caged hens surrounding me. These men knew how to abuse, manipulate, and terrorize to get what they want. They wanted me to leave the shed the quickest way possible, so they abused and terrorized me to get me out. They want the hens' eggs, so they cage and torment them in order to get what they want the easiest and quickest way possible."

Why grab Debra Tranter's breasts rather than more quickly muscling her out the door? The hens and the dairy cows can tell us. To break an animal's spirit, you must first steal from her the sense that she controls her own body. These animals and the more than a million children held in sex slavery are the living legacy of the days when all female animals—human and nonhuman alike—were chattel.

Fat cow. Silly hen. We use animals to insult women and project our ideas about passive femininity onto them. The result is to reduce the female animal to a body whose reproductive powers can be controlled and appropriated by men.

Thanks to thousands of years of using every trick in the book to control the reproduction of other animals, we people have got sex and power all mixed up. Young men confuse rape for consensual sex. Young women see their own bodies as objects to barter and then put themselves down for doing so.

That's one part of the process that leads so many women to believe the lies about themselves and other animals. Women buy the groceries in most households. They're the ones buying the eggs and milk of other females to feed their children, many of whom may themselves be sexually abused.

But some women stand in solidarity with the hens and the cows. They refuse to allow themselves or other animals to be reduced to meat. Like Patty Mark and Debra Tranter, they feel afraid but act anyway. In so doing, they liberate themselves—and us—along with the animals. And they deserve nothing less than our fullest support.

20

"Let's Put on a Show!"

This is one of a series of essays written in fits of frustration about the unwillingness of the US antiwar movement to do anything other than mount futile protest marches in the wake of 9/11, in the run-up to the war on Afghanistan, and then again with regard to the invasion of Iraq. This essay was originally published on the *Common Dreams*, *Dissident Voice*, and *Press Action* websites in 2004. Other essays in the series included "Marching in Circles: The Tactics of Dizziness and Despair" published by *Freezerbox Magazine* and the *News International* [Pakistan] in 2003; "Don't Buy Miss America's Pie" published by *Briarpatch* [Canada] in 2003; "O Tio Sam Precisa de Você Para Boicotar os USA" published by Centro de Midia Independente [Brazil] also in 2003; and "Crisi della Sinistra USA" in *Bandiera Rossa* [Italy] and "Il Pacifismo USA in Cerca di Strategia" in *Capitalismo-Natura-Socialismo* [Italy] in 2001.

I first began worrying about the utility—and possible counter-productivity—of protest marches back in the early 1990s, during the first war against Iraq. As marchers around me shouted awkwardly cadenced variations on the "Hey Hey Ho Ho" chant, I wondered what in the world we thought we were doing. We were in *Ann Arbor*. Most people on campus and in town opposed the war already. Our relaxed stroll through the streets of a small city in no way impeded the war machine. Indeed, as I worried aloud to a fellow marcher, I wondered if we weren't accidentally play-acting the myth of democracy in a way that might be used by the warmongers as evidence of United States superiority. My comrade, an elder member of a communist party, became visibly annoyed with me, and so I let the subject drop. But I never stopped wondering.

I'm not against flamboyant demonstrations of dissent—far from it! At the same time, I know that humans are copy-cats who tend to develop knee-jerk habits rather than thinking each new situation through thoroughly. And I know how easily we can be seduced by the *feeling* of *doing something*, especially when that something allows us to vent our emotions. I know, too, that—as social animals—we like to show off our opinions to each other. In combination, those tendencies can lead to performances of dissent that can eclipse less showy, but potentially more potent, forms of organizing.

In the wake of 9/11, I wished for the US peace movement to set aside parades and shouted slogans in favor of door-to-door conversations about how horrible it feels to be attacked because somebody doesn't like your government and whether we really wanted to do the same thing to the civilians of Afghanistan. Once the Bush II wars had begun, I wished for the US peace movement to call for economic direct action. Peace activists elsewhere were eager to call for a boycott of US products but wouldn't do it without the OK of the US left, which preferred to devote its energy to marching in despairing circles, presuming that resistance was futile and all that remained was to shout into the wind "not in my name!"

"Let's Put on a Show!"

Spectacle vs Reality in the US Peace Movement

Yet again tens of thousands prepare to descend on major metropolitan areas to march in circles through empty streets. We will exercise our legs and our lungs and our egos and then go home again. Nothing will change and nobody will be surprised at that. As usual, exorbitant expenditures of time and money will add up to exactly zero. Meanwhile, people and animals and ecosystems in Iraq and elsewhere will continue to pay the price for our failures of courage and imagination.

The French have a word for it: *spectacle*. Back in the 1960s, Guy Debord and other Situationist theorists and activists described late capitalist culture as "the society of the spectacle." Long before the advent of reality shows and ring tones for disposable cell phones, Situationists were already chafing at the degree to which the lively variety of everyday life had been reduced to a deadening array of things to watch and buy.

Today, consumer culture extends to extremes beyond the most most jaded and surrealistic dreams of the political theorists of earlier eras. Only fictional nightmares such as Karel Capek's *War with the Newts*, Aldous Huxley's *Brave New World*, or George Orwell's *1984* approximate the sinister absurdity of the sociopolitical atmosphere in which we now must find ways to effectively create change.

In the society of the spectacle, there's no business like show business. Image is everything. Even those who actively participate in the events of the day do so as spectators of their own lives, with one eye always looking back at a real or imaginary camera. All actions, including and especially political acts, become performances. Creative resistance is quickly suffocated by incorporation into the show.

Sound familiar? It should. Troubled teens write in weblogs rather than private diaries while television network NBC (owned by military-industrial behemoth General Electric) literally makes a mockery of subversive ideas on comedy programs like Will & Grace and Whoopi.

We must live in a democracy if people are allowed to mock the president on TV. That's what they — including "the president" — want us to think. Do you remember how Bush portrayed the biggest US peace marches before the invasion of Iraq? He said that such demonstrations illustrated the difference between the United States and Iraq, thus turning the protests into one more reason why the people of Iraq needed to be "liberated."

By then it should have been manifestly evident that symbolic demonstrations of dissent no longer shake up the system to any significant degree. Instead of challenging the spectacle of democracy, our protests are incorporated into the spectacle, making it stronger and more compelling. The more spectacular our demonstrations become, the more drums and puppets we deploy, the easier it is for average citizens to see protesters as merely the cast members of an ever-more-colorful reality show.

This bears repeating: The big demonstrations that have become so popular are not only ineffective; they actually make matters worse. By channeling the time, energy, money, and creativity of so many activists into an exercise in futility, these demonstrations and their preparations deflect activist attention from the urgent task of fashioning actual (rather than symbolic) challenges to the corporate world order and the military power that sustains it. Moreover, these demonstrations leave people — activists and regular citizens alike — more rather than less comfortable with the existing order. Watching or reading news reports about the event, citizens feel good about living in "a free country." Mollified by making the news, participants go home feeling like they have done their part. Indeed, judging from the comments they make to reporters, personal comfort appears to be the primary reason many people attend these events. "I know we can't stop the war," goes the usual litany, "but I couldn't live with myself if I didn't show my disagreement." Thus, the performance of dissent becomes an end in itself rather than the means to an end.

When we start from the premise that we can't make a difference, is it any wonder that we don't? When we choose tactics that are spectacular rather than substantial, should we be surprised when we are simply incorporated into the show? Is it true that the best we can hope for is superficial media coverage of the mere fact that some people disagree with the policies of the Bush regime? Might we dare to dream more extravagantly? Dare we risk disappointment by trying to actually stop the crimes that Bush is perpetrating in our name, rather than simply signal our disapproval of them? What might we do to really make a difference?

The first thing we need to do is understand the distinction between direct and indirect action. For too long, too many activists have mistaken drama for direct action. For the record, direct action includes only tactics that have an immediate impact on some element of the problem at hand. Indirect action seeks change via more circuitous routes, such as seeking to change citizens' minds in the hope that they will, in turn, change their voting behavior and that this will, in turn, lead to changed national policies. Rent strikes, boycotts, blockades, sabotage, and demonstrations that substantially interfere with business as usual are direct action. Petition drives, letters to editors, community education, and demonstrations that are limited to symbolic expressions of opinion are indirect action.

Study of successful social change movements reveals that success is most likely when both direct and indirect tactics are coordinated. Needless to say, these must be effective tactics, which means that they must be rooted in accurate perceptions of reality and smart strategic analyses. Want to change the hearts and minds of your fellow citizens? Then you'd better have a clear sense of what they're really thinking and feeling along with at least a rudimentary working knowledge of the factors that lead people to change their attitudes and behavior.

If peace activists feel a little daunted by that list of prerequisites, that's good — they should. Like people in every other field of difficult endeavor, activists are forever making mistakes due to unspoken, and inaccurate, assumptions. Because marches and rallies were so effective during the civil rights and Vietnam protest movements, we assume that they will have the same effect on public opinion today. We forget that times have changed; we forget that people are no longer shocked by the sight of thousands of their fellow citizens marching in the streets; we forget that, for both observers and participants, protest marches have become little more than parades.

We also forget that direct action was an essential element of many of the most effective protests of the past. In the USA, civil rights protesters deliberately got arrested en masse in order to overwhelm the criminal justice systems of small southern towns, thereby literally preventing them from conducting business as usual. Similar tactics had been used in anti-colonial movements elsewhere in the world including, most famously, in South Asia. The leaders of the US civil rights movement learned from what activists in other countries had done, correctly adapting the tactics to suit the circumstances.

In contrast, the current US peace movement functions like a closed-circuit television system, repetitively broadcasting the same old message to its own members. Protest events are highly scripted, with the emphasis on style rather than substance. Activists signal dissent but do not actually rebel. Demonstrators and police officers often engage in highly stylized cooperative ballets wherein a handful of people are voluntarily arrested.

The point of such dramatic scenarios entirely escapes me; certainly, they do not in any way constitute direct action. Direct action is not necessarily dramatic and, in these days of the spectacle, may be most effective when it is not part of any show. Direct action against war must, by definition, in some way impede the march of the war machine. Withdrawing one's financial support from the military-industrial complex is direct action for peace; shouting "Whose streets? Our streets!" on a sunny Sunday afternoon is not.

Emergencies call for urgent action. Killing continues in Iraq and is likely to commence somewhere else soon, if the Bush Doctrine of preemptive warfare remains the foreign policy of the United States. That dramatic violence plays out against the backdrop of everyday environmental mayhem perpetrated by the Bush administration. Now is not the time to indulge our taste for for the spectacular or our wish for self-satisfaction. Now is the time for effective direct action. Specifically, now is the time for economic direct action.

The Industrial Workers of the World used to say that the workers of the world could stop capitalism just by crossing their arms. In today's late capitalism, where few workers are unionized and the franchise is increasingly illusory, our greatest power may be as consumers. The consumers of the world can bring the military-industrial complex to a crashing halt just by keeping our hands in our pockets.

The two ways to withdraw one's financial support from the war machine are to stop paying war taxes and to boycott the corporate profiteers that constitute the industrial side of the military-industrial complex. Both of these strategies ensure that we are not supporting war with money at the same time as we oppose war with words. At minimum, these forms of economic direct action subtract funds from the war machine and its corporate supporters. At maximum, such direct action may impact the foreign and domestic policies of the Bush regime.

Is it possible to make such a sufficiently significant dent in corporate profits? Yes. The majority of people in the world opposed the war in Iraq and continue to resent the current foreign and environmental policies of the United States. Many organizations around the world already have joined together to call for a boycott against war. All that remains is for the mainstream US peace movement to stop marching in circles and get on the peace train. If we agree that everyone should, insofar as possible, shun the shoddy consumer goods of evil corporate behemoths in favor of substantial and sustainable local products, then we will be supporting the regrowth of healthy local ecosystems and economies at the same time that we are weakening the war machine.

If you want peace, don't buy war. There's nothing spectacular about that.

V. ALLSORTS

This section includes a selection of briefs, columns, talks, and other miscellaneous aggregations of words that don't fit into any of the above themes. Unlike the rest of this volume, they appear in chronological order.

21

The African "Queen"

I began writing for publication in the early 1990s, learning along the way. First came one-off opinion pieces and feature articles for local independent newspapers written in the service of my activism. Then, from 1993 through 1995, I wrote a monthly opinion column entitled "Out in Left Field" for Michigan's statewide LGBT newspaper, *Between the Lines*. The practice of churning out a monthly essay was salutary, forcing me to verbalize ideas that might have remained inchoate. Since physical newspapers have strict constraints, I also picked up the handy skill of ruthlessly excising verbiage.

I hesitate to include any of those columns here, in part because they *always* reference then-current events with which many present-day readers will not be familiar. And of course, thirty years later, I find my own past thinking so very, very rudimentary. And yet, because those columns forced me to learn to write vividly and concisely, I feel sentimentally attached to them.

So, I present to you my 1995 commentary on the forced resignation of Surgeon General Joycelyn Elders by President Bill Clinton. Elders served as Surgeon General from September of 1993 through December of 1994, when she was unceremoniously ousted in response to a smear campaign by conservatives who portrayed her views on sex education as dangerous to children and who also seized on her remarks about the potential public health impact of drug legalization as evidence of moral turpitude. Perhaps you will notice that elements of the national conversation that I critiqued in 1995 persist today. Perhaps, like me, you will end up feeling queasy.

OUT IN LEFT FIELD

THE AFRICAN "QUEEN"

The nightmare has begun. Less than two months after the most overtly mean-spirited and covertly racist campaign season in recent history — before the right-wing devils even assumed office — one of the most prominent and outspoken Black women in government has been sacrificed on the altar of bigoted ignorance.

I'm speaking, of course, about the recent firing of Surgeon General Jocelyn Elders, for daring to speak accurately about the educational efforts necessary to halt the spread of the virus associated with AIDS. As the most courageous and visible government official dealing with AIDS, Surgeon General Elders was in the business of saving lives. Her loss of a job is our loss as a country. I have no doubt that, as a result of Clinton's rash actions, some of us will die who might have been saved.

How can we understand what happened here? To even begin to make sense of it, we have to look not only at the new-found power of the far right, but also at the process that brought them to power. The election season was dominated by the far-right agenda, to the extent that even allegedly liberal and moderate candidates agreed that the main issues were crime and welfare. This was, of course, pure silliness — welfare accounts for less that 1% of the federal budget, and the FBI has reported a decrease in crime in recent years. So, why did this rhetoric strike such a chord? To understand that, we have to think about racism.

In an era when it is no longer acceptable to overtly 'play the race card' in seeking white votes, politicians have resorted to images which allow them to do so without ever mentioning race. Despite the fact that most crimes are committed by whites, *crime* has become a code word for *out of control Black men* terrorizing law-abiding (white) citizens. Despite the fact that the majority of recipients of public aid are white, the word *welfare* summons up stereotyped images of *out of control Black women* who just won't stop having sex and getting pregnant. Politicians can safely spout off about *crime control* and *welfare reform*, knowing that the racist images in the minds of their intended audience will take care of the rest. The dominant if unspoken subtext of the recent election, then, was the need for *mainstream*— that is to say, white—Americans to bring *crime and welfare*—that is to say, Black man and women—under control. President Clinton responded to that implicit mandate this week by the symbolic action of bringing a Black woman — Joycelyn Elders — under control.

Of course, we all will suffer as a result of this action, and gay and lesbian teens may suffer most of all. This is yet one more example of the ways that racism and sexism and sexism work together and yet one more reason why gay and lesbian activists can never afford to forget issues of race, class, and sex.

In a column in this paper last year, I discussed the ways that the word *queen* — which summons up images of *queerness* — has been repeatedly used to smear African American women. At the time, I suggested, that gay men join in solidarity with Black women and fling the word back at the forces of evil. Gay men didn't do that, but Surgeon General Elders did.

Referring to jeering right-wing references to her as the "condom queen," Elders said that she would proudly wear a condom on a crown if she thought it would lead even a few teenagers to be more likely to practice safer sex. To her credit, Elders did not balk at the implied queerness of the term, but turned it to her advantage, explicitly including gay and lesbian teens among those who's lives she so valued. Elders, a heterosexual woman, clearly understood something that many gay men and lesbians still do not, namely, that our lives are connected and that an injury to one truly is an injury to all.

Why do I say some of us still don't get this? Well, look at the behavior of local and national 'mainstream' gay and lesbian organizations during and since the elections. Rather than joining in active solidarity with progressive people of color, poverty activists, and others concerned about the hateful rhetoric spewing from the mouths of both Republicans and Democrats, 'mainstream' gay organizations played at being neutral while all too many gay men and lesbians joined the ugly cacophony of voices clamoring for more prisons and less money for the poor. Since the election, the head of a prominent national gay organization has actually bragged about the presence of a few gay men among the new ruling elite led by Jesse Helms and Newt Gingrich. Given that the actions of this elite will undoubtedly result in more than a few gay and lesbian deaths, they should be ashamed of themselves. I'd be embarrassed for them but I'm too busy throwing up.

22

13 October 2000

Daybook was a zine that published hour-by-hour descriptions of days by a wide array of people. On a lark, I wrote up a day at what was then a very new chicken sanctuary. I'm glad that I did so. Not only do I have a detailed record of that one day, but the publication of my log in the zine led to good things for the sanctuary. First, a reporter for the *Baltimore Sun* saw it in the zine and was inspired to write a profile for that newspaper. Then, a producer for the PBS series *In the Life* saw the newspaper article and decided to feature us on the show.[1] That goes to show that you never know what might happen if you go ahead and write something, even if the purpose of doing so is not immediately clear.

---

1. You can watch that episode here: https://tinyurl.com/VINEonPBS

Daybook

13 October 2000

06:15 AM

The daily tragedy of being forced out of bed begins. Gretchen is walking on our heads and Zami is whining pathetically at the back door. Inside of the covers is warm, so very warm. Outside of the covers is oh so cold. Blessedly, Miriam gets up to let them outside.

06:20 AM

Miriam sweetly tells me it's time to get up.

06:25 AM

Miriam sweetly tells me it's time to get up.

06:30 AM

Miriam sweetly tells me it's time to get up. I claim that all I want is "5 more minutes" of sleep. She accedes but then I suddenly remember that I didn't go out to buy more dog food last night. I had planned to make some rice to mix in with the kibble that we do have, but fell asleep before doing so. In my sleepy state, the three hungry dogs outside seem like ravenous wolves or maybe starving kittens. Either way, I must figure out what to feed them. With great regret, I drag myself from under the covers and pile on layer upon layer of mismatched clothing.

06:35 - 07:00 AM

I figure out that by adding some leftover spaghetti and a can of puppy food left over from when we briefly sheltered a pit bull found by the side of the road, I can stretch the kibble to cover breakfast. With great relief, I do so. I then make Miriam's lunch, as I try to do every day. Sandwich, apple, something salty, something sweet, and some sour treats for the work mate who eats lunch with her. As I am assembling the lunch and Miriam is getting ready, we chat about the upcoming day. As usual, the conversation is punctuated by cries of "Gretchen!" and "Gretchen, No!" and "Gretchen, Down!" Going back into the bedroom to put on outdoor clothing, I run into Dandelion and spend some time loving her up. I then pile on more clothing, as though opening up the chicken coop were the equivalent of an Arctic expedition. I am having a hard time with the transition to autumn.

07:00 - 08:00 AM

The sun is coming up later each day. It's downhill to solstice when finally the days will start getting longer again. I wait for a few minutes until sunrise has truly arrived and then go out to open up the converted garage that serves as a chicken coop. On the way from our door to theirs I hear wild bird songs that I haven't heard for a while. I guess many of the birds who over-winter here are back. I am glad of that.

Now comes the morning routine: fill up the water basin in the first hen yard then open up the coop door which opens into that yard, say "good morning hens," climb over the fence into the rooster yard cursing myself for not yet putting in the gate between the yards, fill up the water basin in the rooster yard then open up the coop door which opens into that yard, say "good morning roosters," go through the gate to the second hen yard, fill up that water basin and open up that door saying "good morning hens" again. The greetings are always heartfelt because, no matter how cranky I might be about getting up and out in the morning, I am always so happy just to see them.

And they are happy too — to get out! Don't let anyone tell you that chickens are somehow content to be confined. They want out at sunrise and, except in severe weather, will stay out till sunset given the opportunity to do so. Anyway, back to the routine... but, wait — I notice that two hens from the group that just came in from Ohio have found their way into the rooster yard. They don't realize that these big "broiler" roosters could seriously hurt them just doing what comes naturally. So, I've got to catch them and put them back with the hens.

Then, back to the routine. Next, I have to take any ailing birds to the separate "hospital" area adjoining one of the hen yards. Right now, that's Dolly and Cynthia. Dolly is an indomitable hen recovering from a foot injury. She's affectionate and stubborn and often reminds me of my departed grandmother. She came in last May with a bunch of hens from the same farm and, since they spend all their time together, I am only now getting to know them individually. And, not a moment too soon, since they are reaching the age at which many of these poor "broiler" birds start to experience health problems due to having breasts which are too large for their ligaments and internal organs to comfortably support. We've already lost a few of Dolly's crew and I am grieving them still. Cynthia is a youngster brought to us by a lady who found her by the side of the road. She's almost completely blind, probably from the ammonia fumes at the chicken house in which she spent the eight weeks leading up to slaughter. She's very sweet and has grown very attached to Dolly. We are hoping for a younger bird to come in soon and get attached to Cynthia so that she can have someone to lead her around. Once Dolly and Cynthia are settled, it's time to feed everyone.

As I am distributing the chicken scratch and sunflower seeds, I notice that Railroad Red has found her way into the new hen yard. Railroad, who is a Rhode Island Red we found by the railroad tracks, traditionally has hung out with the roosters and has been allowed to do so because she is quick enough to evade them. "Allowed" is probably the wrong word since Railroad does exactly what she wants regardless of any efforts on our part to sway her.

I also notice that a couple of roosters are sneezing. That means they've picked up the bronchitis that hit some of the hens earlier in the week. It's a good thing that I decided to medicate everyone's water. Now, I just have to watch and worry and hope that everyone recovers. Since some of the hens who are already improving, I am hopeful that the course of treatment will work for the roosters too. While all of has been going on, I have been keeping up a running commentary aloud, addressing myself to any bird nearby.

Now it is time for the individual greetings for the birds who expect them. Scout, Fanny, and Simone are just three of a host of red hens who expect some hand feeding and individual attention every morning. They all came from the same North Carolina egg factory, where they endured truly horrific conditions. I am amazed that they want anything to do with humans, since they are still visibly marked by those experiences. But they do want, indeed expect, attention from me. Scout is truly intrepid and will climb all over me, peering intensely at anything new. Fanny seems to think of me as a walking tree and is pretty sure that, if she scratches at me just right, the seeds will pour forth from me. Simone de Beauvior is an independent egghead, with her own strange beauty; of all the birds, she is the one who is most tuned into my feelings. She comes around to comfort me when I am sad. But I am not sad this morning. It is a beautiful day. After all of the feeding is over, I pause for a few moments just to soak up the atmosphere of the peaceful morning light. Then, after saying a gentle hello to shy giant Iris, I go back inside.

08:00 - 08:20 AM

Per usual, Dandelion and Gretchen demand to be let out immediately. Per usual, I fulfill their demand, reminding them not to harass the chickens on the other side of the backyard fence. Then it is time to love up Zami. Every day at this time, she brings me a toy and we play a little fetch. Playing fetch is how we have always reaffirmed our relationship. Just a few tosses suffice to soothe us both. Now comes breakfast with the morning paper. I am craving a sandwich like the one I made for Miriam's lunch so I go ahead and make one for myself, contemplating the fact that what I am really eating is a soy sandwich. Those vegan 'deli slices' taste great as long as you don't think about the fact that you are really eating a slab of soy. But I am happy to have them. It's not so easy being vegan here. The food coops and other natural food outlets I had come to take for granted in the city simply do not exist.

The local paper is usually a source of grim amusement. Today, however, it is just grim. Buchanan is coming to speak in a nearby town; Ralph Reed was here just last week. And then there's the Middle East. As soon as this round of fighting broke out, I knew that it would be more than just another skirmish. I take no satisfaction in being right.

08:20 - 08:30 AM

Jot down notes of day so far.

08:30 - 09:20 AM

Attend to my personal e-mail. Try hard not to get annoyed with Reuven, who wants to lay on the keyboard and who will not be dissuaded by gentle persuasion. I get a lot of e-mail. On purpose. I know it is fashionable to complain about too much e-mail but here in rural America, it is a lifeline. For one, I conduct most of my business via e-mail, getting assignments from clients and editors and then sending the completed jobs as attachments. I also have signed up for a great number of individualized news and press release services. Today is a mixed e-mail news day. I read some good news about non-genetically modified maize crops but then read some bad news about the ethnic nationalism of Kostunica, who was supposed to be such a wonderful replacement for Milosovic. I worry. I let the dogs in.

09:20- 10:25AM

I hurry up and pay some bills before the mail carrier comes. I take a nice hot shower with peppermint soap, which takes the edge off the chill in the house. I check to make sure that Dolly and Cynthia are okay and briefly greet the other birds.

10:25 - 11:50 AM

Time now to check the e-mail for our editing business. There's a note from a regular client asking us to please rush and edit a report for her. (English is not her first language, so she sometimes has us edit important reports that she will turn in at work.) I am happy to oblige but it turns out that the 'document' she attached is a Windoze .exe file rather than a .doc file. This is not the first time this has happened with this client. I call her and she promises to get a friend to help her send the document the right way. While waiting, I go looking (online) for information about an international women's march that Miriam read about in the latest *Off Our Backs*. The march is the day after tomorrow. I hurry up and put a notice about it on the web site for our chicken sanctuary and then start thinking about what to put on a sign that would explain, in ten words or less, the connections between women's liberation and hen liberation. Meanwhile, I check the e-mail for the sanctuary. Often we get very interesting inquiries but today there is nothing very interesting.

11:50 AM - 01:15 PM

I still haven't received the document from the editing client so I turn my attention to a contract writing job. In addition to the editing and freelance journalism, I also write reports for a company in New York. Today, the company's client needs me to visit several health care web sites and write up reports on them. Easy! I complete the job and send it off then check my personal e-mail again. I also jot down more notes about the day so far.

01:15 - 02:20 PM

I go to the mailbox with anticipation but return with disappointment. Living here, the daily mail is a big event. We make sure that we get a lot of interesting mail. But today there are no packages, no personal letters, no surprise donations to the sanctuary, not even any good magazines, just junk mail and bills. On the way back from the mailbox, I visit with the chickens.

Back inside, I think about lunch then dance with the dogs. Still wanting lunch, I look vaguely into the refrigerator but find nothing of interest. At loose ends, I pick up a harmonica and start what we call a "concert," since both Dandelion and Gretchen join in whenever I play. Bored of that, I give them a treat and decide that I really must eat. I grab a box of cornbread mix (cornbread mix?!? whatever possessed me to buy that when making cornbread from scratch is so easy?), follow the directions, and toss the resulting glop into muffin tins and then into the oven. I read magazine articles printed out from the internet while waiting for it to bake.

When the corn muffins are ready, I eat them while brooding about pastoralism and its connections to patriarchy. I try to convince myself that eating anything freshly baked is a delight but, truly, these muffins from a mix are wretched. I put on a big pot of eggs to boil for the chickens and return to the computer.

02:20 - 02:50 PM

The printer is acting up. I've been avoiding admitting that there is a problem but now I have to fix it. I start trouble shooting and think that I may have found the problem when I smell something funny. Oh no! I turned on the wrong burner. Again! One more scorched burner cover for Miriam to mourn.

Now Zami and Gretchen want to go out. I let them out the back door then go back to the computer to retry my print job. I am trying to print out some background information for an article that I want to pitch to a magazine. The first page prints okay but then the problem happens again. The client from this morning calls to say she has resent the document. I go into the printer again, finally finding a tiny piece of paper that was causing the problem. The cause of the paper is Sheena the cat, who loves to tear paper into tiny pieces with her sharp little teeth. Any unguarded paper in the house ends up with little bite marks. Now we will have to remember to guard the printer paper too.

02:50 - 03:25 PM

I go online to get the document for the editing job, morbidly reflecting on my recurring sinus infection as I wait for the evil Internet Explorer to initialize. (I am a MacAddict. IE is my only concession to Microsoft and only because it is free.) I get the document and sign off. I turn off the eggs, run some cold water over them, and then leave them to cool. I hurry up and edit the document and send it back to the client.

03:25 - 04:25 PM

I let Zami and Gretchen back in and then take fresh water to the chickens. Now it is time for their afternoon fruit and egg treat. While cutting up apples and tearing up eggs, I think about a talk that I am going to have to give next month in California. I need to figure out how to explain to gay men and lesbians why they should care about animal liberation. It's not so hard with lesbian feminists, since they recognize homophobia as a weapon of sexism and the connections between sexism and and animal abuse are pretty well established. But gay men and non-feminist lesbians (my mind reels at the thought)... I test out a few ideas in my head but am not satisfied. I take the treats out to the chickens and also fill up their regular food containers. I visit with the hens and note that my beloved Iris seems to be recovering nicely from the bronchitis. Visiting with the roosters, I notice that Viktor Frankl — our first chicken and, hence, the real founder of the sanctuary — is resting, which is unlike him at this time of day. Also little Lucky (the mama's boy of the rooster yard) is rasping. Again I am glad that I decided to put them all on the antibiotics. Up till now, I have relied upon natural means of health promotion but this clearly is a time when medications are warranted. I am not going to let myself worry about Viktor. But I do worry.

04:25 - 05:45 PM

I rest on the porch for a few minutes, thinking of nothing, then bestir myself to clean the coop. That involves using the pitchfork and wheelbarrow to cart out the soiled straw, scraping the floors and perches with a sharpened hoe, spraying water laced with essential oils to keep down flies and kill germs, and then putting in fresh straw. In the middle of all this, Miriam arrives home from work. She is crying with frustration and anger. She teaches in a different but still very rural school district. She loves the kids (and, if I may brag, she is an excellent teacher) but many of her coworkers are bigoted jerks. The racism among the white teachers is only barely suppressed and the homophobia among almost all of the teachers is overt and unabashed. In addition, everyone is so very Christian that they seem not to even understand that other religions exist. Forget about them understanding paganism... they seem not to even understand that there might be Muslims or Jews among their students or coworkers. After Miriam finishes telling me about the latest outrages, she goes inside and I hurry up and finish cleaning the coop. I note that little Cynthia now follows me, apparently using her sense of hearing. That's a good skill for her to have if only we can find a hen to be her special friend. I go inside and let Gretchen and Dandelion out.

05:45 - 06-40 PM

I plop down on the hammock in Miriam's work room (we share a bedroom but each have our own work rooms), talking with Miriam while Sheena stalks and then sits on my lap. [I'm not sharing the intimate details of our conversations because she's not the one who agreed to catalog her day.] I start sorting the socks that remain from when I did laundry earlier in the week. My back starts to hurt. I let Gretchen and Dandelion in and then sort more socks.

06:40 - 06:45 PM

Miriam points out that sunset is upon us, which I had neglected to notice due to my obsessive concern with properly matching the white socks. I rush outside to close up the chickens. This entails carrying Dolly and Cynthia back in, standing around while the last few stragglers (generally, Simone and Lucky) enjoy the evening for a few moments before retiring, and then closing each of the three doors to the coop. Of course, I always say "good night" to everyone. Tonight, I also suggest that they "cuddle up" because it's going to be a cool night. Then I have to go looking for any eggs laid outside. A few of the hens use a hollowed out tree trunk as a nest but the number of eggs there has been declining. That might be because it's getting cooler (hens naturally stop laying for the winter) but might also be because a new and improved hiding place has been found. I speculate where that hiding place may be. I suspect that Simone and maybe Railroad have been jumping the fence to lay their eggs in or around the front yard but I can't catch them at it or find the hiding place. I give up and go in. Per usual, all the dogs then rush out to see what all the commotion was about (chickens are pretty noisy when they are settling in for the night).

06:45 - 07:15 PM

I finish sorting the socks, joke around with Miriam, and then lounge on the couch deciding what to do next.

07:15 - 08:45 PM

The dogs come in and we go out. We get in the pickup with Miriam driving. The moon is huge. We love and adore the moon. We drive along in silence then turn on 91.3 to listen to Fresh Air. Miriam is annoyed, per usual, by Terry Gross. She wonders, per usual, why Terry Gross chooses to interview so many more men than women. We change stations. We stop for beer at my favorite roadside spot. The owners have been totally screwed by the Fruitland town council at the behest of the new Walmart. So, I buy my beer from them whenever I can. But, today we need dog food too, which means Walmart. I wait in the truck suddenly so sleepy that I must lay down on the extremely uncomfortable seat. I drift off and then feel very vulnerable when Miriam wakes me up. We drive to the local Chinese/Japanese (yes, both) restaurant for take-out vegetarian sushi. Again I wait in the truck and again I am so sleepy that I have to lay down. When Miriam gets back, I jump up like sleeping is a crime or maybe the crime would be to make her wait even a moment to get in. Probably I am just very hungry and sleepy, the combination of which tends to make me feel like a very vulnerable child. Miriam drives us home.

08:45 - 09:00 PM

We lug everything in and put away away the purchases while also setting up the table for dinner and feeding the dogs. Miriam remarks that she likes it how we automatically cooperate on such daily tasks. It is nice.

09:00 - 09:45 PM

We eat and talk. I worry about all of the things I have left undone.

09:45 - 09:55 PM

I have a smoke and jot down notes. [I've been smoking all along, just not noting it.] While I'm at it, I check my e-mail and check the latest news from Palestine. I really am very worried about this war.

09:55 - 11:30

Miriam and I play scrabble. Because I concentrate so fiercely, I don't think of anything else. That is relaxing for me. I win but, for the first time in my life, am truly uncomfortable with that. I keep going over my math just in case I can find some more points for Miriam. Instead, I find that I made a mistake in her favor. I try to hide that from her but she figures it out anyway. We laugh and have a pretty good time. We pack up the game and go to bed.

23

The Power of Grassroots Movements

The Grassroots Animal Rights Conference, or GARC, of 2005 convened for a weekend in April in New York City, bringing together grassroots animal advocates of every persuasion, from the most moderate to the most radical, working to end any kind of animal exploitation. Intended to be an antidote to the annual animal rights conferences that, then as now, were dominated by national organizations dedicated to an ever more narrow range of aims and tactics, GARC aimed to be a true conference, where local activists from all over the country working on a wide array of problems using a wide array of tactics shared ideas and information with each other. I felt proud to be invited to give one of the opening speeches. Here it is.

The Power of Grassroots Movements

Power

Power is the capacity to do things.

Power is neutral, like electricity.

Malcolm X thought that power deployed in service of freedom is naturally stronger than power deployed in the service of repression.

I agree. Power spent in the service of repression is like fossil fuel — unsustainable and destructive — while power spent in the service of liberation is like photosynthesis — renewable and creative.

Most movements focus on how to get and use power but our task is more nuanced because, while we have much less power than the institutions and cultural practices we oppose, we already have too much power over those for whom we purport to act.

Thus we must ask both how to get power and how to give it back. We also are obligated to think deeply about how best to deploy the power that we have and obtain.

People acting on their own behalf have the right to let foolishness or vanity or knee-jerk preferences for this or that tactic impede their own progress toward freedom but we have no such right in relation to the animals. We must constantly, rigorously, and unflinchingly seek the truth about the efficacy — or lack thereof — of our efforts so far. And we must have the courage and the capacity to make changes as needed.

We do have power already and as we work together we are sure to get more. That means that we are not meeting in a vacuum here. The decisions that we make about what to do for the animals will have real impact on the physical lives of actual animals.

We must never forget that. As we argue for this or that analysis or action, we must always be asking ourselves, "Is this really true? How do I know? What if I'm wrong?"

I'm reminded of the phrase "more power than we want," which was phrased by men in the anti-rape movement. That phrase often comes into my head when I'm making decisions at the sanctuary. Sometimes, I have to make a decision that could have life-or-death consequences for a bird. That makes me feel uncomfortable — and it should.

You should feel uneasy too. Your decisions about targets and tactics must be just as carefully considered as my decisions about which medication to give a sick bird. In both cases, somebody other than the decision-maker will pay the price in the event of a poor choice.

Grassroots

Five years ago, only a few weeks after accidentally landing in an epicenter of poultry production, my partner and I found chicken in a ditch. Now, five years later, 200 or so birds call our place home.

Every morning at sunrise one or both of us is outside, opening the coops and doing the morning chores. Every evening at sunset one or both of us is outside, doing the evening chores and making sure the ducks and chickens are closed up safely for the night. Every day at midday — whether it's raining or snowing, whether we're slogging through the mud on a cold grey day or sweating and squinting in the hot summer sun — we're out there checking on the chickens. Like so many others who run small sanctuaries, we draw no salary, live at edge of poverty, and often have to cover sanctuary costs out of our own pockets. When I get back home after this conference, I'll actually be sowing grass seed in some of the foraging yards. So, you might think, "it doesn't get any more grassroots than that!"

But you would be wrong. We are not the grassroots. You are not the grassroots.

The animals struggling for their own freedom — the free elephants trampling genetically modified crops in South Asia; the captive elephants who turn on their trainers; the monkeys in India who recently jeered US Secretary of Defense Donald Rumsfeld so loudly that they interfered with his press conference; the free cats and dogs who establish colonies not unlike those of escaped slaves; the baboons who are biting back in South Africa; the sharks who bite back along the shores of the USA; all of the animals who, like Nana, use their brains and their brawn in the service of freedom — they are the grassroots animal liberation movement. We are just their allies.

And then there are the actual grass roots, the so-called weeds growing where they don't belong, the plants who have evolved resistance to our most poisonous pesticides. They, rather than EarthFirst! or the Earth Liberation Front, are the grassroots environmental movement. We are just their allies.

We must take responsibility for ending human exploitation of the earth and other animals, just as men must actively support women in the struggle against sexism and white people must work hard to divest ourselves of the illegitimate power and privilege that come with being white. Of course, feminists would never tolerate men trying to run the movement against sexism. And, could you imagine what would have happened if, when I was doing anti-racist work, I had run around saying "I am the voice of the Black man"!?

There are no such natural checks on self-importance in the animal liberation movement. We have people running around claiming to be "the voice of the voiceless" as if animals don't have voices of their own. That heroic attitude makes it easy to assume that you know what's best for the animals without stopping to wonder what they might say if you asked them and were able to understand their answers.

That said, of course the organizations represented at this conference are grassroots organizations in structure, as distinguished from the big national groups. Grassroots groups have great potential, as evidenced by the success of various anti-colonial movements that actually succeeded in overthrowing illegitimate governments.

Grassroots groups may be less prone to the kinds of hierarchy and hubris that beset big organizations. But don't think that grassroots equals good. There are grassroots hate groups and grassroots campaigns to roll back civil rights initiatives. The power of popular opinion is formidable and, like any electrical current, can be used for good or ill

So, again, we end up having to think about what to do with power. And again we must remember that we are making decisions for beings who ought to be free to determine their own destinies. I suggest that, instead of considering ourselves "the voice of the voiceless," we think harder about how to listen to the animals for whom we purport to speak.

That may require us to make some changes.

Movement

Which brings us to movements: A movement is a process, not a thing. In other words, movements are actions not objects.

That means that, if we want an effective movement, we all have to be willing to change.

We have to see our efforts as an ongoing experiment in effective activism. We have to use trial-and-error, understanding that we might be in error and being willing to change our ways if that proves to be true. We cannot let our egos or ideologies keep us from seeing what we need to see and doing what we need to do.

Finally, let me draw your attention to the fact that motion always requires emotion. That means that all of our rationality must flow from and feed into our empathy.

We must have empathy for animals and for ourselves, because we're animals too. Our own animal selves have been squelched in the process of socialization into dominance over non-human animals. Part of the process of freeing the animals thus must be freeing ourselves to be just one animal among many. Because that's what we are.

Our reward for doing that hard work will be an end to the estrangement from nature and other animals that leaves us all feeling so lonely.

Thanks for listening to me this evening. As you move through this exciting weekend, I hope you will think about power, grassroots, and movement. Most importantly, I hope you will always remember that we are not alone.

24

Honk for Peace

For some years during my decade-long sojourn on the Eastern Shore of Maryland, I set myself the task of using holidays to write, revise, and submit what I called "one-day essays." Thus, I wrote this in a burst immediately following the events it describes, which occurred on Christmas Day of 2005. It was published as "What's So Patriotic About Peace" by the now-defunct *Freezerbox Magazine* in January of 2006 and reprinted, in whole or part, in the newsletters of various antiwar organizations over the next few years.

Honk for Peace

Grey rain hangs in the sky. Translucent drops splash on the blacktop, sluicing like a summer thunderstorm on this Christmas Day. I gaze with glazed eyes at the glassy surface of the water until the blare of a car horn blasts me back into my body. Heart pumping, I wave weakly. I'm cold and wet.

Six of us stand in a line with picket signs. One of the signs says HONK FOR PEACE.

The Peace Alliance of the Lower Shore (PALS) has moved its weekly vigil to noon in hopes of catching churchgoers after Christmas mass. Not being Christian, I don't have anything better to do, so I drag myself out of my warm house and along miles of rural roadways to stand at an intersection of the small city that calls itself "the crossroads of the Delmarva."

"Thought you might need some help today," I say after selecting a sign that says MOTHERS MOURN ON BOTH SIDES.

"Yes," says Jackie Fritch in her jolly red sweatsuit, juggling an American flag along with her sign, "we do."

Not sure where all of this is happening? Start at Washington, DC. Drive east until you hit the Chesapeake Bay. Cross the bay. Drive south to Salisbury. If you come on Sunday, you'll see the PALS standing in line with their signs, urging you to HONK FOR PEACE.

The PALS are Unitarians, mostly. They believe, as the sign carried by the woman in the bright blue rain boots says, that PEACE IS PATRIOTIC. I disagree. I'm pretty sure that governments always carry guns.

Jackie's sign says SUPPORT THE TROOPS and urges us to BRING THEM HOME. I don't support the troops. I want the US out of Iraq but I'm not so eager to see the soldiers return. I wonder what the torturers of Abu Ghraib and the snipers of Fallujah will think they have the right to do when they get home. Shoot down anybody who lives in a house they would like to occupy? Waterboard their wives?

I keep such thoughts to myself. I resist the urge to make my own sign. The PALS would not approve of any of the wry, snide things I'd like to say on this Christmas Day.

But these PALS are my tribe, I realize. As the existentialist philosophers say, you are what you do. And here we are together. We are the ones who stand in the rain, asking people to HONK FOR PEACE.

Some people do honk, waving and grinning in their Santa caps as gaily wrapped presents bounce on their back seats. Others drive by quickly, eyes straight ahead, gripping their steering wheels tightly. Either way, I wonder what they think of our bedraggled line of rain-drenched signs.

Here, where even the children instinctively sneer at anything different or new, symbolic actions like vigils and picket lines still have the shock value that big-city protest marches lost long ago. Like us or not, the people driving by can't not notice us.

My own mind wanders then gets stuck. At a silent vigil, there's nothing to do but brood. Luckily, I'm good at that. Three years ago, vigil musings led to an essay—"Who Would Jesus Kill?"—that ended up in publications ranging from a major Pakistani newspaper to a little Hawaiian newsletter.

Three years ago?!? How long has this vigil been going on? How long has this war been going on? Was there ever a time when I wasn't standing on some street corner with clean needles, vegetarian literature, or a picket sign? What time is it? Why do I always forget gloves? When will we be allowed to go home?

Before I start to feel sorry for myself, I remember: My home hasn't been bombed. My t-shirt, flannel shirt, and sweater are torn but warm. My cheap vegan shoes (hope they weren't made in a sweatshop) keep out the rain. There's food at home and I'm not in a cage.

Driving home, I see 30 wild turkeys hiding from hunters amidst hundreds of geese. Startled by my pick-up truck, the gawky yet graceful black turkeys flutter and move more deeply between the geese.

The geese, they honk for peace.

25

Truth Against Trash

From 2005 to 2007, I contributed a regular opinion column to *Satya* magazine. As with my previous column, the intent was to inspire readers interested in one thing to notice conjunctions with other things. In the previous column, I prompted readers of an LGBT newspaper to pay closer attention to harms caused by racism, sexism, and capitalism. Now, writing for a vegan magazine, I hoped to prompt readers to simultaneously deepen their own anti-speciesism and attend more closely to social and environmental injustices.

Again, I found the pressure of a regular deadline to be both bracing and taxing. Always needing fresh copy, I fleshed out ideas that might have remained unformed. On the other hand, I was always behind. Sometimes, deadline + word limits led to half-baked ideas in print. Still, there's something to be said for getting ideas out there for other people to play with.

Learning to live with imperfection is one of the themes of the essay from that series that I have chosen to reproduce here. I wrote this piece under deadline pressure while coping with a devastating personal trauma in 2006. There are many aspects of it that I would change today. The wording is at times over-heated, and some sections are overly simplistic. Still, I feel proud of producing a piece so forgiving while coping with having been deeply harmed. And so I will forgive myself for its many flaws.

Truth Against Trash

Every day I ask myself *why?*

I live on a dead-end rural road. Each week more litter materializes on the roadside. Fast-food bags and wrappers appear and disappear, disintegrating with every rain. Waxy cups linger longer among the wild weeds. Soda bottles and beer cans move in to stay, permanently defacing the landscape.

This road is not a thoroughfare. Rush hour for us is three cars and a school bus within 30 minutes. The friendly UPS guy certainly isn't the one dropping beer bottles into our drainage ditches. It's not the mail carrier or the school bus driver or the farm supply truckers either. It's got to be the people who live here.

Watching dog Dandelion snuffle a coffee cup or cat Dodici delicately step over sticky liquid, I struggle to imagine the impulse to toss trash out a car window anywhere, much less on your own street. Why would anybody want to do that? What does it feel like to do?

Could it feel like freedom to spit in the eye of the crying Indian from the Keep America Beautiful campaign? Does it feel deliciously wicked to defile Mother Nature? Or does it feel clean, like shedding something sinful, to get that garbage out of your car?

Or does it feel like nothing at all?

Disposable Bodies

Dandelion and Dodici themselves were discards. Dandy was dropped off at a shelter when she grew too big and boisterous for people who wanted a very different sort of dog. Dodici was left like litter in a carrier on the side of a highway.

We kill three or four million unwanted dogs and cats every year here in the U.S. Meanwhile, more than 200 million male chicks are trashed annually—often literally thrown into dumpsters where they suffocate or starve—by an egg industry that has no economic use for them.

Worldwide, about a million newborn babies are murdered each year by parents who have no economic use for females. According to Amnesty International, more than 60 million girls and women are "missing" from the world right now thanks to sex-selective abortion and female infanticide.

Also among the missing are the girls and women who disappear into the global sex trade every day. Here in the U.S., runaway children fleeing abuse and "throwaway" teens who have been abandoned or told to leave home are the 'fresh blood' upon which the prostitution and pornography industries depend.

Here and elsewhere, rape and murder are occupational hazards for workers in these flesh trades. Both perpetrators and police tend to consider sex workers to be "unrapeable"—as if their bodies are already so polluted that they cannot be defiled. Once sold, according to this logic, the body no longer truly belongs to the prostitute. She's forever lost the right to say "no."

Mass murders of women who were (or were mistakenly believed to be) sex workers in British Columbia, Guatemala and Mexico have made the news in recent years. But it's the everyday attrition everywhere that leads some experts to believe that murder is the top cause of death among prostitutes. Facile post-feminist talk about women empowering themselves through erotic dancing at high-class clubs aside, the fact is that most prostitutes have been raped at least once and everybody in the street sex trade knows at least one women who's gone missing.

The dangers are even greater for the two million women and children trafficked into servitude in brothels every year. These women and children endure unspeakable physical and psychic anguish that often ends only with death. Like egg factory owners tossing "spent" hens into wood chippers, the gangs that run the brothels in which women and children are enslaved do not hesitate to kill any captive whose upkeep is no longer profitable. Those who aren't killed may die anyway due to untreated HIV or other sexually transmitted diseases.

This is happening right now. Governments routinely launch rescue missions for even a handful of hostages. Why isn't anybody rushing to rescue these children and women? Why haven't we who shun sweatshop products also worked to shut down the travel agencies that ferry our fellow citizens to sex tourism destinations? Why haven't we who free hens from battery cages also staged open rescue actions to expose the enslavement of women in brothels in our own backyards? Can it be that we too see captive sex workers as unsalvageable?

From the Dump to the Salvage Yard

Worldwide, 250 million children live on the streets, and 115 million children never have stepped inside a classroom. A third of all children in Africa live with hunger every day.

From the ranks of such cast-off, orphaned and impoverished children come hundreds of thousands of child soldiers in dozens of countries. Captured, sold or recruited into rag-tag armies, boys and girls are forced to commit horrific acts that leave them estranged from their families and convinced of their own venality. They often become the most ruthless killers of all, deployed to commit atrocities when they are not used as cannon fodder in wars of attrition.

The same dynamics twist the psyches of abused children everywhere. Abusers commonly force or trick children into hurting others, thereby convincing them that the badness is within themselves.

They may grow up believing themselves to be poisonous or unworthy of love. They may consequently treat themselves or others like trash.

We commonly speak of the "stolen innocence" of abused or exploited children. Innocent means blameless. What might a child who has lost his or her innocence be? Guilty?

When we say that children have lost their innocence, aren't we relegating them to the realm of trash, treating them like spoiled produce good only for the compost heap? Aren't we using the same logic that leads us to kill rather than rehabilitate the dogs and roosters who have been tricked and twisted by fans of animal fighting?

Knowing things can change you. Abused and exploited children are marked by the things that have been done to them, the things they have done, and what this has taught them about people and the world.

Nonetheless they retain their animal innocence. Habits of belief and behavior developed defensively can be changed through a long hard process of recycling undertaken in an atmosphere of safety and empathy. The first step is seeing the salvageable goodness underneath the debris of anger and fear.

The Tao of Trash

I used to live across the street from a crack house on a block where the Neighborhood Watch was losing the war on drugs. There, the drifting plastic bags and candy wrappers seemed a natural part of the cityscape. I grew organic vegetables in the backyard and unsuccessfully sought to protect the abused children next door.

Then, as now, my house-proud neighbors thought I was crazy or lazy for not mowing my lawn.

The only white person on the block, I was acutely aware that the words "white trash" are often associated with weedy yards like mine. More than once, I allowed myself to be shamed into paying someone to waste fossil fuel trashing perfectly good plants.

Like many people, I struggle with shame. A throwaway teen myself, I had been luckier than most but had become entangled for a time in sex work, in the course of which I was sexually assaulted. Years later, as the weeds were rising and the neighbors were once again casting reproachful glances at me in my garden, I sought solace in chapter 13 of the *Tao Te Ching*, which talks about accepting disgrace willingly.

Crouching amidst the denigrated plantain and pokeweed, my mind drifted to the rest of that chapter, which talks about loving the world as your self so that you can be trusted to care for all things. Suddenly, I saw the flip side of the golden rule: as long as I exempted aspects of myself from compassion, I could not be trusted. Always, there would be the question: Who else is exempt? Always, there would be the risk of dumping the despised aspects of myself onto somebody else.

I now teach speech at a historically Black university. One day I met a student[1] in the library to talk about why he was missing class and not doing his work. He explained without self pity that he came from a dangerous neighborhood in a dangerous city with dangerous relatives who expected him to protect them from disrespect. Sometimes he had to go home to take care of things. His hands were scarred from fighting.

As we spoke, a dam broke and emotions rushed in. "I just want to know," he said, stretching out those marred hands as tears streamed down his contorted face "if it's too late for me to be forgiven for what I've done?" He was 19 years old.

Later, he told the class about an incident of betrayal and life-threatening injury. His classmates listened with evident empathy. When asked at the end of the term, "What's the most important thing you learned in this class?" he said that hearing his female classmates talk about rape and homophobia awakened him to the struggles faced by Black women. Having experienced empathy, he was eager to extend it.

---

1. When asked after he was no longer my student, this young man readily gave me permission to share his story.

Refusing to be Refuse

We're all tainted by the things that have been done to us and the things that we've done. Our bodies are contaminated by pollutants that poison our bloodstreams and corrupt our DNA. Our minds are full of received ideas and our hearts are clogged with accumulated hurt. We spew waste into the waters and shoot junk into space.

It all goes back to treating the earth like dirt and animals (including ourselves) as if they were inert. It stops when we see the world as a quivering living thing and realize that we are a part of—not apart from—the breathing biosphere that sustains us all.

It's time to go dumpster diving within ourselves. It's time to refuse to be garbage, to find new uses for old feelings and recycle our energy into effective activism.

We've got to see and salvage the animal innocence in ourselves and each other. If former child soldiers and sex slaves can do it—and they do—we can too.

There's no time to lose. Every year, more species of plants and animals end up in the dustbin of history. Every day, more children are thrown away. What will you pick up off the roadside today?

26

Gays at War

I wrote this in the midst of a trip down memory lane that reminded me of the conversation that begins this piece. As is often the case with these brief pieces, I was supposed to be writing something else but had to get this out of my system first. It was published on *Znet*, the website affiliated with *Z Magazine*, in July of 2006. *Adele* and *Trey* are pseudonyms for real people.

Gays at War

In the summer of 1979, I was enraptured by the sunny smile of an erotic dancer called Adele. I never saw her at work, only around the neighborhood and at the local lesbian bar, where she and I routinely danced ourselves into a mutual trance, spinning and sweating hip to hip, ignoring the hoots and hollers of the old-school butches who just didn't understand girls like us. When the songs stopped, we'd scoop up the change that they threw at us and buy ourselves a drink.

Adele had a surly girlfriend who didn't like to dance. I had an older and ostensibly heterosexual lover who couldn't afford to be seen with me in public. Wednesday nights left us both at loose ends on cheap drink night at the bar, where some kind of alchemical reaction conjured up a protective bubble between us and the rest of the world, wherein we were safe until the arrival of her girlfriend or the too-bright lights of "last call for alcohol."

To understand the import of what I'm about to impart, you need to understand this: Adele's smile taught me the meaning of "weak in the knees." I loved her with a fierce tenderness that still makes the base of my throat ache. But when her girlfriend Trey stopped by my apartment to say she was going away to join the army, I spent the next several hours trying to talk her out of it.

No matter how much I wished she would go away, I couldn't bring myself not to say the things I thought Trey needed to hear about what she was planning to do. Like many young Black women who don't conform to either European or African American notions of femininity, Trey saw the army as both a refuge and a way out. She couldn't imagine anyplace else where she could both make money and be herself. The costs—conformity, possible combat, and certain collusion with a government she hated —seemed small in comparison to the freedom it felt like subordination would buy.

In the end, nothing I said made a difference and Trey sold her youth to the US army. I never did work up the nerve to tell Adele how I felt, even when she came to me for protection from another surly girlfriend. Years later, I learned that she had had a crush on me too but by then it was too late.

But that's another story and there's no time for such silliness these days. The movement for gay liberation long ago stopped being about freedom for superfluous love and crushes on all the wrong people. Now we want the right to get married and join the army.

We had a big victory recently, when the ban on homosexual soldiers was set aside to allow gay and lesbian reservists to go to Iraq. The Center for the Study of Sexual Minorities in the Military uncovered a regulation holding discharges for homosexual conduct in abeyance when a unit is scheduled to be deployed. In such cases, the homosexual soldier is to enter active duty along with the rest of the unit.

Now that we know that US soldiers routinely use homophobia to humiliate prisoners of war, aren't we proud that gay men and lesbians are part of it all? Of course, forcing hooded and naked Arab men to simulate oral and anal sex is just one highlight in the great gay Iraqi adventure. During the invasion, gay and lesbian soldiers were right there with the rest of the troops, attacking a disarmed country without UN sanction and despite the desperate pleas for peace by the majority of people in the world. Doing their part by helping to drop cluster bombs on children, terrorize elderly civilians into abject submission, and occupy a nation under the guise of liberation, the unasked and untold soldiers of the rainbow brigade proved once and for all that the gay men and lesbians of the USA pose no threat whatsoever to the patterns of power and privilege that shape the domestic and global socioeconomic order.

Why then, I wonder, do so many Americans feel so profoundly threatened by the idea of gay marriage? Focus on the Family president James Dobson says that "civilization will go down" if efforts to ban same-sex marriage fail. He means it. Unlike George W. Bush and other slick politicians who don't really care about the issue but are happy to manipulate it, Dobson and his ilk really do fear that their world will come crashing down if girls are allowed to say "I do" to each other. Thus RenewAmerica columnist Fred Hutchinson writes that "The defense of marriage is on the front line of the war to defend civilization."

My question for him is: Will gay soldiers be allowed to fight in that war? My question to all of the would-be gay soldiers and brides is: What are you thinking?

Let's get one thing perfectly straight (yes, straight): Heterosexual marriage really is a cornerstone of Western civilization. Historically and continually, the patriarchal power that constructs the governments that armies defend is obtained, in part, by marriage.

You don't need to read complicated feminist histories to see that men have and continue to be aided and comforted by the labor and property brought to them by the marriage ceremony. Think of the ceremony itself, in which the echoes of the days when women were chattel still reverberate. The original owner (aka the father of the bride) transfers his property to the new owner (aka the husband of the wife). Think about the word "groom," which is used for both tamers of horses and takers of wives. Understand why the words "bride" and "bridle" are so similar.

Did you know that, in many countries, married women still may not work, travel, or get medical care without the permission of their husbands? Even married women in modern democracies are less free than they believe. There are still plenty of places in the world where marital rape is not a crime and husbands thus enjoy the right to enter their wives at any time, with or without consent. Cross the border into one of those places and you are your husband's sexual slave. Maybe you're right in thinking tha—even though one in seven married women is raped by her husband—your man wouldn't ever assert his legal right to rape you while visiting one of those places. But he could. So, I have to ask heterosexual women who are or hope to be married the same question I asked queer would-be soldiers and brides: What are you thinking?

Male-headed nuclear families are, indeed, the building blocks of industrial countries with atom bombs. It's only when we understand the role of marriage in male rule that certain seeming absurdities start to make sense. Suddenly, we can see why conservatives will use any means necessary—including the punitive welfare reform measures that have hurt millions of children—to coerce teen mothers and impoverished women to marry men but cannot abide the idea that women might marry each other. We can see why the Christian right is so keen to convince African American mothers that their children need a father in the home—even though the extended family structures and communal child care practices common in many African cultures offers children many more adult role models and sources of support than the European marriage-based family—but so determined to keep African American gay men from marrying each other.

It's not monogamy or stability or child-friendly families they seek. A personal patriarch for every woman is what they want and need to ensure the continuation of male rule in this country. And—make no mistake—we do have male rule in this country. Look at the Senate or the list of state Governors if you have any doubts about that.

If Dobson and Hutchinson were right, I'd be all for gay marriage. This so-called civilization is sick and anything that might bring it down would be okay by me. But I fear that, if achieved, gay marriage would be, like gay soldiers in the military, a boon to the powers that be. Like those futile protest marches that reinforce the myth that we live in a democracy but do not in any way impede the war machine, same-sex marriage would prop up a dangerous institution by making it look less oppressive than it is.

But—wait—maybe I've missed something. Maybe we're smarter than that. Maybe the gays in the military movement has been a sham all along. Maybe all the patriotic fervor has been a ruse to trick them into giving us the guns so that we can melt them down in a frenzy of nonviolent noncompliance, one aim of which would be getting the government entirely out of the business of legitimizing families. That would be a truly queer coup!

27

The Turtle Talk

This speech was delivered at the "Paths to Animal Liberation" plenary session at the National Animal Rights Conference in Arlington, Virginia on Friday, 11 August 2006. Earlier that year, the SHAC 7[1] had been indicted for conspiracy to violate the Animal Enterprise Terrorism Act (AETA), which made it a federal offense to interfere with the profits of any animal exploiting industry. While none of the defendants had been charged with engaging in violence or property damage themselves, these indictments stirred up debate within the movement concerning tactics such as liberating animals or protesting outside the homes of vivisectors.

As I planned this talk, I recall being appalled both by the indictments for what ought to have been recognized as free expression protected by the First Amendment *and* by the lack of solidarity shown by some movement leaders who rushed to distance themselves from activists who were facing the terrifying prospect of years in prison. So, in addition to wanting to weigh in on the tactical controversies upon which I had been invited to opine, I also wanted to both express my own solidarity and encourage others to develop their own feelings of kinship with our endangered comrades, all of whom did end up having to serve prison terms for their sincere efforts to end the torture of more vulnerable others.

While many of the points in this talk are covered elsewhere in this volume, I include it because so many people engaged in many different forms of activism have told me that it was meaningful to them—for some, so much so that they hung onto the photograph that I gave out as part of the talk for many

1. The SHAC 7 included my beloved friends Lauren Gazzola, Josh Harper, Kevin KJonaas, and Andy Stepanian as well as Jake Conroy, Darius Fulmer, and the organization Stop Huntington Animal Cruelty itself.

years—and so I think it might serve as an example of how to talk about "radical" ideas in commonsense terms that everybody can understand.

The Turtle Talk

This photograph was taken in 1971 in Baltimore City. The turtle was called Timothy. The little girl was called Patti-Lee. She grew up to be me.

One summer day not unlike today, little Patti-Lee was standing in front of that row-house with one foot on the sidewalk and one foot on the postage-stamp sized front yard, shifting from leg to leg and saying "our property, not our property, our property, not our property, our property, not our property."

She was troubled. She was trying to figure it out. But no matter how hard she thought, she couldn't make it come out fair.

She knew that her grandparents had bought the house from somebody who had bought the house from somebody who bought the house from somebody going back to when it was built. But how did that little bit of land come to belong to one person rather than another in the first place?

She thought back to what she learned in school about the Pilgrims and the Indians. She imagined a Pilgrim with his musket building a fence and threatening to shoot anybody who trespassed onto what had become his "property."

It didn't seem right that the trees and the squirrels who used to belong to themselves belonged to him just because he had a gun. And if that wasn't right, she wondered, how could it be right for the people who bought the land from the people who bought the land from the people who brought the land from him to say "that's my property?"

And so it came to be that, in those childish musings, little Patti-Lee happened upon a truth that many adults never get around to figuring out: Property is violence.

So it's apt that this grown up girl is here to convince you that breaking locks, tearing down cages, disabling bulldozers, and other ways of interfering with property are *anti-violent* activities. I also aim to convince you that demonstrating on public sidewalks is always okay, no matter what the defenders of the sanctity of the private property bounded by those sidewalks might say.

The division of the world into countries with borders policed by armies has been and continues to be a violent process that hurts both human and non-human animals.

The subdivision of the natural world into disconnected bits of private property hurts animals too.

Fences interrupt ecosystems, breaking up homes and families while blocking off resources like watering holes. Fences enclose animals, making them into captives and ultimately into bits and pieces of property to be bought and sold.

It's time to tear down the fences, freeing the animals and restoring their habitats to them.

Of course, violence is never okay since that is the root of all of our problems.

Violence is unjustified or excessively injurious use of force.

Many uses of force are not violent. How can you tell the difference? It's easy in context.

One day, Patti-Lee was standing at the top of a flight of stairs, facing an angry and out-of-control adult not unlike those we've seen in undercover videos from vivisection labs. All of a sudden, the screaming grownup gave her a short, sharp shove to the shoulders, sending her tumbling down the steps. That was violence.

But the exact same muscular action—a short, sharp shove to the shoulders—would have been justified and even heroic if she had been standing in the path of an onrushing truck.

I tell you these details from my life so you will know that I know what violence really is.

Take it from an animal who knows what it's like to be hit and hurt and hope, hope, hope for somebody to come to the rescue: Breaking locks isn't violence, tearing down cages isn't violence, tossing a monkeywrench into the works of a machine that kills animals isn't violence, carrying a hurt and terrified animal to safety isn't violence, and—certainly—using public sidewalks to denounce abuses that occur behind closed doors is not violence.

Look at the picture:

What if that little girl was trapped inside that row-house and being burned by a fire?

Wouldn't you break down the door to help her escape?

What if she saw that turtle being tortured in her neighbor's basement? Wouldn't she climb in the window to help him escape? Wouldn't she break that window if she had to? Wouldn't she match her little muscles against those of the torturer if that's what it took to make the violence stop?

What if the torture was happening in a vivisection lab?

What if that little girl learned that the homes of that turtle and his whole family were going to be bulldozed to make room for fancy houses for people who already have perfectly good places to live? If she could, wouldn't she put a little sugar in the gas tank of that bulldozer or maybe take a monkey-wrench to its engine? I think she would.

What if that little girl learned that her neighbor was torturing puppies at his job? Can't you just see her marching up and down the sidewalk with a picket sign? Of course she'd be very careful not to do anything that might scare the dogs, cats, or children living in surrounding houses. But wouldn't she want to tell the world: "This man hurts animals!" And wouldn't that be her right?

I made 300 copies of a picture of myself to give out tonight not because I'm so egotistical but because I want you to have something to hang onto to help you remember what I said tonight.

I want you to remember that there's a difference between force and violence and that the context often determines the difference.

I want you to remember that violence is never okay but force is sometimes necessary.

I want you to remember that property is violence and that we can—and must—interfere with that violence if we want a world in which little girls and turtles can be safe, happy, and free.

Not everybody has to do that work but we all have to be in solidarity with those who do.

So, if you ever find yourself getting ready to denounce or distance yourself from the brave and loving activists who risk their own freedom to free animals and protect their habitats, I want you to look at this picture and remember what I said tonight.

If you are one of those brave and loving activists, well, you know who you are and you know what you need to do. What I want you to know is that you're not alone. Wherever you go to take truly nonviolent direct action for earth and animals, that little girl goes with you.

28

Axioms

At the 2008 National Animal Rights Conference, I distributed a white paper entitled "Strategic Analysis of Animal Welfare Legislation: A Guide for the Perplexed."[1] The aim of that paper, the entirety of which is available online, was to intervene in the toxic *abolition vs welfare* war that was roiling the animal rights movement, demoralizing activists while diverting their energies into arguing about a false dualism. The paper goes into great detail concerning the situation of hens in egg factories, which is used as a case example of how to carefully assess proposed tactics and strategies. If those details interest you, you can find the whole paper online. Here, I have excerpted the section in which I sketched out basic principles from which to begin thinking more productively and care-fully when considering possible actions to be taken on behalf of animals. I share it here because, as *Zoopolis* coauthor Sue Donaldson recently has said, the idea that animal advocates ought to consult the animals for whom they purport to speak "was quite a radical proposition at the time, and indeed continues to be."[2]

---

1. You can find the full paper from which this section is excerpted at https://vinesanctuary.org/wp-content/uploads/perplexed.pdf

2. Donaldson, Sue. 2021. "Agency in Community." Presented at A Celebration of the Work of pattrice jones, Wesleyan University, November 5.

Strategic Analysis of Animal Welfare Legislation

A Guide for the Perplexed

Axioms

1. Animals[1] exist

Actual animals live in the material world and experience real pleasure or pain depending upon what happens to them. The actions or inactions of animal advocates help to determine what happens to actual animals. Thus, what we do (or don't do) *matters* to animals. We must assume that what *actually happens* matters more to animals than our theories, motives, or purposes. Thus, actions undertaken for the sake of animals ought to be guided by careful assessment of what is likely to actually happen rather than by inclination, theory, or habit.

2. Nothing happens in a vacuum

Nothing actually happens except in a particular context. Thus proposed actions for animals ought to be analyzed individually and in their relevant material contexts rather than condoned or condemned in the abstract. Thus, rather than condoning or condemning "direct action" or "welfare reforms" we ought to ask what the outcomes of a particular type of direct action or welfare reform would be likely to be at a particular place and time. Contextual analysis of proposed tactics may, in addition to providing a more valid method

1. People are animals. As I have argued elsewhere, full recognition of this fact mandates changes in the way we think about the project of "animal liberation." However, in order to avoid excess verbiage, I am using "animal" here to refer to nonhuman animals unless otherwise specified.

of assessment, reveal consequences and possibilities that otherwise might be missed.

3. Animals are the subjects of animal liberation

Every day, in a multitude of ways, animals resist not only captivity and subjugation by humans but also the intrusions of humans into their habitats. Thus, animals ought to be recognized as the subjects, rather than the objects, of animal liberation. In order to avoid reproducing the dynamics of animal oppression, in which animals are seen as the objects of human agency, animal advocates must learn to see themselves as the allies of animals who are seeking their own liberation and to accord to animals the same deference accorded to people seeking their liberation. Just as heterosexual people rightly cede to gay and lesbian people the right to determine the course of the gay liberation movement, animal advocates ought to recognize animals as the most legitimate leaders of the animal liberation movement.

4. Liberation includes self-determination and freedom

Liberation means not only freedom from captivity, forced labor, and the like but also freedom to determine one's own fate insofar as possible within the natural constraints imposed by the material world and social life. Among people, self-determination means making one's own choices about personal matters such as health care and having an equal voice in collective decisions about social matters such as governance. True allies of subjugated or otherwise oppressed people respect their right to self-determination, working for what they say they want rather than imposing other goals on them. Thus, if a community of refugees from racial persecution say that what they need most is a maternity clinic, it is not for their allies to insist that the limited resources available to them be used to build an elementary school instead. Similarly, allies of animals ought to respect their right to self-determination about such matters as whether to endure extreme suffering that might be relieved.

5. Animals may want more than liberation

We tend to think of liberation in terms of the things most people want for themselves, such as legal recognition of rights. Nonhuman animals as a class (or subsets of nonhuman animals) may want more or different things than human animals. For example, while the concept of "environmental justice" is relatively new and not widespread among people, many animals are more troubled by water pollution and depletion by people than they are by their lack of rights within our legal system. If they are troubled by our legal system at all, it is by the very existence of a network of laws backed up by guns that reduces all of the natural world to "resources" to be exploited by groups of people. Thus free fish who do enjoy self-determined movement through unbounded but poisonously polluted waters have legitimate demands that go beyond liberation as it is commonly understood. Similarly, free birds facing starvation due to climate change have different, although equally urgent, demands than their caged counterparts facing starvation due to forced molting.

6. Animals have voices

However much animal advocates may enjoy calling themselves "the voice of the voiceless," the fact remains that animals can and often do express their wishes quite clearly. Animals cry out in distress, snarl in self-defense, and flee from captivity. Animals also coo in contentment, relax in circumstances that feel safe, and move toward things they want. Whether expressed vocally or behaviorally, the wishes of animals are often quite easily discerned through casual observation. More subtle indications often may be accurately read by those with expert knowledge of the animal in question.

7. Animal advocates ought to listen to animals

If we truly believe that animals deserve self-determination then we must listen to them when they say what they want. This does not mean that we must accede to all expressed wishes regardless of circumstance — the feral cat who wants to run onto a highway, not understanding the concept of tractor-trailer, may be rightfully restrained from doing so — but does mean that we cannot in good faith make decisions that impact the lives of animals without due consideration of the opinions of those animals.

8. Actions taken on behalf of animals ought to be taken for the sake of animals

Just as trial lawyers must do what is best for their clients, even if this goes against their own inclinations, the decisions of animal advocates must be guided by what is best for animals rather than by their own desire for cognitive consistency, emotional ease, or feelings of moral purity. This is not to say that animal advocates should never use rhetoric that appeals to the self-interest of people. Such rhetoric may be a very effective method of obtaining substantial gains for animals. However, our own thinking about what to do (or not do) for animals ought to be guided by their interests rather than our own. Since animals deserve self-determination and animals have voices, the interests of animals ought to be discerned, insofar as possible, by consulting them.

9. Animals are different from one another

Thanks to our common ancestry, all animals share certain characteristics and needs. Even animals who seem very different often share important physiological characteristics, such as the basic brain structures shared by reptiles, birds, and mammals. Still, due to the many branches on the evolutionary tree, cold-blooded reptiles have very different needs than hot-blooded birds. They also might have different priorities in the struggle for freedom from human hegemony.

10. Different animals may want different rights

People differ from one another in the rights they claim for themselves and the emphases they place on various rights. For example, the right to housing is asserted in the United Nations Declaration of Universal Human Rights but is neither codified in the U.S. Constitution nor recognized as an entitlement by most U.S. citizens. U.S. citizens tend to highly value political rights such as freedom of expression but have shown a willingness to forgo such rights at times of perceived crisis. People also vary in the individualist *versus* collectivist nature of their conception of rights. For example, Native Americans strongly asserted a collective right to land while strongly resisting the imposition of the individual land ownership rights that are so highly valued by many people of European descent. Given so much variance across time and space within a single species, it stands to reason that there may be even more variance across different species. Furthermore, just as humans do not always agree with each other, animals within the same species may have differing perspectives depending on their circumstances.

11. The interests of different animals may be contradictory

The legitimate interests of different animals may contradict each other. Natural conflicts, such as the struggle between predator and prey or competitions among insects who make different uses of the same plant, are beyond the purview of this paper and tend to balance themselves out in ecosystems that have not been deranged by human intrusions. However, human exploitation of animals sets the stage for anomalous conflicts of interests, as when the right of minks to be freed from captivity conflicts with the interests of animals who would not naturally confront predation by minks. Since such contradictions raise especially complex ethical questions for animal advocates and since what we do (or don't do) matters to actual animals, it's important to distinguish between certain contradictions and those which are merely possible and to be very careful in assessing the probability of possible contradictions.

12. Animals value their own lives and the lives of some known others

Unless they have been traumatized into submission, animals flee or fight against efforts to end their lives, thereby demonstrating that their lives matter to them. Animals also demonstrate by their behavior that the lives of known relatives and companions matter to them. In various ways, many animals indicate by their actions that the lives of family members, flock or herd members, and even companions of other species matter to them. Animals sometimes do sacrifice their own welfare, and even their lives, for other animals who matter to them.

13. Animals do not sacrifice their lives or welfare for unknown others

We cannot know if the lives of unknown other animals matter to animals and thus cannot assume a willingness to sacrifice their lives or welfare for strangers of other species.[2] Similarly, we cannot know if the lives of possible future animals matter to animals. While some animals care for their young, thus demonstrating a behavioral concern for the existence of future generations, others do not. While some animals care for the young of other conspecifics and

---

2. We can speculate that animals known to adopt members of other species would care about other animals if they knew about them but such speculations do not justify the assumption that lab rats in New Jersey would be willing to delay their liberation in order to improve the welfare of chickens or that chickens in California would be willing to be tortured in order to hasten the liberation of rats.

even sometimes for the young of other species, most do not. Forced to guess, "does the life of an unrelated animal who might or might not exist in the future matter to any given currently existing animal?" we would have to say that the likelihood seems low. Thus we cannot assume that currently existing animals are willing to sacrifice their lives or welfare for the sake of future animals.

14. Animals are not objects

To sacrifice the life or welfare of one animal for the sake of another animal in the absence of evidence that the sacrificed animal consents to the arrangement would be to treat the sacrificed animal as an object in relation to the other animal. To treat one animal as an object, as a mere means to an end, in relation to another animal is no less morally repugnant than to treat an animal as an object or means to an end in relation to a human.

15. Harm happens

Driving to a demonstration creates greenhouse gasses that endanger animals other than those we hope to help. Taking action against one kind of animal abuse always takes time that might have been devoted to fighting another kind of animal abuse. Time spent on current crises is time not spent on long-term aims and *vice versa*. It's simply not possible to do everything that ought to be done. Nor is it possible to do almost anything without inadvertently causing some harm to someone. Hence the importance of both careful assessment of tactics and cooperative association among animal advocates, including those who focus exclusively on liberation and those who include efforts to improve animal welfare in their work.

16. Animal welfare is a component of animal liberation

Animals want freedom and well-being. Since animals ought to be the bosses of animal liberation and since actually existing animals have clearly expressed the wish for relief of their own suffering, we cannot justly ignore current animal welfare even if we believe that ultimate liberation is the more important goal. Due to pain's evolutionary role as a signal of emergency, acute pain tends to block out all other considerations. Animals in acute pain undoubtedly want the relief of that suffering more than anything else. If the acute pain of actually existing animals can be relieved, then we must do so — or, at least, not interfere with others who are doing so — unless we are certain that the means of doing so will cause harm to other actually existing animals. If harm might be caused to actually existing animals, then probabilities must be assessed and ethical decisions made. We may not refuse to relieve suffering of actually existing animals — and certainly may not interfere with others who are doing so — for the sake of possible future animals for whom the existing animals have not consented to be sacrificed. Whether or not a particular effort to improve animal welfare will improve welfare without causing harm and whether or not that effort might also be a component in a long-term strategy for animal liberation can only be determined by analysis of that particular effort.

29

In Defense of Actual Animals

As a companion to the *Strategic Analysis of Animal Welfare Legislation* paper from which the axioms in the previous chapter were abstracted, I distributed this short paper offering guidance to activists ensnared or confused by the raging movement debate between self-styled *abolitionists* and the so-called *welfarists* they derided. Since similarly inane and vituperative disputes continue to distract activists who might otherwise be working for the freedom and well-being of animals, I include it here.

In Defense of Actual Animals

Moving Past the Welfare-Abolition Impasse

Let's face facts: The whirlpool of controversy swirling around the question of whether current efforts to relieve the suffering of existing animals help or hurt the long-term struggle for animal liberation has descended into a death spiral that itself hurts the struggle for animal liberation, demoralizing activists and inhibiting many from taking any action on behalf of animals other than argumentative efforts to promote ethical veganism. Meanwhile, worldwide meat consumption is at an all-time high and rising, vivisectors call on governments to protect them by prosecuting animal liberationists as "terrorists," and climate change threatens the health and habitats of an ever-increasing number of species.

We can get past this impasse if and only if we are willing to learn to argue constructively, use words carefully, respect tactical biodiversity, and analyze actions strategically within an accurate understanding of psychology, history, and economics. Let's look at each of those in turn, because the animals need us to be better allies to them and each other.

Creative Conflict Resolution

The point of argument among allies is, or ought to be, the identification of larger and larger areas of common ground by means of careful examination of the sources of disagreement. Consensus, rather than victory for either "side," is the goal.

To achieve that goal among allies in the cause of animal liberation, we must bring to our discussions the assumption that all of us are acting in good faith, trying as hard as we can to do what's right, and that disagreements among us are due mostly to different ideas that we have about the best way to achieve our shared aim. Those different ideas may be rooted in divergent understandings of relevant facts or in different theories of social change.

It is essential to distinguish between questions of fact and questions of theory, favoring fact over theory and avoiding the use of analogies, which always tend to be interpreted differently by different people and which do not constitute proof in any case. For example, the idea that welfare reforms open the door to the attainment of more substantial legal rights is a *theory* of social change; the idea that such reforms will slow the effort to obtain legal rights also is a *theory* about social change. Neither can be proved to be true or false on the basis of available facts and, thus, moderation rather than dogmatic assertion is mandated when arguing from them. Analogies such as slavery do not aid in clarifying the question.

What are the available facts? What do they collectively suggest? The shared quest to discover this, if done in an open-minded spirit of cooperation, can lead to new and more nuanced theories that can guide future strategies. For example, consideration of the fact of the finite and declining availability of agricultural land suggests not only that fears of increased animal product consumption due to welfare reforms such as abolition of battery cages are unfounded but also that any reforms forcing more space-per-animal are likely to be strategically useful by both significantly raising costs and physically limiting production.

Sometimes, what seem to be deep disagreements turn out to be confusion due to imprecise use of language. Therefore, it is especially important to speak clearly, to listen carefully, and most especially to ask questions in order to ensure that you truly understand what those with whom you seem to disagree are saying. React only to what people actually say, not what you infer they believe or feel, as you may be very much mistaken. Trust that people are telling the truth when they say their beliefs and feelings. Be honest yourself. Begin sentences with "I" rather than "you." Begin discussions by affirming the good faith and shared purpose of all. These and other facets of constructive conflict resolution can turn fractious and frustrating arguments into fertile fields of creative problem-solving.

Clarification of Terms

Much of the current crisis is rooted in imprecise use of words to describe other activists and their tactics. This clarification is offered in hopes that the terms "abolitionist" and "welfarist" will either fall out of use among animal liberationists or begin to be used much more honestly and precisely.

There are organizations and people who believe that animals are rightly considered property but who believe that animals ought to be treated humanely.

Those holding that belief are rightly called "welfarist." They are careful to distinguish themselves from those who work for animal rights and, thus, there ought to be no confusion between them and those who seek the ultimate liberation of animals. Unfortunately, such confusion has arisen due to the rhetoric of self-identified "abolitionists" as well as due to the behavior of some organizations that work for both animal rights and animal welfare.

Activists working for legal rights and ultimate liberation of all animals do sometimes advocate for improved welfare for currently existing animals. Some do so as part of a strategy for more substantial change while others do so due to ethical considerations. Some argue from a mixed position including both strategy and ethics. Thus, Ingrid Newkirk of PETA has argued that any recognition of any animal rights by legislators is a step toward the recognition of full rights. Karen Davis of United Poultry Concerns has argued that individual animals ought not be treated as unimportant objects to be sacrificed for the good of the class of animal to which they belong. I have argued that we have an ethical obligation to listen to animals and that we can respond to their clearly expressed wish for immediate relief of suffering in ways that make their continued exploitation unprofitably costly.

It is perhaps not an accident that the three of us are women who have taken actions such as hunt sabotage, vivisection lab infiltration, and open rescue while the most mocking condemnations of welfare reforms have been inspired by the writings of a male scholar who argues from an abstract ethical perspective not rooted in engagement with actual animals. Women tend to work from what feminist scholars have called an "ethics of care" while men are sometimes dismissive of arguments falling outside of abstract systems of rules. Some feminists have identified that preference for abstraction as an element of both speciesism and sexism. Opponents of animal welfare should take care to respect different methods of moral reasoning, being especially careful to not mock women for expressing and acting on their concern for the actual experiences of existing animals.

This is not to say that advocates of animal welfare bear no blame for the dreadful state of the current debate. While most take care not to cross the all-important line between opposing particularly hurtful practices and promoting "humane" animal exploitation, a few high profile slip-ups have given an aura of legitimacy to the mistaken equation between the abolition of specific factory farming practices and the promotion of "happy meat." The opacity and lack of accountability of the upper echelons of some national organizations have, like the stridency of some "abolitionists," make productive dialogue difficult.

All sides can help to move the debate past the present impasse by being more careful with language, being especially careful to avoid derogatory uses of the term "welfare" (and derivatives thereof), being especially careful to avoid blurring the line between support for welfare reforms and support for the products thereof, and being more open to engagement with critiques that are respectfully and accurately expressed.

Respect for Tactical Biodiversity

Self-styled "abolitionists" sometimes disdain all tactics other than argumentative promotion of ethical veganism. At the other end of the spectrum, some proponents of welfare reforms have gone out of their way to denigrate those who take direct action on behalf of animals. Neither side in what has become a dangerously demoralizing debate seems to appreciate the fact that significant structural shifts in national or international politics or economics have only ever happened following a period of unrest during which different actors press for the same change from different directions, for different reasons, and by different means. Never in history has a shift as significant as the one we seek been achieved. Surely, it cannot possibly be achieved by *less* comprehensive strategies than those that were needed to win votes for women or the eight-hour workday in a single country.

In a world where people go to war with one another over what seem (to outsiders) to be relatively minor religious differences, the idea that everyone in the world can be converted to veganism by means of ethical arguments is unrealistic. It is similarly unrealistic to assume that amoral corporate profiteers will change their ways in response to moderate arguments not accompanied by more direct efforts to reduce their profits. Only by recognizing and respecting the importance of tactical diversity can we cooperate with one another in comprehensive strategies might actually achieve what we say we want.

Strategic Analysis in Context

The liberation of animals from all forms of human encroachment and exploitation will require a fundamental restructuring of the world economy as well as revision of all existing systems of government. People who earn their own bread through the exploitation of animals will have to, somehow, find other livelihoods. Local economies rooted in the exploitation of animals or their habitats will have to, somehow, be restructured from the ground up.

Powerful corporations that profit from the exploitation of animals will have to, somehow, be forced to give up those ill-gotten gains. The governments that support those corporations will have to, somehow, be convinced to dissolve or reform themselves to serve people, animals, and ecosystems instead. Human attitudes about animals also will need to be reshaped, somehow, despite the fact that all but a few cultures assert human superiority.

How, exactly, will all of that happen? What are the steps by which even a single community might be converted to a cruelty-free economy? By what means might exploitive industries be driven out of business? How might even a single government be restructured to truly represent the animals under its dominion? If animals gained "rights," how would these be enforced? How, exactly, will the currently quite small and unrepresentative animal liberation movement achieve a worldwide change in human psychology?

In the interim, rather than condemning or supporting "welfare reforms" in the abstract, animal advocates ought to analyze proposed reforms strategically and contextually, holding the interests of actual animals uppermost in mind and remembering that factory farms are for-profit enterprises that go out of business when costs rise too high. Total animal liberation may be a long time coming, but factory farms can be driven out of business right now, though a concerted effort to simultaneously reduce demand while raising the costs of production. Welfare reforms such as the abolition of battery cages can bring real relief of suffering while also raising costs.

Conclusion

Animals exist and have the right to self-determination. Animals want to be free *and* to be relieved of suffering. Actual animals suffer actual harm when we don't respect their self- determination in this regard. We *can* work toward the ultimate liberation of animals *while also* caring for existing animals, using ethics and strategy rooted in reality rather than theory.

30

PEACOCKS, PARAKEETS, AND THE TWO SIDES OF STYLE

This brief piece was written for the Montreal magazine called *Versus* in 2015. This is the first time that it appears in English.

Peacocks, Parakeets, and the Two Sides of Style

Here at VINE Sanctuary, there is a peacock called Rocky who likes to display his fabulous tail feathers to a rooster called Sharkey. Of course, we cannot be certain what he intends by this gesture, but Rocky seems to be courting or trying to attract Sharkey — obviously not for reproductive purposes. Speciesist discourse explains every animal behavior by way of reproduction, as if animals were automatons mindlessly intent on getting their genes into the next generation. This grim and falsely "reprocentric" conception of nature contributes to the subordination of both LGBTQ people and nonhuman animals.

University of British Columbia biologist and linguist Bruce Bagemihl proposes that we see same-sex affection, coupling, and courtship displays among nonhuman animals as "biological exuberance" — a function of the surplus energy that shines down from the sun every day. When male griffon vultures soar together in the pair bonding display called tandem flying, riding thermal currents one atop the other, this reflects the abundance of energy and creativity that *is* life.

I see style in the same way. When we paint our walls pretty colors, just for the fun of it, or when we adorn ourselves with scents and sparkling objects likely to bring pleasure to others, we realize our own animal gifts for generosity, superfluous creativity, and purposeless joy.

That's beautiful, yes? But consider this: The only parrots native to eastern North America, Carolina parakeets, were driven to extinction by consumer demand for their colorful feathers, with which stylish people decorated their hats. Replacing feathers with vegan equivalents does not solve all of the problems with what might be called the ugly side of style, which emerges when our animal instincts for beauty, pleasure, and communion express themselves in the context of elitism and capitalism.

Capitalism began with captive cattle, the heads (or *capita*) of whom were the original capital. The mathematics of this inherently hurtful economic system require more and more consumers to buy more and more things. This is, of course, destroying the planet upon which all animals depend. In order to fuel consumption, capitalism promotes style. Advertisers convince people that embellishments are necessities and encourage people to display elite status by means of stylish purchases.

Style serves not only as a means of self-expression but also as a marker of group membership. As social animals, we sometimes use style to place ourselves in one or another social group. This may be inoffensive or even valorous, as when people flaunt rather than hide signs of their membership in a denigrated group, but styles meant to signal group membership very often are colored by cliquishness or conceit. When the group in question is a high-status group such as an economic elite, style serves to exclude rather than embrace.

And so we can begin to see the two sides of style: On the one hand, nourishing joy abides in the flourish, the gesture performed only because it is beautiful. On the other hand, danger lurks within the empty commodity, especially if it serves as a symbol of membership in some sort of elite.

This tension within style becomes even more evident when one thinks about *vegan* style.

As more and more companies, large and small, begin to court vegan customers, I've become increasingly worried about what I call "commodity veganism" — a way of being vegan that focuses on and fetishizes vegan products, including not only foodstuffs but also clothing and adornments. I've also grown alarmed by the self-regard implicit in the idea that veganism is an identity rather than a practice. Those concerns collide when I imagine people purchasing expensive products that in some way showcase their identities as vegans.

On the other hand, I love the idea of people from many different stylistic communities not only figuring out how to "veganize" their wardrobes and furnishings but also finding ways to display the joys of plant-based living to their peers. I'm also interested in efforts to show that full-on veganism (by which I mean rejection of any product that exploits any animal —human or nonhuman— along with an ecological commitment to reduce, reuse, and recycle) can coincide with boisterous beauty.

Let's all embrace the ethos of exuberance and generosity that Rocky demonstrates whenever he displays his fine feathers to the whole wide world. That, to me, would be truly vegan style.

31

SELFIES AND SANCTUARIES

This brief piece was written for the Montreal magazine called *Versus* in 2016. This is the first time that it appears in English.

Selfies and Sanctuaries

This week in Argentina, a crowd of tourists on a beach removed two young dolphins from the water, passing them around to be touched and photographed. Many took the opportunity to snap a "selfie" with a dolphin, perhaps as a keepsake but also possibly with the idea of sharing the photos on social media.

Dolphins cannot live for very long outside of the water. One of the dolphins died.

Of course, every animal advocate views this event with horror. I personally cannot stop thinking about that poor dolphin, imagining how she or he felt, passed from hand to hand among land mammals, dying of dehydration as the oblivious killers crowded and cheered.

But are we really so different from the people on that beach? Do we never become so preoccupied with our own pleasure or vanity that we allow those shallow considerations to eclipse the vital needs of nonhuman animals?

Critiques of the unhappy event on the Argentinian beach have focused on the egocentrism of people so intent on taking photographs of themselves that they did not notice that the dolphin was dying. Narcissism, in the sense of self-centered focus on image combined with radical lack of empathy for others, appears to be an apt focus for our ire in this case. The idea that this dolphin died for a "selfie" seems to say something very significant about the culture of today.

But I am interested in different questions: Why were those people so eager to take selfies with a dolphin? How did they feel when the dolphin died? What can we learn from this?

Like the two dolphins, many of the land mammals on the beach were juveniles. In photographs taken before the dolphin died, the children's faces are bright with eager excitement.

When I was a child, about nine years old, I had a pet turtle called Timothy. I don't recall the day Timothy came to live in our urban backyard, but I must have brought him home from a nearby creek. Like those adults on that beach, nobody told me to put him back. As summer faded into fall, Timothy disappeared and the adults assured me that he must have burrowed into the ground to hibernate.

He must have tried. The next spring I found his shell, with a desiccated body inside, shallowly buried under a barren plum tree. I told no-one. I didn't want to be soothed. I knew it was my fault.

What we can learn from that story is this: I loved that turtle with an open heart. And I killed him. Both are true.

So let us return to the beach in Argentina and ask: Why were those people so eager to take selfies with a dolphin? Was it merely to have a unique photograph to share on social media, or was something more primordial at play as the people crowded around the dolphin, reaching out their hands, hoping to make contact?

And let us return again to the question: Are we really so different from the people on that beach?

I once spent part of an animal rights conference in the company of a dog called Babe. Like most of us, Babe did not like to be touched by strangers. In this crowd of vegans, Babe became more and more uncomfortable as person after person touched or tried to pet her. Her body language expressed her preferences clearly. She pulled away, ducked her head, and moved closer to her human companion for protection. Again and again, her human companion said things like, "Babe doesn't seem to want to be touched right now." Caught up in the certainty that they were somehow special, or perhaps so wrapped up in their own desires to hear or see anything else, animal advocates continued to try to touch Babe anyhow. It got so bad that Babe and her human companion had to leave the area so that she could have some peace.

At VINE Sanctuary in Vermont, we do not put residents on display by staging tours for the general public. Again and again, we have faced complaints about this from vegans who have become accustomed to treating sanctuaries like petting zoos. At one U.S. sanctuary last year, hundreds of visitors to an annual Thanksgiving event sat on hale bales encircling a turkey to watch the show of the bird being fed. Another sanctuary brought turkeys to a vegan festival where, predictably, they became exhausted and stressed.

Feeling ourselves so estranged from nature, we long to be close to nonhuman animals. We wish, deeply and sometimes desperately, to feel connected to them. That wish is healthy but goes wrong when it overwhelms our empathy or overrides the wishes of the animals with whom we wish to commune.

And so this is our challenge, made most evident by the tragedy on beach: How can we tap into that healthy impulse for closer relationships with non-human animals to motivate truly animal-friendly activities?

At VINE, we offer would-be tourists the opportunity to come for a day of volunteer work, thereby to truly join our multi-species community rather than simply looking at the animals. We are right now trying to figure out how to steer the impulse that leads people into backyard hen-keeping into activities such as wildlife rehabilitation or creating refuges for wild birds. How might you work with, rather than against, the impulses that lead people to inadvertently harm animals while trying to appreciate or be close to them?

32

Dodos and "Dodos"

This essay recaps a talk I delivered in August of 2022 as part of a panel on *The Human Propensity for Error* at the annual meeting of the North American Association for Critical Animal Studies, the theme of which was extinction.

Dodos and "Dodos"

Ableism, Speciesism, and Human Error in an Era of Extinction

I join you today from the grounds of VINE Sanctuary in what is now called Vermont, which is the traditional homeland of the Abenaki people. The sanctuary stretches over more than a hundred acres, half of which is reserved for as a wildlife refuge and the other half of which is is occupied by our our multi-species community.

Among the denizens of the forests surrounding VINE Sanctuary are wild turkeys, who evolved in the forests of North America more than 20 million years ago. That's so much earlier than our species evolved on another continent! I can't imagine, and I don't think any of us can imagine what these forests were like back then or even a few hundred thousand years ago. What birds filled the trees?

I can maybe catch just the slightest glimpse when I see flocks fluttering through the forest: crows, bluejays, redwing blackbirds, and—seemingly incongruously—pigeons. Pigeons are among the animals who find refuge at VINE: survivors of vivisection, survivors of canned hunts, survivors of squab farming, and more. Many of their descendants have rewilded themselves, and so there are huge flocks of the descendants of human captives sharing the forests with the wild turkeys and the other birds I named.

The dodo was a pigeon, about three feet tall and plump, living on the island of Mauritius, where they co-evolved with a particular tree. They ate the fruit of this tree, their digestive processes helped the seeds to germinate, and their perambulations spread the seeds all around. But then came Dutch sailors who discovered a taste for dodos, mocked the dodos for being easy to catch, and then ate them to extinction. The trees disappeared too.

The moral of this story of human hubris and cluelessness is, evidently, that *dodos* were dumb.

In English, as you probably know, the word *dodo* has been and sometimes continues to be used as a slur to denote that the person you're insulting is in some way inane or unintelligent. Making fun of people by mocking their intellectual capabilities or lack thereof has a long trajectory that continues to this day. I'm old enough to remember joke books that featured what were called *moron jokes*. 'Moron' is one of many terms now considered slurs that doctors actually used to describe people with intellectual disabilities.

I can remember reading joke books with those slurs in them. I cannot know the degree to which such jokes wormed their way into my brain. Of course, I've done my best to divest myself of such ideas, but they go deep. We see it every day. People on the left and the right take evident pleasure in casting aspersions on the intelligence of those who disagree with them politically, often using terms associated with cognitive or perceptual disabilities as slurs.

And that's ableism. But if you remember the dodo and notice the definition of our species as *Homo sapiens*, the wise ape, then you can see that this way of thinking about intelligence or the lack thereof—and, more broadly, about abilities or the lack thereof— is not only ableism but absolutely central to speciesism. By defining *human* by way of the ostensibly superior cognitive capabilities of our species, European men like Aristotle and Linnaeus simultaneously denigrated both animals and people with disabilities while creating a category of sub-human into which humans of any group might be consigned due to real or imagined deficits of ability.

While thinking about what to say on the topic of extinction, I asked myself: *How can you center absence?*

And so, here we are not quite at the middle of my time, and what I would like you to do is join me in imagining and mourning each of these extinct members of the pigeon family:

Bonin Wood Pigeon
Choiseul pigeon
Dodo
Mauritius blue pigeon
Norfolk Island ground dove
Passenger pigeon
Red-moustached fruit dove
Reunion Pigeon
Rodrigues blue pigeon
Rodrigues solitaire
Ryukyu Pigeon
Saint Helena dove
Spotted Green Pigeon
Tanna ground dove

Thick-billed ground dove

In the words of Samuel Beckett: "I can't go on, I'll go on."

Two-thirds of North American bird species are currently at heightened risk of extinction due to climate change. That's some 389 species, each with their own unique ways of being feathered beings. I do feel that it's necessary to try to hold those who are no longer with us in mind, to have them with us in our thoughts as we think about what to do while also attending closely to those who are currently endangered. The book *Extinct Birds* by Erroll Fuller offers a litany of birds whose demises echo that of the dodo: The soldiers or sailors arrived, they discovered a taste for these birds, they hunted these birds to extinction and/or hunted these birds while destroying their habitats and were surprised by the ensuring extinction.

Over and over and over again: the same mistakes. And now here we are, and I don't think any of us could deny that decades of sincere and intent efforts by many humans—including some of the most educated and, in some cases, politically powerful among us—have made nearly no impact on the escalating emergency of human-engendered climate change. And so I think we have to concede that there's some substantial problem with our collective problem-solving capabilities.

And so, I'm not even joking when I say that instead of *homo sapiens*, we should turn to another Latin phrase, *errare humanum est*, to define our species. What if, instead of thinking of ourselves as especially wise, we thought of our species as an animal that is especially prone to error? We are, after all, animals who have—again and again and again and again and again in many different times and places—destroyed our own habitats, necessitating migration, only to eventually run out of planet.

What if we considered ourselves more likely than not to be wrong in any given situation? How would this change how we interact with each other, how we struggle together to solve problems, and how we communicate our ideas to others? I think that might be helpful, but of course, that's just my idea and more likely than not to be wrong.

Still, there is broad agreement among scholars from many different fields that it's a fairly necessary and urgent task to deconstruct *human* as it is currently constituted because this way of thinking of ourselves is not only linked to ableism and speciesism but also plays a foundational role in racism and in the treatment of the larger-than-human world as mere resource. I completely agree, and I do see the deconstruction of the category *human* as among our more urgent tasks. At the same time, I think we must come to terms with who we might actually be. The flip side of dismantling the false ideas about our species is making a good-faith effort to discover what might be true about us. If we're not the superior lords of the universe who always behave rationally, then what kind of animal *are* we?

This could be tricky right now because one way that politically progressive people have pushed back against very dangerous forms of essentialism has been to embrace the fantasy that we are blank slates who can, by virtue of our omnipotent minds, be anything at all. From that perspective, it feels wrong to suggest that our material bodies exercise any meaningful influence at all on our thoughts, feelings, or behavior. Nonetheless, I do feel that we must figure out how to talk about and work within an awareness of the material parameters of our own animality.

Let me explain why: We're not only in the midst of an escalating climate emergency but also in an escalating emergency of ethno-fascist nationalism or whatever else you want to call the rapid rise of right-wing populists in the USA, Brazil, India, the Philippines, and too many other countries for me to list. These authoritarian populists are *actually popular.* Their followers perceive them to be strongmen who will protect them. They tend to be climate deniers who embrace what some have called "petro -masculinity."[1] Their rise coincides with a terrifying upsurge in wildfires, floods, and other frightening catastrophes associated with climate change. Their followers are *afraid*. The strongmen soothe the fear by saying, "You don't have to worry about climate change" and "I will protect you from those scary monsters," whether those monsters be immigrants, LGBTQ+ communities, or merely people who disagree with them about tax policy.

We cannot understand, much less intervene, in this dynamic unless we are prepared to confront the fact of our species as profoundly emotional animals for whom reasoning often fails and who tend to take refuge in identity. All of us, left and right, are that kind of animal. We're all in the midst of multiple disorienting crises. The weather is awry! Our bodies know this. Even if they didn't, we are besieged by news of truly terrifying happenings every day.

And so, I think that we will need to take feelings into account more than academics tend to do because rational argumentation is not going to save us or anyone else. And yet, this raises a new difficulty: How do you work within emotions without manipulating emotions as the strongmen tend to do? And

---

1. Cara Daggett, "Petro-Masculinity: Fossil Fuels and Authoritarian Desire," Millennium 47, no. 1 (September 1, 2018): 25–44.

so, the question becomes: How can we work with and call to emotions in a way that's transparent and non-manipulative?

OK, this has all been very grim. Or, rather, much of this has been just terribly sobering and chastening. But one thing about me that may be constitutional, and which has been the source of many friendly arguments with my fellow panelist Lori Gruen, is my tendency always to be looking for that upside of any situation. So, for whatever it's worth, here's where I see hope in this situation: The mistaken elevation of rationality and language as defining features of humanness has tended to suppress all of the other ways that human beings can think and communicate, *but those all remain available to us* if only we can summon them up. The larger-than-human world is always *right there* for us to rejoin and learn within if only we step down from our self-constructed pedestals and look around.

I know we are not *the* rational animal, but I would not argue with someone who said that a defining feature of our species is its behavioral plasticity. I'm pretty sure that there's not another species that has so many different kinds of homes in so many different places and is able to eat so many different kinds of food. We have a tremendous capacity for behavioral flexibility. So that means—as Angela Davis is always reminding us—that it's important not to falsely assume that whatever happens to be the case right now will always remain the case.

In closing, let me return to the pigeons at VINE sanctuary, who fly free. You've seen pigeons too, I know it, no matter where you live. I have seen them everywhere I have ever gone. I've seen them in Rome, which is in the Mediterranean, the homeland from which pigeons were carried all around the world by humans in the course of multiple waves of imperialist and colonial excursions. Most evocatively, I saw pigeons in Christchurch, New Zealand, when I was at an animal studies conference there. Those pigeons had made their homes in a cathedral destroyed by an earthquake. No humans were anymore using this building, which had become entirely occupied by pigeons, who flew in and out and in and out and in and out all day long.

When I dare to predict one fact of the future, it is this: Whatever humans do or don't do, pigeons will persist. That does not obviate our obligation to them, to other birds, and to other animals (including humans) to do absolutely everything we can. Still, it does hearten me and make it more possible for me to go on to know that they will go on even in the eventuality—the very likely eventuality—that we fail to do the things we're trying to do. And so I share that with you in the hopes that it will also hearten you to do the things that that you're trying to do.

33

Otherwise

Invited to contribute to a series of talks entitled *Animal Politics: Utopian and Dystopian Visions of Multispecies Society* at the annual *MANCEPT Workshops* aggregation of political theorists in September of 2022, I encountered a call for papers in which questions of optimism, pessimism, utopia, and dystopia were juxtaposed. In response, I wrote this abstract for a talk to be entitled "Otherwise":

Utopia or dystopia? Other. Optimistic or pessimistic? Other. Politics? Otherwise. But, given the colonization of our brains and bodies by human supremacy, it may not be possible to imagine that otherwise unless we ***become*** *otherwise. Sanctuaries conceived as multispecies communities can be catalysts for such transformations, but it is also possible to become other-wise, and therefore otherwise, in other ways and places by mindfully queering ourselves and our relations with(in) the larger-than-human world.*

In the days leading up to the talk itself, events at and around VINE Sanctuary took a decidedly dystopian turn. People called us about an emu loose in the woods and then disregarded our advice to avoid stressing her. By the time the head of our animal care team arrived on the scene, the emu was dead. An effort to rescue hundreds of roosters bred for cockfighting went sideways, with the birds scheduled for execution on the day of the talk.

At the time I spoke, I believed they had already been killed. (In truth, they had been spared, and we would be able to rescue a subset of them.) Grief-struck, I did my best to stick to the outline from which I have written this piece. However, I cannot say with any certainty whether this in any way reflects what I actually said. Many thanks to Eva Meijer for inviting me to speak at this event and to Will Kymlicka and other attendees who extended sincere empathy to me on a devastating day.

Otherwise

We must become otherwise and can do so, in part, by becoming other-wise, by which I mean wise to the ways of others. Sanctuaries can be sites at which such transformations may be enabled.

This week, I have had experiences that have turned my mind toward the dystopian side of the optimism vs pessimism question. I've been thinking about dystopias I have known and wondering what the animals entangled in them might know or want us to know.

VINE Sanctuary began as the Eastern Shore Sanctuary, a 2.5-acre refuge for chickens surrounded by factory farms. On the Delmarva peninsula, where they kill and cut up more than a million birds every day, families play pick-up games of baseball in the shadows of sheds housing tens of thousands of suffering birds. An annual festival features an area where children can pet newly hatched chicks side-by-side with the "world's largest frying pan," in which chicken parts are sizzling.

In that place, Miriam Jones and I founded a refuge for chickens, declaring our motto to be "Let birds be birds." We did what we could to set up a suitable habitat for refugees from the local poultry industry as well as survivors of egg factories and cockfighting. In the spring and again in the fall, this region is a flyway for migrating birds. When wild birds passed overhead, the chickens often paused what they were doing to send up a keening song, as if they wished they could join them.

At present, more than a third of the migratory bird species in the Americas are at risk of extinction.

Not long after founding a chicken sanctuary, Miriam and I welcomed a group of ducks rescued from a foie gras factory. None of us can imagine, not really, what it might be like to be a duck—a waterbird!—caged in such a place, enduring twice daily force-feedings via pneumatic tube. But please, stop now and try to imagine it.

Ducks are delightful. Ducks are so sociable. Ducks go their own way but also commune readily with members of other species. If you pay attention, you can catch ducks talking about you when you have disappointed them, and this will disabuse you of your human hubris.

Two of those ducks, Jean-Paul and Jean-Claude, initiated our now decades-long exploration of the intersections between queer and animal liberation. I've told their story in detail elsewhere. In short, they were a bonded pair, but I initially mistook their sex for fighting and kept separating them. Each time I did, Jean-Claude went to extraordinary lengths, climbing fences and walking through woods, to return to his partner. Imagine that, too: A duck so determined to be with his beloved that he defies a giant ape and navigates strange terrain to return to him.

Together with us and other birds, those foie gras factory refugees co-created a quasi-utopia within the dystopia that humans had established on that peninsula. They extended care to incoming chickens, once adopting a rooster with a poorly healed broken leg into their clique. They talked with each other incessantly, discussing and negotiating everything. They mostly ignored humans, especially when it served the needs of the avian community to do so.

I remember one evening when it had gotten quite dark, but they refused to go into the barn, ignoring my entreaties. It turned out that they were hanging back to allow newly arrived chickens to enter first, having perceived what I had neglected to see: The new birds were afraid of the larger ducks and would be hesitant to brush past them into the barn. As soon as the new chickens entered and settled themselves, the ducks rushed in behind them, eager to settle down for the night.

This is what I have called 'Natural Anarchism.'[1] At the sanctuary, again and again, I have seen true mutual aid across species in action. As Kropotkin[2] knew, we have so much to learn from other species.

When confronted by questions such as those in the call for papers for this session, I often ask myself what various animals at the sanctuary might say in response. One of the people whose opinion I often try to imagine is Jan.

Jan jumped a "beef" farm fence while pregnant, gave birth to her calf in the freedom of the forest, and then found her way to friendly people who conveyed her to a sanctuary. She turned out to be too fierce for that sanctuary, which regularly gives tours to visitors, because she would charge at anyone who even

---

1. See "Free as a Bird: Principles and Practices of Natural Anarchism" in this volume.

2. Petr Kropotkin, Mutual Aid: A Factor of Evolution (1914 Edition) (Boston: Porter Sargent, 1976).

looked at her calf Justin too long. So, the two came to VINE, where semi-feral bovines conduct their own affairs in the freedom of the back pasture, and we humans keep our distance when we count the cows twice daily, clean the barns, and deliver hay.

Years later, Justin is nearly twice Jan's size, but she still eyes strangers with evident suspicion if they show too much interest in him. I don't think she trusts us very much, either. She escaped from a "family farm" where cows were slaughtered on-site. She's seen what humans who act friendly one day can turn around and do the next.

I suspect that if we were to consult Jan about her opinions concerning multispecies societies, she would say: "Leave us alone." And so, we must remember that some animals will not want to engage with us in any sort of negotiations and have every right to insist that we do the work of changing the behavior of our species ourselves.

We must do so unheroically, remembering that we know next to nothing. This past weekend, we got a call about an emu in the forests of Vermont, exhausted and panting in the heat after being chased by people who wanted to "rescue" her. We begged them to stand back until we could get there, but they could not stop themselves from continuing to try to intervene. By the time we arrived, she was dead. Like foie gras factories, her death was awful beyond imagining and yet summoned up by human imaginings.

That forest was co-created by turkeys and beavers, in association with countless other flora and fauna, millions of years before modern humans existed. Although regularly chased by hunters and displaced by developments, wild turkeys still inhabit North American forests today. For me, that raises the question of what it might mean to take the decolonial principle "land back" seriously. This would require us not only to honor the claims of those who were first-among-humans to venture into a place but also to recognize the claims of animals to their own homelands.

This reminds me to remind you that you are someplace. Every place has a unique history and ongoing ecology. One-size-fits-all remedies are unlikely to succeed. This is another reason I reject blanket optimism or pessimism, preferring to assess probabilities for particular interventions more ecologically.

But let us return to ducks. Ducks are both otherwise and other-wise. Ducks apprehend the world differently than we do. For example, the tips of their beaks can discern minute gradations of nutrients in sedimented water. They are also, as their behavior at the sanctuary has repeatedly shown, wise to the ways of others. I recall a time when a Muscovy duck called Seagull inserted herself into a dispute between roosters, interrupting a fight and then scolding the aggressor so thoroughly that he thereafter refrained from attacking others.

Blue-green algae are also otherwise, both in the sense of not conforming to our categories and in the sense of being capable of things we cannot do. Their exhalations of oxygen, across time spans that stretch our imaginations, created the conditions for plant and animal life to evolve. At present, due to a combination of pollution and warming waters, their aggregations create dead zones.

We cannot solve this or any other problem unless we ourselves become otherwise. I mean this literally. We must become able to imagine things we cannot yet imagine and do things we are not yet able to do. Due to the extreme behavioral plasticity of our species, this *might* be possible. If so, becoming more other-wise, in the sense of learning with and from other animals, may be an essential part of the process. Sanctuaries can be places at which such transformations can occur, but you need not visit VINE or any other formal sanctuary to begin becoming otherwise yourself. Any place can become a sanctuary, and the process of transforming your own neighborhood into a safer and more equitable place can transform you. If there were one one-size-fits-all political praxis worthy of optimism, it would be this: Get to know your neighbors of all species and improve your relationships with them. Doing so will help you become both other-wise and otherwise.

Afterword

Consider This Alongside Genocide

Riding the eastbound #46 bus through Minneapolis one early spring evening, I heard the bus driver call out the window to someone he hadn't seen in a long time. They exchanged shouted greetings across traffic until the light turned green. The driver shifted the bus into gear, clearly reluctant to go. "I hope you and the family are doin' good," he hollered as he drove on, away from the setting sun.

And he *did*. He wished that, so sincerely. You could hear it in his voice. He would feel sad to hear of their hardship or ill health.

The date was March 2nd of 2012. I know that, and the exact words the bus driver used in extending his heartfelt well-wishes, because I pulled out my notebook and recorded what I had witnessed, appending a prompt: *Consider this alongside genocide.*

Again and again, in reviewing the essays included in this volume (and in rereading those I chose not to include), I have been struck by the never-ending nature of the struggle and the seemingly bottomless human capacity for cruelty and rapacity. In 1993, I now see, I wrote about racist tropes that remain potent in 2023. In October of 2000, I wrote that I was worried about Palestine. Right now, in October of 2023, Israel is openly committing genocide in Gaza with the enthusiastic assistance of the USA. Everywhere I look online, I see words, words, words that do nothing to stop the bombs that kill children and animals indiscriminately, poisoning land, sea, and sky along the way.

In that context, I have fought with the feeling that nothing I or anybody else might say could make any difference at all. The antidote to that feeling of futility has been awareness of the extraordinary behavioral plasticity of our species. We humans *can* both behave and become otherwise, but only if the social and environmental circumstances are right. If the tactics we've been using to shift those circumstances haven't worked, that doesn't mean that the cause is lost, only that our strategies have been mistaken.

I think, I hope, I believe that we can arrive at more accurate analyses, and therefore more useful strategies, if we set aside the myths of human supremacy, eschew posturing in favor of action, and work in solidarity and sympathy with the larger-than-human world. Perhaps I am wrong. Either way, if anything in any of these essays helps you with your projects, I will be glad about that. Let me know.

Acknowledgements

If you want to blame somebody for this book, start with Janelle White, who has been encouraging me to collect my essays into a book for close onto two decades. Next, blame Leah Garces, who more recently encouraged me to make chapters hidden away in obscure, expensive, or out-of-print collected volumes more accessible to activists. Blame Lori Gruen for finding that to be such a good idea that she retracted her demand that I pour all of my writing energy into a book-in-process about queering animals liberation in order to focus on making this one happen first. Blame Sarahjane Blum, who—like Lori and Janelle—knows how to be a true friend, for insisting that it is not hubristic to collect your own essays if people have been asking you to do it. Most of all, blame VINE Sanctuary co-founder Miriam Jones for persistently and patiently encouraging me to write, year after year after year, despite my tiresome claims of incompetence and complaints about how much I hate writing.

Speaking of Miriam, she is also first among the many people with whom I have conversed so extensively over the years that I cannot claim any of the ideas in this volume to be mine alone.

I cannot hope to compile a complete list of the people whose insights have inflected my thinking, but here is a partial list of people who commented on one or more of the pieces collected in this book:

Carol J. Adams, LoriKim Alexander, Mignon Anderson, Sarahjane Blum, Melissa Boyde, Gay Bradshaw, Michelle Carrera, Dany Celermajer, Marinella Correggia, Karen Davis, Greta Gaard, Lori Gruen, Breeze Harper, Sangamithra Iyer, Miriam Jones, Lisa Kemmerer, Marti Kheel, Syl Ko, Gorgo Losi, Patty Mark, David Nibert, Fiona Probyn-Rapsey, David "Dandelion" Rosenberg, Adam Weissman, and Janelle White.

All of those people also contributed to these essays in other ways, such as by encouraging my writing or engaging in generative conversations with me. Others who contributed to these particular essays in those ways include but are not limited to:

Nekeisha Alayna Alexis, Liz Anderson, SA Bachman, Batya Bauman, Sayoko Blodgett-Ford, Anna Boarini, Miko Brown, Bede Carmody, Julia Caruk, Darren Chang, Kevin Cudabac, Sue Donaldson, Kay Evans, Ryan Fletcher, Larry Fox, Leah Garcés, Lauren Gazzola, Nella Giatrakou, Katie Gillespie, Josh Harper, Audrey Haschemeyer, Nancy Heitzeg, Julian Johnson, Seba Johnson, Anita Krajnc, Indra Lahiri, Wendy McGovern, Christopher-Sebastian McJetters, Jess Maurer, Erica Meier, Dawn Moncrief, Namita Money, Lynn Mowson, Unny Nambudiripad, Yamini Narayanan, lauren Ornelas, Aram Polster, Annie Potts, Michelle Rojas, John Sanbonmatsu, Brenda Sanders, Jeri Schneider, Lisa Shapiro, Kim Stallwood, Rachel Stratton, Corvus Strigiform, Amy Trakinski, Yvette Watt, Susan Weingartner, Sister Mary Winifred, and Cheryl Wylie.

Recognition is also due to all of the attendees of all of the *Queering Animal Liberation* workshops I have facilitated over the years as well as the students in the *Cultural Politics of GLBT Sexuality* course at Metropolitan State University in Fall of 2011 and Spring of 2012 for participating in processes of collective cognition with me. Similarly, I owe gratitude to all of the members of the VINE Book Club and attendees at book club meetings for joining me in invigorating and thought-provoking discussions every month.

Finally, you and I both owe deep debts to the librarians who ensure free and equal access to books and ideas. I would not be as able to write, or to think, were it not for the existence of the Enoch Pratt Free Library in my hometown of Baltimore. Support your public library, wherever you are!

www.ingramcontent.com/pod-product-compliance
Lightning Source LLC
Chambersburg PA
CBHW070054030426
42335CB00016B/1886

* 9 7 9 8 9 8 9 6 1 7 2 0 3 *